Y Tymbl

The Tumble – the Growth of a Gwendraeth Valley Mining Village

Cover image - Great Mountain Colliery No. 2 Slant by Fred Roberts of Tumble (1933).

Jeff Alexander

Printed by Biddles Books Limited

Y Tymbl Ddoe a Heddiw

Hen bentref yng Nghwm Gwendraeth, cartrefle'r llwch a'r glo,
Lle cafwyd sant a meddwyn a chymeriadau bro;
Lle tarddodd caredigrwydd, dihafal ar bob llaw,
A goddefgarwch ingol yng nghanol mwg a baw.

Yr hen gymdogaeth annwyl: lle magwyd cerwi lu,
Lle cafwyd pur Ddiwylliant yng nghrombil ddaer ddu;
Y tlodi cyffredinol yn rhwymo pawb yn un,
Mewn trallod a llawenydd 'roedd ffrindiau yn gytun.

Brawdgarwch yn teyrnasu a chydymdeimlad pur,
Tosturi yn feunyddiol at frawd oedd dan ei gur;
Cymydog yn gymydog, yn barod ar bob pryd,
I gynorthwyo cyfaill oedd ddwfn yng nhorsydd byd.

The first three versus of a poem by Lilian Rees published in 'Y Tymbl Ddoe a Heddiw' (Cyfle i Bawb).

Contents

Rhagair - W. Gareth Davies

Pryd bynnag y gofynnlr i mi, a gallaf eich sicrhau bod hy' yn rheolaidd, - 'ble yng Nghymru ydych chi o Gareth?' - fy ymateb ar unwaith yw 'Tumble, pentref gwaith glo balch yn Nyffryn Gwendraeth.'

Mae arwyddocâd yn yr ymateb hwnnw, gan fod y pentref, Tumble, ac yn ail Ysgol Ramadeg Gwendraeth, fy alma mater, ochr yn ochr â fy rhieni gofalgar, efallai wedi fy llywio yn ddiarwybod am beth bynnag oedd o'n blaen yn fy mywyd. A'r cyfan wrth dyfu i fyny yng nghysgodion y tomenni glo enfawr ochr yn ochr â Glofa Great Mountain a oedd yn dominyddu'r dirwedd I bawb, rwy'n ddiolchgar yn dragwyddol, gan fod fy nhaith, er fy mod yn siŵr na gynlluniwyd wedi bod yn antur ryfeddol, gyda llawer mwy atgofion pleserus na anfanteision ac mae wedi fy ngalluogi i greu cyfeillgarwch a phrofiadau ledled y byd sy'n dal i fod yn ei lle.

Roedd y pentref yn cynnwys dwy gymuned, Tymbl Uchaf a'r Tymbl Isaf, nid y byddai unrhyw ymwelydd sy'n mynd drwyddo yn sylwi, gan y byddent trwy Uchaf, Canol ac Isaf mewn fflach! O amgylch Tymbl mae cefn gwlad bryniog, lle mae ffermydd, caeau a ffermydd bach yn ein hatgoffa o sut oedd bywyd cyn i'r daearegwyr ddatgelu'r cyfoeth a oedd oddi tano. Rhoddodd y ffordd o fyw a ddaeth i'r amlwg o amgylch cymunedau cloddio glo Dyffryn Gwendraeth ymdeimlad dwfn o ffydd i lawer ohonom o fy nghenhedlaeth i, gwleidyddiaeth flaengar barhaus, ymdeimlad angerddol o fod yn Gymro a phryder am chwarae teg a chymuned.

Talodd fy nhad ac yn wir berthnasau a thadau eraill ffrindiau'r pris am weithio o fewn pyllau glo caled y Great Mountain a Cynheidre, gan anadlu llwch ac yn ddyddiol yn gwynebu ei beryglon niferus. Ni fyddaf ar fy mhen fy hun oherwydd dyled enfawr o genhedlaeth cenhedlaeth fy rhieni. Roeddent yn bobl eithriadol. Mae wedi fy helpu weithiau i feddwl fy mod wedi gallu byw bywyd i'r eithaf: fel pe bawn i'n byw i ddau berson arall, yn llai ffodus na fi. Rwyf wedi elwa ar fy magwraeth, ac wedi bod yn ffodus ac yn hapus. Yn y dyddiau tywyll a rhyfedd hyn byddem yn gwneud yn dda i werthfawrogi bywyd i'r eithaf.

Mae Tumble yn cynrychioli, mewn microcosm, y profiad Cymreig sydd wedi gadael ei ôl ar bob un ohonom. Byddai'r cwm wedi ei faichio a'i gyfoethogi gan y Chwyldro Diwydiannol, ac yn wrthdaro mewn radicaliaeth a chrefydd, byddai'r pentref wedi bod yn od pe na bai wedi cofleidio'r traddodiad mwyaf Cymreig ohonynt i gyd - rygbi. Mae'r gêm wedi'i gwehyddu'n annatod i myafrif cymdeithasau pentrefi Cymru. Yn sicr nid yw Tymbl yn eithriad.

Gall bywyd pentref fod yn anodd, yn enwedig rhai sydd wedi gweld dyddiau gwell o gyflogaeth llawn a gweithgaredd economaidd bywiog, ond mae pobl Gymru wedi arfer delio ag adfyd. Pan fydd popeth arall yn ymddangos yn ddu, mae rygbi bob amser i godi'r ysbryd, i gael calonnau'n dymchwel ac i symud y cylch diddiwedd hwnnw o ddadl, dadl a sylw sef gwaed bywyd cymuned.

Diolch i un o fy ffrindiau cynharaf Jeff Alexander am ymchwilio ac ysgrifennu'r hanes rhagorol hwn o Tymbl, ac am fy ngwahodd i ddarparu'r nodiadau yma i'r llyfr - braint fawr. Diolch – Gareth.

Foreword – W. Gareth Davies

Whenever I am asked, and I can assure you that I am quite regularly, -"where in Wales are you from Gareth?"- my immediate response is "Tumble, a proud mining village in the Gwendraeth Valley."

There is significance in that response, as firstly the village, Tumble, and secondly Gwendraeth Grammar School, my alma mater, alongside my caring parents, perhaps unknowingly steered me for whatever lay ahead in my life. And all whilst growing up in the shadows of the huge coal-tips alongside the Great Mountain Colliery that dominated the landscape

To all, I am eternally grateful, as my journey, whilst I am sure not planned has been a marvellous adventure, with far more ups than downs and has enabled me to create friendships and experiences around the world that still endure.

The village consisted of two communities, Upper Tumble and Lower Tumble, not that any visitor passing through would notice, as they would be through Upper, Middle and Lower in a flash! Tumble is hemmed in on all sides by rolling, hilly countryside, where farms, fields and small holdings are reminders of what life was like before the geologists uncovered the wealth that lay beneath.

The way of life that emerged around the coal-mining communities of the Valley gave many of us of my generation a deep sense of faith, enduring progressive politics, a passionate sense of being Welsh and a concern for fair play and community.

My father and indeed other relatives and dads of pals paid the price for working within the shining anthracite pits of Great Mountain and Cynheidre, breathing in its life-shortening dust and each day facing its many dangers. I will not be alone in owing my parents' generation a huge debt of gratitude. They were exceptional people. It has helped me sometimes to think that I have been able to live life to the full: as if I lived for two other people, less fortunate than me. I have benefitted from my upbringing and have been fortunate and happy. In these dark and strange days, we would do well to value life to the full.

Tumble represents in microcosm the Welsh experience which has left its mark upon us all. Both burdened and enriched by the Industrial Revolution, and strident in radicalism and religion, the village would have been odd if it had not embraced the most Welsh tradition of them all- rugby football. The game is inextricably woven into the fabric of most Welsh village societies. Tumble is certainly no exception.

Village life can be tough, especially ones that have seen better days of full employment and vibrant economic activity, but Welsh people are used to dealing and coping with adversity. When all else seems black and doleful, there is always rugby to lift the spirits, to get hearts thumping and set in motion that endless cycle of argument, debate and comment which is the life blood of a community.

Thank you to one of my earliest friends Jeff Alexander for researching and penning this excellent history of Tumble, and for inviting me to provide the foreword to the book – a great privilege. Diolch – Gareth.

Preface

I grew up in Tumble from the late 1950s until leaving the village in 1974. Even now, nearly half a century later, if anyone asks where I am from, my answer is *Tumble*. In Sussex, where I have lived for many years, that can get me some strange looks, but I am always proud to explain my roots. If, as I occasionally do, I bump into someone from closer to home, the next question will invariably be 'Upper or Lower?'. The answer is 'Lower'. My family came to Tumble to live in one of the first new National Coal Board houses built in Maesgwern. Our back garden looked up at the two sets of headgear of Cwm Colliery, where my father worked alongside the German contractors developing Cynheidre shafts three and four. The field behind our house bordered the *venetian blind* factory in Bethesda Road, where my mother worked in the 1960s.

Early on, the Great Mountain Colliery was still open, and I have vague memories of miners on their way home from the morning shift past our school - the fathers of nearly all my friends were colliers, either at the Great Mountain or increasingly at Cynheidre. But my best memories of the colliery are from a few years after it closed. As many boys of my generation have commented, there could be no better adventure playground than an old colliery. In Tumble we were spoilt for choice – we had two waste tips to scramble up and slide down. We could stand at the forbidding entrance to No. 2 Slant and dare each other to walk down the steep steps to the gates that secured it – a descent so many Tumble men had made on the primitive *spake* some never to return to their families. But to us it was just a place of adventure!

The pit-head baths, opened in 1936, seemed very modern compared with most of the other buildings, many dating from 50 years earlier. They included a large, open area (the former canteen) which provided the perfect inside arena for five-a-side football on a rainy day. No.1 Slant was still in operation as a pumping station for Cynheidre and we stayed well clear of it, but the rest of the colliery was our domain.

As well as exploring the old colliery, I loved to roam the countryside with a group of friends or our spaniel for company. The two *Graigs* were favourite haunts as were the *cwms* with their red, iron-stained streams. My favourite led from the lower end of Bethesda Road, via swing gates, toward the Dynant area and beyond to an old ford and lane that led up to Cwm Colliery. I had no idea then that the path I had followed once formed an extension of a tramway (or *horseway*) that connected the coal mines of the Bethesda Road area to the canal and railway near Pontyberem. I remember grassy areas to the side of the path that were great for picnics but may well originally have been passing places.

Turning left up the steep lane to Cwm Colliery, unknown to me I was following close to the line of the rope-worked incline up which trams were pulled, connecting Dynant Colliery with the L&MM railway. Once, I carried on walking beyond the colliery onwards and upwards to an area of heathland with gorse and heather and views of the sea. I knew vaguely about Jac Ty-isha and the Rebecca Riots but was totally unaware that I had reached the location of the landmark meeting on Mynydd Sylen in 1843 reported in the Times of London.

On most of these walks I would have an impression of features – such as dips and hollows and deposits of grey shale - that were not part of the natural landscape. The two railway lines also offered great walks dodging the occasional coal train. I particularly liked walking along the line from Cwm-mawr to Pontyberem (not knowing that it was also the line of the old canal). Closer to home, in the field behind our house, there was a copse just outside the factory fence where we built dens around a bottomless, black, water-filled hole which I now realise was a remnant of one of the many former coal mines alongside Bethesda Road, long before it was given that name.

Shopping and entertainment were very local affairs. Siop Harold in Bethesda Road met most of our grocery needs supplemented by the occasional visit to the Co-op in Upper Tumble. Typical of shops and other businesses outside of the village centre, Siop Harold was housed in what was little more than a corrugated zinc shed. Trips to town on the bus for clothes shopping and the market or, much better, to Stradey Park were a treat. The Village Hall was a centre for entertainment – for me that mostly meant Saturday morning and Friday evening pictures and later the billiards room and library. In my last couple of years in Tumble the Rugby or Workingmen's Club in Lower Tumble played an important role - particularly the Friday night discos.

So, as a youngster in Tumble I was aware of features of the village's past but made little or no connection between them. There was the old colliery of course – with the somehow related large, ugly, brick building above the church - and the Tumble Hotel, Ravelston (so different in style to any other house in the village), the terraced houses of High Street and Railway Terrace, Pownd Bacs, the railway lines and the paths through the *cwms*. It was much later that I started to be intrigued by these features and the stories that connected them.

This curiosity led me to some excellent sources that have both inspired and informed this book. It started with Phil Cullen's *Gwendraeth Valley Coal Mines*. From there I drew the wider context from *Hanes Plwyf Llan-non* by Noel Gibbard, and *Hanes Cymoedd y Gwendraeth a Llanelli* by D. Huw Owen. For learned analysis I could do no better than the excellent articles published in the Carmarthenshire Antiquary. A special mention must also go to four books that breathe life into the story of Tumble by connecting with the people: Wilfred Timbrell's invaluable *Reminiscences of Tumble from 1886*; *Coal Dust & Dogma* by Glyn Anthony; *They Gave me a Lamp* by Phyllis M. Jones; and *Y Tymbl Ddoe a Heddiw (Cyfle i Bawb)*.

I have also drawn heavily from contemporary newspaper accounts, partly because they are such a good (but not always unbiased) source but also because the way events were reported at the time can be as interesting as the events themselves. Perhaps a little unusually, I would also like to acknowledge a social media group – *Memories of Gwendraeth & Amman Valley*. At those inevitable times when I questioned whether my work would be of interest to anyone other than myself, a post would appear demonstrating that the people of Tumble, wherever they now live, have a deep interest in the unique story of their village.

My thanks to Tumble RFC for allowing me to draw extensively from John Myrddin Davies' booklet - a real treasure of village history - *Tumble Rugby Football Club – 1897-1949*. Also to Phil Cullen who, as well as being generous with his own publications, provided invaluable advice on the sections dealing with coalmining, and to John de Havilland for his expert guidance on the transport section, including drawings that he adapted to meet my particular needs. Caru James of Llanelli Library was also always ready to help.

I was particularly pleased to be in touch with the descendants of two Tumble characters who shared their family stories with me: Lynette Griffiths, granddaughter of *Bryn y Barbwr,* and Janine Wood of Melbourne, Australia – great-great-great granddaughter of Jac Ty-isha.

I am also grateful to Mike and Rosanne Alexander for their help and encouragement.

Wherever possible I have acknowledged the sources of the images I have reproduced. In some cases, despite making what I believe to be every reasonable effort, I have been unable to identify any owner. I have made the judgement that these are too valuable a record of the village not to be included in a book of this kind, but I apologise if I have transgressed in any way.

I do not claim to have written a history of Tumble. What I have attempted is to bring together particular events that have intrigued me and set them in the context of a hamlet that almost over-night developed into a large village, with one of the most productive collieries in the Gwendraeth Valley. I have concentrated on the period from the Rebecca Riots to the closure of the Great Mountain Colliery with particular focus on the earlier decades. I have not done justice to many aspects of Tumble's story – including the art and science of coalmining and the richness of cultural and religious life. I also hold my hands up to any accusation of a Lower Tumble bias. I offer in mitigation my roots in that part of the village and the extent to which the events I have covered connect to the Great Mountain Colliery.

Finally, and above all else, I must pay tribute to the men and women of Tumble who through their work, hardship, achievement, sorrow, independent spirit and humour created this story. It is a mistake just to express admiration for the miners themselves without embracing the families and community that supported them. Nevertheless, they do have a special place in Tumble's history and I know that I will have fallen short in capturing the daily dangers and life-destroying disease they faced in earning a living and building our village.

Jeff Alexander, October 2020.

1.Origins and Early Growth

Village names in Wales tend to be rooted in local features, either man-made or natural, and are obviously Welsh. Tumble, or Y Tymbl, is different – the name sits oddly with those of other villages in the Gwendraeth Valley such as Pontyberem, Cefneithin and Cwm-mawr. By coincidence, one of Tumble's near neighbours, Cross Hands, also stands out from the norm - but that is another story.

So, a good place to start the story of the village is with the name itself. Sadly, there seems to be no evidence to back the once popular view of Tumble school children that it honours a local hero - Twm Bwl. That leaves two main theories. The first that it comes from the description of the geological fault that runs through the village bringing coal seams close to surface; and the second that it derives from the name of the local inn.

In his history of Llannon Parish (*Hanes Plwyf Llan-non*), Noel Gibbard refers to the name *Tumbledown Dick* (or *Tumble Dick Down*) appearing in the Llannon Parish records from around 1817. He recognises the contending claims to the origin of the village name but concludes that there is clear evidence that there was an inn of that name in the parish. It seems that these very early records may have been lost. However, the inn does feature in the parish records of 1828, referred to simply as *Tumble* (the home of Samuel Howel *publican* and his wife Catherine). Though not conclusive, the view that the inn gave its name to the village carries considerable weight and is consistent with the common and long-standing practice of referring to the village as *The Tumble* or *Y Tymbl*.

Tumbledown Dick might seem a strange name for an inn located in a remote almost totally Welsh-speaking area, but it was not unusual for Welsh public houses to have English names (there are several other examples in the Gwendraeth Valley). The name is linked to Richard Cromwell, son of Oliver Cromwell, who succeeded his father as Lord Protector in 1658. He was in power for just nine months and his enemies, who were glad to see him go, gave him the satirical nickname of *Tumbledown Dick*. When Charles II became King, several inns and taverns took the name in celebration of the coronation of the *Merry Monarch*, and their optimism for a return to jollier times.

So, the origins of the name *Tumbledown Dick* are clear, but why would it have been given to a remote Gwendraeth Valley inn? There is a possible intriguing connection with the onetime landowners - the Earls of Balcarres and Crawford, a Scottish aristocratic family. The family archives, held at the National Library of Scotland, record that Alexander Lindsay, 6th Earl of Balcarres (1752-1825), had acquired Carmarthenshire estates in 1819. These estates included coal mining interests in the Tumble area. A survey undertaken in 1876 for the Llanelly and Mynydd Mawr Railway identified that Danygraig Farm in Tumble (along with Tyryrbryn, Ty-issa and Garnfach) was owned by Lord Crawford (the earldoms of Crawford and Balcarres were combined). In the English Civil War, the family had been staunch supporters of Charles I – to the extent that the first Lord Lindsay of Balcarres died in exile during the rule of Oliver Cromwell. Despite the passage of time, it is possible that the name *Tumbledown Dick* was given to the inn by the *Royalist* landowners of Danygraig Farm in mockery of the son of the family's former bitter enemy.

The debate on the origins of the village name may continue but, whatever the outcome (if there ever is one), it is sad that the Tumble Hotel has been demolished - it was at the heart of so much of Tumble's story.

The Tumble - early references

Farms and families in the area that later became Tumble date back many centuries. Noel Gibbard notes, for example, that the Treharne-Thomas family was associated with Llety-mawr at least as far back as the 16th century (they could trace their line back to Sir Hugh Treharne who was killed in the battle of Poiters in 1356). Tumble appears by name in the Ordnance Survey Map of 1831 (fig. 2), but the names of farms and other features are given equal prominence, so the map could be identifying the inn rather than a recognised settlement. In 1825, the Llannon parish records show *Samuel Howel* as *publican* and his *abode* is simply given as *Tumble*. Earlier still, in 1813, the Ordnance Survey Map of Llannon Parish (fig. 1), while not identifying Tumble by name, does show an inn at the location later occupied by the Tumble Hotel. The origins of this inn may go back further, but its identification in 1813 as *New Inn* and its precise location suggest a connection with the opening, just a few years earlier, of the Carmarthenshire Rail Road (a tramroad with horse-drawn waggons).

Located at the intersection of the railroad and the turnpike road to Nantgaredig, it would have been well-placed to serve hauliers and other travellers as well as the local farming and mining communities. Were it not for the railroad, the junction of three turnpike roads in Upper Tumble (later known as the *Square or Sgwar*), with its tollgate, would have been a more obvious location for an inn.

In 1833, the company engineer for the planned extension of the Kidwelly and Llanelly Canal to Cwm-mawr, a mile or so from Tumble near the Gwendraeth Fawr river, made an early reference to Tumble. As part of the case for extending the canal, he referred to the opportunity to make connections by railroad 'near the Tumble Colliery' (he may have been referring to mining in the area of Tumble more generally rather than a specific colliery of that name). There are also early references to Tumble in newspaper reports on the Rebecca Riots dating back to 1843, but it was yet to be formally recognised as a village of that name. For administrative purposes at least, Tumble was identified as falling within the *Hamlet of Glyn* described in the 1844 Topographical Dictionary of Wales as:

A hamlet in the parish of Llannon, hundred of Carnwallon, county of Carmarthen, South Wales, 12 miles (S.E. by S) from Carmarthen: the population is returned with the parish. A branch of the Gwandraeth-Vawr river passes through the hamlet, the inhabitants of which are chiefly engaged in agriculture.

Figure 1. Llannon Parish Map, 1813 Ordnance Survey. The location of the future Tumble Hotel is identified as 'New Inn'. The Tollgate (T.G.) in Upper Tumble is shown at the junction of the Turnpike Roads. The 'Old Rail Road' is also identified.

Tumble grew around the inn of that name. Noel Gibbard notes that in 1833 it had only two or three houses, with Hirwaun Forge nearly half a mile away towards Cwm-mawr. The Census records, starting in 1841, were recorded by parish and enumeration district. The districts do not coincide neatly with the boundaries of today's village – hardly surprising as settlements like Tumble were growing from a few scattered farms and other dwellings. The inn, under various names and publicans, is a common reference point in the early census records. In 1841 it is recorded as the Tumble Tavern alongside three other properties with Tumble in their name: *Bank y Tumble*, occupied by a collier and two others; *Tumble Shop* with Evan Treharne identified as grocer; and *Tumble Glyn* occupied by 20 people of whom only two have recorded occupations - a collier and an agricultural labourer. The existence of a small cluster of *Tumble* properties around the inn suggests that a distinct settlement of that name was taking shape. By the mid-1800s, *The Tumble* was being used to describe the growing community and not just the inn and the local mining activity. Arguably, however, Tumble did not become a true village until the surge of growth brought by the opening of Great Mountain Colliery in 1887.

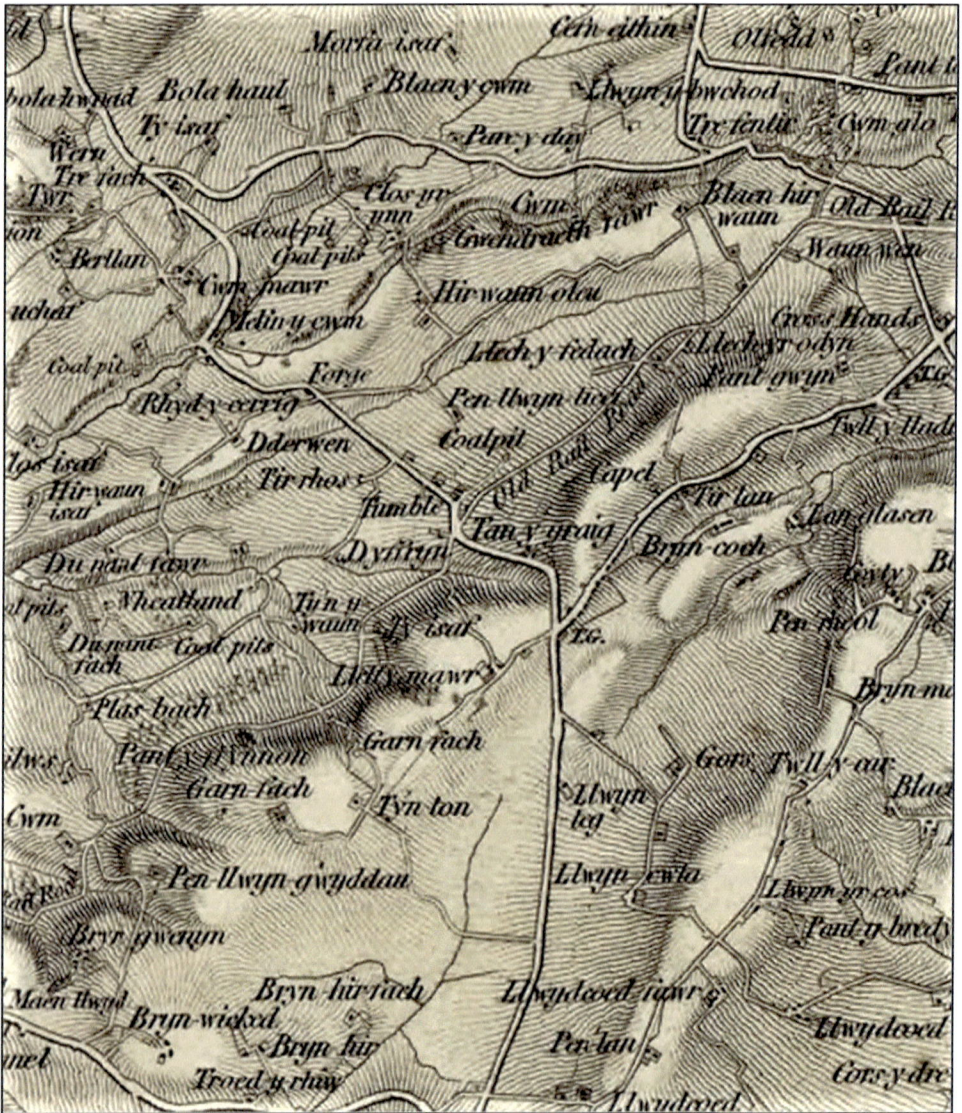

Figure 2. Extract from 1831 Ordnance Survey map of Carmarthenshire. Interesting features include: the identification of Tumble (not necessarily as a recognised village); the location of the Tollgate in Upper Tumble (T.G.); the location of Bethania Chapel; and the line of the Carmarthenshire Tramroad (Old Rail Road).

Figure 3. Tumble Hotel and the road later named Heol-y-Neuadd

Impact of the Great Mountain Colliery

By 1892 the Great Mountain Colliery, established and owned by the Waddell family from Scotland, had grown to employ some 600 workers and had demanded an influx of men and their families. But how were they to be housed in what had, until then, been little more than a rural hamlet, remote from the nearest concentrations of labour in Llanelli and Carmarthen? The colliery owners' answer was to build terraced housing, quickly and cheaply (though the homes were described in one local newspaper as 'comfortable .... with very extensive' gardens'). This expansion began with Tumble and Tan-y-Graig Rows, later renamed High Street, followed by Railway Terrace and Railway Place (also both since re-named losing a bit of their historical connection in the process).

Looking down on the colliery from the lower end of High Street, the imposing *Model Lodging House* was built by the colliery owners in around 1892. Originally housing mostly Scottish mining experts and skilled workers brought in by the Waddells, in 1893 it was to play a central role in the Tumble *riots*. Glyn Anthony (*Coal Dust & Dogma*), drawing from his memory of Tumble in the 1920s, gave this description of how turning off the railway and heading along a back lane behind the High Street he and his friends passed a huge building:

> *... specially built in the early days of the colliery by its owner for his technicians and experts, but later, when these people had moved into more luxurious and better situated houses, the building was handed over for the use of English families who had arrived in search of work from across the border. It gradually deteriorated into a drab, dilapidated building, an isolated enclave for poor people.*

13

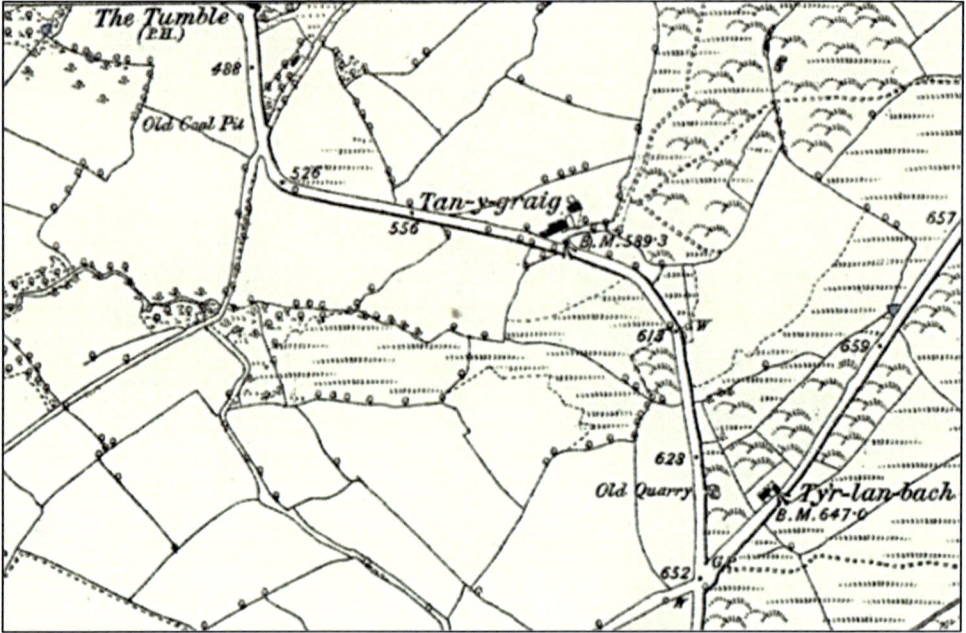

Figure 4. Maps illustrating the rapid growth of the village. The top map was surveyed in
1878. The lower map, revised in 1905, shows the growth of the village including Tumble
Row, Railway Terrace, the L&MM Railway, Church and Chapel (the Great Mountain
Colliery is to the north of this extract). OS maps with permission of NLS.

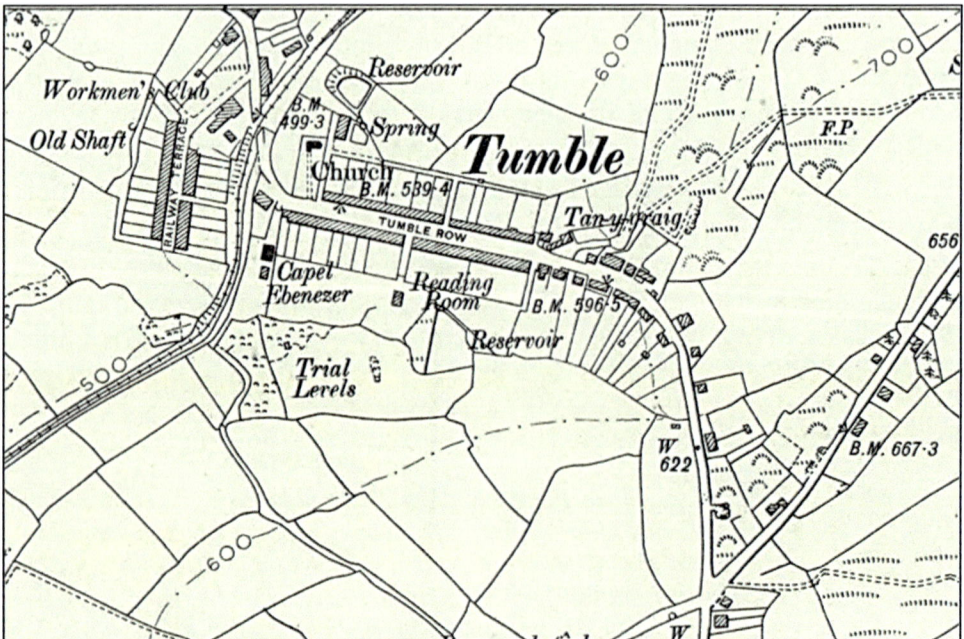

Figure 5. Heol y Neuadd (Caldy View) looking up at the colliery entrance, railway line and the Lodging House, before the construction of St David's Church.

High Street, Tumble

Figure 6. High Street (Tumble Row) – before the rendering of the front facades in the mid-1920s. A lamp stand (oil) provides street lighting.

Before the building of their homes in Tumble, Waddell family members had a suite of rooms in the Lodging House reserved for their use when they visited the area. In stark contrast to the houses in High Street, the building had a hot and cold-water system serving baths. By 1911, John Waddell (grandson of the founder of the Great Mountain Colliery) was living with his family in Ravelston. Two other grandsons, George and James, were living at nearby Merkland.

Figure 7. Ravelston in Lower Tumble bult by the Waddell family (author's collection).

Where did the people come from?

Within three years of the Great Mountain Colliery opening in 1887, the village had grown, from a few dwellings around the inn and scattered farmhouses, to have a population of around 500. By 1894 Tumble was a village of 135 homes – all within a half mile radius of the new Workingmen's Club. The 1891 census, the first after the opening of the colliery, records a street of 104 colliery-owned houses in Tumble and Tan-y-Graig Rows. At the time, numbers 1-38 and 78-104 were identified as Tumble Row, and the remainder as Tan-y-Graig (the naming and numbering suggests that the street name transitioned halfway up the hill leading to Upper Tumble). The Model Lodging House, with accommodation for 60 people, housed men and their families mostly from Scotland. Noel Gibbard identifies the impact of this rapid growth on Llannon parish. Between 1901 and 1910 the population of the parish, with Tumble being the main driver, grew by 78%, and between 1891 and 1911 it doubled.

Of the heads of household recorded for Tumble and Tan-y-Graig Rows in 1891, 75% had been born in Carmarthenshire, many in local, very rural parishes (including those within the neighbouring Gwendraeth Fach valley); 24% had been born in other parts of Wales (predominantly Pembrokeshire and Glamorganshire); and just one head of household in England (and even he is shown as speaking both English and Welsh, suggesting that he was not a newcomer). Of the heads of household, 73% identified themselves as Welsh speakers, 8% as English speakers (mostly born in Pembrokeshire); and 19% claimed to speak both languages. So, some 92% were Welsh speakers. This profile remained much the same at the time of the 1901 census.

By 1910 the number of houses in Tumble and Cwm-mawr had risen to 263. With the ever-increasing demand for labour, further terraced housing was developed in the early 1900s at Railway Terrace and Railway Place (Pen Parc and Park Place). Here the colliery company built and subsidised the development but, rather than becoming the landlords, offered the houses for outright sale or for occupation on rent-purchase terms - a building society was established to support private ownership. Railway Terrace and Railway Place feature in the 1911 census and present a far more cosmopolitan profile than *High Street* from two decades earlier. Of the heads of household identified, just 37% had been born in Carmarthenshire, with 34% in other parts of Wales. Most of the remaining 29% had been born in England. With 21% of heads of household identifying as Welsh speakers and 50% as both English and Welsh, that left a significant proportion of non-Welsh speakers – quite a contrast to the almost complete dominance of Welsh in *High Street* just 20 years earlier.

The 1911 census record for Railway Terrace and Railway Place also stands out for the large number of boarders from other parts of Wales and, in very significant numbers, England. One property in Railway Terrace housed 9 family members and 4 young boarders from Yorkshire and Birmingham. In another, 9 family members shared with 5 boarders. It is difficult to imagine what the living conditions must have been like which would have been mitigated only a little by the colliery workers in the household working different shifts.

One of the newcomers to the village was Wilfred (Wilf) Timbrell. His father, David, had moved to Wales from Gloucestershire after his wife had died and when his son was aged just two. After a time in Ammanford, David Timbrell re-married and, as his new wife originally came from the parish, they moved to Tumble in 1896 to be nearer her family and friends. Aged over 80, Wilf Timbrell wrote his memoirs, *Reminiscences of Tumble from 1896,* covering the period from his arrival in the village through the first two decades of the next century. His account is fascinating as it brings to life the bare facts of the rapid growth of the village. One of the last acts of the Llannon Parish Council in 1974 was to publish the memoirs and in so doing preserved an invaluable first-hand account of this period. Timbrell, aged about 15, is in the 1906 photograph of Great

Mountain Colliery workers at (fig. 42). He also features in the photograph of the 1911-12 Tumble rugby team (fig.114).

Figure 8. Railway Terrace – possibly showing electric as well as oil street lighting.

Wilf Timbrell recalls arriving in Tumble for the first time in 1896 on a *gambo* (a horse-drawn cart) owned and driven by John Evans, Dynant Farm. He was impressed by the newly rebuilt Bethania Chapel and the fresh appearance of Llechyfedach School. His first impression of High Street/Tumble Row was equally vivid but less positive. He was puzzled as to why some of the houses were empty, with broken windows, while others were undamaged. He later discovered that the damaged houses had been the homes of blacklegs during the 1893 strike. Describing the appearance of the village around 1900, he refers to the houses of High Street as being built of rough stone and mortar and looking very ugly. (In 1926, following a campaign by Tom Nefyn, the houses were rendered to improve their appearance and make them less prone to damp.) There was no street lighting at the time but Timbrell does acknowledge the foresight of providing such a wide road. He also refers to the square in Upper Tumble as *Finger Post Square* and comments that there were just three buildings on the side of the main road to Llannon – Brynteg Farm cottage, the old Bryndu Board School and the old Tollgate House (at the junction with the road to Pontyberem).

The caretaker of the Lodging House, Captain Braven, gets special mention. He was a retired ship's captain who had brought copper ore into Llanelli for smelting. Timbrell describes him as a 'striking figure dressed in frock coat and tails with a top hat on Sunday.' (His heavy-drinking brother would enthral local children with tales of shipwrecks off the Cefn Sidan.)

Figure 9. Tumble 'Square' with Siop Annie, Upper Tumble Club and the Post Office.

Figure 10. A view from Heol y Bryn, down High Street/Tumble Row to Greenhill.

From its *Wild West* days Tumble emerged as a strong community – mostly, but not exclusively, nonconformist and Welsh speaking. With its rapid growth and terraced housing, perhaps more so than any other Gwendraeth Valley village, Tumble shared characteristics with contemporary mining communities that had sprung up almost overnight in the Rhondda and other valleys to the east. The difference was the extent to which Tumble was able to absorb the influx of new settlers while retaining its language and culture. It remained connected with its rural Carmarthenshire heritage most obviously in the continued dominance of the Welsh language but also its village identity – one of a string of distinct villages, separated by farmland, along the length of the Gwendraeth Valley.

These villages were bonded by a shared heritage - language, chapel, choirs, coal mining and rugby (village rivalry but also shared devotion to Llanelli Rugby Club). Later, the secondary schools in neighbouring Drefach, Pontyberem and Cefneithin and the Cynheidre super-pit maintained a strong link between Tumble and its fellow Gwendraeth Valley villages. Despite this shared heritage, from the early days of the Great Mountain Colliery, Tumble developed a distinct personality and reputation - perhaps a bit *tougher* than other villages that had grown at a gentler pace from more established settlements. Tumble's dramatic growth, punctuated with riots and religious schism, shaped that reputation for several decades. A particularly uncompromising rugby team may also have been a factor!

Figure 11. Tumble (pre-1910). Key features (from left) include the colliery reservoir, Reading Room (later the Tivoli), High Street, Railway Terrace, Ebenezer Chapel and Lodging House (author's collection).

Figure 12. Upper Tumble from Graig Llechyfedach (author's collection).

Perhaps because of this reputation, there were at least two serious attempts to re-name the village. In March 1907, a well-attended meeting held at the Reading Room located behind High Street, chaired by Mr John Davies the colliery manager (a local man), unanimously agreed to petition the Postmaster-General to 'discard the old name, "Tumble,", and to substitute the characteristic place-name, "Arfryn", as the future appellation of this growing colliery centre.' The clerk to the Parish Council was duly instructed to inform the Chief Postmaster of this change. For whatever reason – possibly wider public opinion in Tumble - this change was not made. Fortunately, a later proposal to change the name to Waddellston (after the Scottish owners of the Great Mountain Colliery) was soundly rejected by the people of Tumble who were clearly attached to their village name despite any negative image it had acquired.

With its chapels, church, schools (Bryn-du and Llechyfedach), shops and other businesses, by the end of the 19th century Tumble had grown from a hamlet into a vibrant village with a major colliery connected by a railway to international markets. The speed at which the community spirit developed, as evidenced by Wilf Timbrell, must reflect a strong common culture (particularly language and chapel) and the camaraderie from working and living together in a demanding environment. Coal mining continued to dominate through the decades of the 20th century. An industrial survey, undertaken for the County Development Plan in 1951, recorded that 2,872 men of the village were employed in coal mining – 76% of the total male workforce.

2.Jac Ty-isha – A Reluctant Hero

In October 1843, John Hughes of Ty-isha Farm Tumble was tried with two companions at the Cardiff assizes. Jac Ty-isha, as he was known locally, was found guilty of having shot at Captain Charles Fredrick Napier, Chief Constable of the Glamorgan Constabulary, 'with malice aforethought to kill and to murder him', during the attack on the Pontarddulais gatehouse. The Jury recommended mercy on account of his good character, but Jac was sentenced to twenty years transportation to Tasmania. He was just 25 years old and, after his transportation, he would not see his homeland again. Jac had pleaded not guilty to the specific charges against him. His sentence was harsh, but he did not deny his involvement at Pontarddulais and he was undoubtedly one of the leaders of the Rebecca Riots.

Born in 1819, Jac was the oldest of seven children of Morgan and Mary Hughes who were tenant farmers at Ty-isha – a substantial farm in Tumble of some 142 acres. Morgan Hughes was a deeply religious man and did not support his son's involvement in the riots, but he was strongly supported and encouraged by his mother. Jac had the qualities of a born leader and, unusually for the time, he was literate in both English and Welsh. The London Times reporter who attended his trial described him as 'a hale, powerful, and good-looking young farmer.'

Figure 13. Mary Hughes, Jac Ty-isha's mother.

The Rebecca Riots

The Rebecca Riots began in the summer of 1839 and, having died down for over three years, broke out again in 1842, with greater violence and lasting through to the following year. Jac Ty-isha features in this second phase. The rioters became well-known for wearing costumes, whether as a disguise or for effect, including women's clothes. They rode their farm horses across the countryside at night leaving the police and military dumbfounded as to when and where they would strike next. Their chosen name, the children of Rebecca, possibly drew inspiration from the Bible: *And they blessed Rebekah and said unto her, let thy seed possess the gates of those which hate them. Genesis, xxiv, 60.*

The underlying causes of the riots went deeper than just a dislike of the tollgate system. In the early to mid-19th century small farmers in west Wales were hit by bad weather at harvest time, increasing rents and taxes raised to pay for workhouses, all causes of discontent. In his definitive account of the Rebecca Riots and the circumstances leading up to them, David Williams (*The Rebecca Riots*) describes how the early 19th century had seen a breakdown in the social structure of rural Wales with government and administrative systems that were no longer fit for purpose. The hated network of tollgates, set up by the Turnpike Trusts to raise funds for the provision and upkeep of roads across the country, gave a tangible focus for this more general discontent and sense of unfairness. There were some 11 different Turnpike Trusts operating around Carmarthen alone, with tolls levied every time someone passed through one of the several gates.

The cost of moving livestock and essential faming supplies, such as lime and animal food, became more than impoverished farmers could bear and discontent inevitably turned into anger. A cart load of lime costing 2s 6d or 3s at the kiln could incur tolls of 5s or 6s for transporting less than 8 miles. The carts carrying the lime did do considerable damage to both the turnpike roads and other local roads that carters used to avoid paying tolls. Much of the anthracite mined in the Tumble area (including at the Ty-isha mine) would have been used to burn limestone in kilns to make the lime much needed as a fertiliser on the heavy soils on the Gwendraeth Fawr Valley. Considerable quantities of lime were produced just a few miles from Tumble in the parish of Llanddarog, on the turnpike road from Carmarthen to Swansea.

The second phase of unrest came to a head on 19 June 1843 when a crowd of over 2,000 marched to attack the Carmarthen workhouse where they were dispersed by charging Dragoons. The following month, the distinguished Colonel Love, veteran of Waterloo, patrolled the countryside of Carmarthenshire. He had been warned that the Porthyrhyd gate and the house of Mr Thomas at Cwm-mawr would be attacked on the night of 21 July. These attacks did not happen, but the patrol's movements were watched closely by locals in the villages and hamlets they passed through, with guns fired to let others know the patrol had moved on. One of these hamlets was Tumble. David Williams records that 'Within an hour after the troops had passed the spot, the colliers of Tumble destroyed a gate near the village' – the likely gate in Upper Tumble is shown on the 1813 and 1831 maps marked T.G. (figs. 1 and 2).

On 25 August 1843, 3,000 men and women congregated on Mynydd Sylen just five miles from Tumble. As well as farmers, the crowd included hundreds of colliers who had sacrificed a day's pay to be there. The meeting agreed a series of resolutions on tolls but finally 'pledged itself to discountenance all nightly meetings [euphemism for the tollgate attacks] by every means in its power.' The sincerity of this pledge was questioned not least because of the vociferous support it had received from the notorious ruffian Shoni Scubor Fawr. Whatever the intention, it did not have the stated effect. The London Times journalist present at the meeting reported sympathetically on the plight of the small farmers who, in many cases reluctantly, saw no option other than to rise against the inequities that were challenging their ability to make an even modest living.

The attack on the Pontarddulais gatehouse

On Wednesday 6 September 1943 in the afternoon, the local magistrates received a tip-off that there would be an attack on the Pontarddulais and Hendy

gatehouses. This came from Miss Hannah Edwards of Gelliwernen who, on hearing that the attack was to take place that night, had sent a servant on horseback to Llanelli with a note to the magistrate, William Chambers Junior, who in turn sent a messenger to Swansea to inform Captain Napier, Chief Constable of Glamorgan, of the impending attack, and a further request to Major Parlby in Carmarthen for cavalry support. Chambers Jnr., with 20 men of the 76th Regiment of Foot, set out to defend the Hendy gate apparently without knowing that Captain Napier was going to lead his men to Pontarddulais.

Figure 14. Captain Napier. Courtesy of Glamorganshire Archives and South Wales Police.

The Rebeccaites arrived sometime after 12 o'clock, on a clear moonlit night, accompanied by bugle calls and the firing of guns (probably not loaded with shot) and rockets. They numbered some 100-200, mostly on horseback and in disguise with blackened faces. Captain Napier and his officers and men arrived at Pontarddulais at about half past twelve and waited in a field about 400-500 yards from the gatehouse from where they could hear horns blowing and see flashes of guns. They were accompanied by the Penllergaer brothers (members of the influential Dillwyn Llewellyn family) – John Dillwyn Llewellyn, who became a pioneering photographer, and Lewis Llewellyn Dillwyn, a magistrate and later Swansea MP for 37 years, along with their brother -in- law, also a magistrate, Matthew Moggridge. Both the Dillwyn family and Moggridge had interests in turnpike trusts.

Figure 15. Commemorative plaque on Mynydd Sylen (author's collection).

GREAT MEETING ON MYNYDD SYLEN MOUNTAIN, CARMARTHENSHIRE, ON FRIDAY. —See next page.

Figure 16. Mynydd Sylen meeting, Aug 1843. London Illustrated News (author's collection).

THE PONTYBEREM GATE, DESTROYED.

Figure 17. The Pontyberem Gate, Destroyed. London Illustrated News 1843 (author's collection).

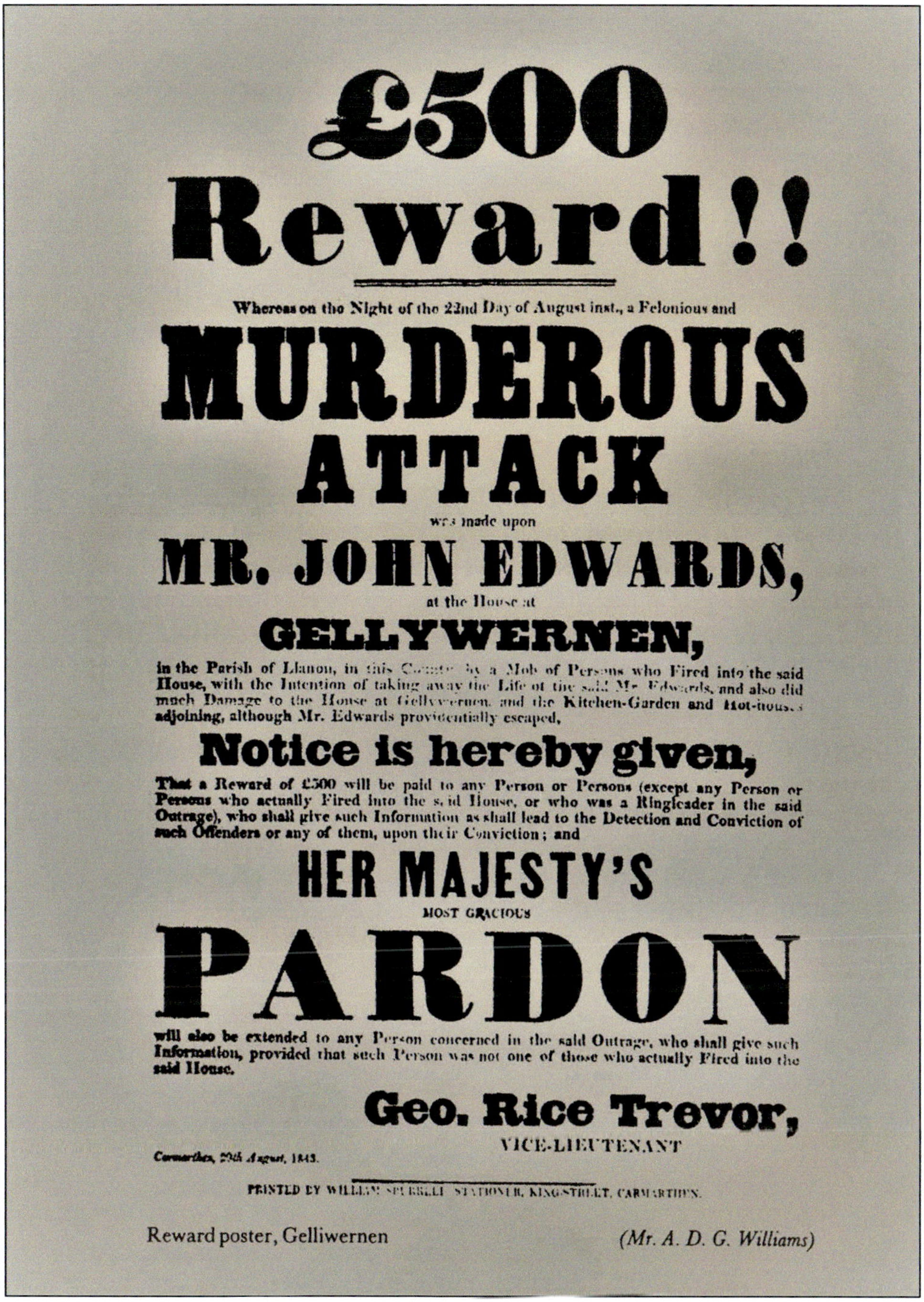

£500
Reward!!

Whereas on the Night of the 22nd Day of August inst., a Felonious and

MURDEROUS
ATTACK

was made upon

MR. JOHN EDWARDS,

at the House at

GELLYWERNEN,

in the Parish of Llanon, in this County by a Mob of Persons who Fired into the said House, with the Intention of taking away the Life of the said Mr. Edwards, and also did much Damage to the House at Gellywernen, and the Kitchen-Garden and Hot-houses adjoining, although Mr. Edwards providentially escaped,

Notice is hereby given,

That a Reward of £500 will be paid to any Person or Persons (except any Person or Persons who actually Fired into the said House, or who was a Ringleader in the said Outrage), who shall give such Information as shall lead to the Detection and Conviction of such Offenders or any of them, upon their Conviction; and

HER MAJESTY'S

MOST GRACIOUS

PARDON

will also be extended to any Person concerned in the said Outrage, who shall give such Information, provided that such Person was not one of those who actually Fired into the said House.

Geo. Rice Trevor,

VICE-LIEUTENANT

Carmarthen, 29th August, 1843.

PRINTED BY WILLIAM SPURRELL, STATIONER, KING-STREET, CARMARTHEN.

Reward poster, Gelliwernen   (Mr. A. D. G. Williams)

Figure 18. This reward notice effectively put a price on Jac Ty-isha's head.

It was about 12.50pm before the police and magistrates moved towards the gate which they found already being destroyed. Napier claimed he shouted 'stop' several times. There was then a general skirmish between the police and the Rebeccaites, with shots fired by both sides. (The police, supported by the magistrates, claimed to have found evidence of shot marks – 'one charge of gun-shot' - in the window frame of the gutted toll house.) The important and highly controversial issue to emerge was - who had fired the first loaded shot? The London Times correspondent reported the view of local people that the police had started the shooting, but the police evidence consistently pointed the finger at the rioters. Captain Napier claimed that volleys were fired at his men, yet no policeman was hit or wounded by shot and only two guns were taken from the rioters.

In his accounts of events, Napier described how the alleged three leaders (later identified as Jac Ty-isha, John Hugh and David Jones) had ridden towards him firing their guns, and that the person he believed to be Jac (Napier's identification of the *Rebecca* is qualified at best) had shot directly at him. In response, he had shot Jac's horse causing him to be thrown to the ground. Napier then claimed that on moving closer to the tollgate he encountered the man who he believed had fallen off his horse and attempted to take him into custody. The two scuffled and one of the police sergeants, Jenkins, intervened and shot the *Rebecca* in the arm from about a yard away. Napier failed to take Jac (if that is who he was) into custody at this point giving the reason that he had been hit on the head. Jac's two companions were also wounded with David Jones (aged just 20) suffering sabre cuts to the head and John Hugh (a married man a year older than Jac) badly shot in the arm. All three men were arrested.

The police and accompanying magistrates had clearly been expecting a gunfight. One of the magistrates, Lewis Llewellyn Dillwyn, proudly gave evidence that he had entered the field with four pistols (two loaded in his hands), had shot a horse through its ribs at point-blank range, and struck the rider - later identified as David Jones - with his pistol. In Court, Sergeant Jenkin produced as evidence a gun loaded with powder and large shot which he said had been taken off an unidentified man during the fight. Following a second volley from the police, other than the captured men, the 'mob' had fled.

Ivor Griffiths (*Pontarddulais Town Council, Local History*) describes how William Chambers on hearing gunfire from Pontarddulais took his soldiers to the Black Horse Square to intercept rioters. This almost ended in an incident of *friendly fire* as his contingent met a troop of the 4th Light Dragoons on their way to the Hendy gate. William Chambers' soldiers formed a line across the road ready to fire. Fortunately, the moon emerged from behind clouds illuminating the uniforms of the advancing cavalrymen and disaster, or at least huge embarrassment, was avoided.

This is how Lewis Llewellyn Dillwyn described the events of the day in his diary:

> *Last night in consequence of information we received of an intended attack upon the Pontardulais gate I drove over to Penllergare at ½ past*

8 o'clock with M Moggridge – there we met Napier with Peake & 5 Policemen – at ½ past 10 J.D.L, M Moggridge, Napier, Peake, 5 Policemen & myself set out & went along the common to Pontardulais when within a short distance of the Gate we waited under a hedge and a little before 1 A.M. a Rebecca mob attacked the gate & tollhouse –our party upon attempting to seize some of the rioters met with a desperate resistance but soon put them to flight capturing 3 of the rioters from ½ an hour to an our afterwards the Dragoons came to our assistance from Swansea,& a party of infantry from Llanelly arrived having taken 4 of the Rioters who were escaping –the 3 prisoners we had taken were after some delay placed in a Phaeton as 2 of them were very badly wounded and escorted by the dragoons into Swansea – I then returned home to P between 6 & 7 A.M. ... at 11 A.M. I went into Swansea to a turnpike meeting.

Figure 19. Commemorative plaque at Pontarddulais bridge (author's collection).

Examination by the Swansea Magistrates

On 12 September, the accused men were taken from Swansea gaol (*House of Correction*) to be examined by magistrates at the Town Hall. The Times reporter described their appearance: 'Jones, who appeared in a dying state on Thursday, seemed to have recovered surprisingly. Hughes (the Rebecca) was pale and thoughtful; while John Hugh, who stood before the court in a dress he had on at Pontarddulais at the riot, seemed very alarmed, and apprehensive of the consequences which would probably be the result of his unlawful conduct.' Captain Napier had made this detailed deposition which was reproduced in the Times:

> *In consequence of information I received, I proceeded, accompanied by Superintendent Peake, two sergeants, and four police constables, to Pontardulais. We arrived a little before 1 o'clock on Thursday morning. Just before we entered the village, I heard a noise as if of a body of men on the other side of the river, which separates the two counties. I also heard horns blowing and a great many guns fired off. I also heard a voice like that of a woman call out – "Come, come, come," and a voice like the mewing of cats. Those sounds appeared to proceed from the direction of the Red Lion Inn, which is at a short distance from the Pontardulais turnpike-gate. Immediately after this I heard a voice call out allowed – "Gate," and in a very short space of time afterwards I heard a noise as if the gate was being destroyed. I then proceeded with my officers and men towards the gate, on coming in full view of the gate, I observed a number of men mounted on horseback and in disguise. Some had white dresses over them; others had bonnets on. Most of them appeared to be dressed like women, with their faces blackened. A portion of the men were dismounted, and in the act of destroying the gate and toll-house. About three of the number, who appeared to take the lead, were mounted having their horses' heads facing the gate with their backs towards me. At this time there was a continuing firing of guns kept up by the parties assembled. I immediately called to my men to fall in and proceeded towards the parties who were on horseback and who appeared to be taking the lead and called upon them as loud as I possibly could to stop. I used the word "Stop" three or four times. Upon coming up to them one of the mounted men, who was disguised as a woman, turned around and fired a pistol at me. I was close to him at the time. I moved on a few paces, and a volley was then fired by the parties assembled in the direction of myself and my men. I should say the volley was fired at us. This was my impression at the time. I then endeavoured to take the parties, the three mounted men in particular, into custody, and myself and the men met with considerable resistance from them and other parties. The three men on horseback road at us as if they intended to ride us down, and get us out of the way. The three prisoners, John Hughes, David Jones, and John Hugh were amongst the parties assembled on this occasion, and were*

taken into custody after very considerable resistance on the part of John Hughes and David Jones. When taken into custody John Hugh was dressed in what appeared to me to be a gown and a bonnet, having something stuck in it, which then had the appearance of a feather, and his face was blackened. The other two prisoners were dressed in white. I saw the prisoner David Jones with a stout stick in his hand, with which I saw him aim a blow at Mr. Lewis Llewellyn Dillwyn, a magistrate, who had accompanied us; but whether the blow took effect or not I cannot state. After the pistol had been fired at me and the volley in the direction of myself and my men, I discharged a pistol at, and shot the horse upon which the man was mounted who had fired his pistol at me; my men returned the fire of the parties and a general skirmish then took place, in which a number of shots were fired on both sides, but in a short space of time the rioters dispersed. Three of the horses ridden that night by some of the parties assembled were detained and are now in my custody. After the parties had dispersed, I found that the turnpike-gate, with the exception of the posts, had been broken down and destroyed. The gate-house was gutted, the windows, window frames, and door driven in, and a portion of the wall of the house pulled down. I found the marks of small shot on the sash of one of the windows of the toll house. I also found on the ground near the toll-house, amongst the ruins of the gate, two sledge-hammers, two crowbars, a pickaxe, and a number of sticks, which I directed my men to take possession of.

Cross examined, he maintained that:

To the best of my belief the prisoner John Hughes is the person who fired at me. I believe him to be the man who took the most active part in the commencement of the affray, from his dress and the appearance of his figure altogether. There was but one man completely covered with white that I saw, and that one was the prisoner John Hughes, to the best of my belief. To the best of my belief, the prisoner John Hughes is one of the three persons who rode at us.

Sergeant Thomas Lewis corroborated Captain Napier's version of events adding that when he had searched the captured John Hughes he had found two powder flasks, each half full of powder, a shot-belt containing a quantity of shot, and 5 shillings sealed in a piece of paper addressed to 'Mrs or Miss Rebecca'.

PC Peter Wright described how he had seen John Hugh fire a gun at the police, 'He was the first man I saw fire.' (At the trial, he confirmed that the man was not Jac.) Like Jac, Hugh fell from his horse and, according to PC Wright, threw his gun to the ground before leading his horse away. PC John Price said that he 'took the prisoner John Hugh off his horse and gave him in charge of Sergeant Jenkins.'

PC William Williams described his altercation with David Jones in the tollhouse claiming that the prisoner had hit him with an iron bar and that he had responded by striking him on his head with his cutlass (he later managed to injure himself with his own cutlass), and went on to give evidence in court that he had been ordered by Napier 'to notice this man *[Jac]* above the rest' suggesting that Jac had been singled out early during, or even before, the confrontation. PC John Price described how he had arrested Jac:

> *John Hughes was on horseback in front of the mob when I reached the gate. He had a white cloak over his body, a white cloth over his hat, and a red handkerchief tied around his neck. He had a gun in his hand, which I saw him fire towards us. He had also a tin horn. I was from 10 to 15 yards distant from John Hughes when he fired. The mob ran away and I followed and took Hughes into custody, just by Pontardulais-inn.*

The magistrates concluded (probably correctly) that Jac Ty-isha, was the leader of the rioters – the *Rebecca*. The authorities claimed that, as well as ammunition, Jac was carrying a threatening letter and five shillings wrapped in a piece of paper indicating that it was intended as a contribution to Rebecca and other sums of money possibly intended to pay the rioters. He was charged with shooting at Captain Napier with intent and his two companions with aiding and abetting him. All three were refused bail and committed for trial at the assizes.

Jac's arrest did not bring an end to the disturbances. The Rebeccaites returned to Hendy just three days after the Pontarddulais attack and set fire to the tollhouse, a thatched-roof cottage. Sarah Williams, the elderly gatekeeper, either intentionally (to stop her identifying one of the perpetrators) or inadvertently, was shot and died while trying to save her belongings. Local sympathy remained with the Rebeccaites and the old lady was accused of having behaved foolishly. The coroner's jury delivered the verdict that she had died from her injuries but that the cause of those injuries was unknown. The local reaction to this incident, with the continuing support for the Rebeccaites despite the possible murder of a 75-year old woman, was one of the reasons why Jac's trial was moved to Cardiff.

Trial and Sentencing

The capture of Jac, a Rebecca leader, caused great interest. Rather than the usual criminal process, the government appointed a special commission to try the prisoners. The members of the commission were an elderly judge, Baron Gurney, who was known for taking a hard-line, and a more sympathetic and younger man, Sir Cresswell Cresswell. The trial took place on 26 October 1843. The seriousness with which the government viewed the disturbances is clear from the Attorney General, Sir Frederick Pollock, personally leading the prosecution accompanied by the solicitor general. Jac and his companions were ably defended by Matthew Davenport Hill, Recorder of Birmingham, noted law reformer and radical (he had armed himself with a gun in 1832 in case he needed it against the Duke of Wellington's men) supported by two other barristers and Mr Hugh Williams, a Carmarthen solicitor, a radical and Chartist.

Figure 20. Sketch of Baron John Gurney (1832, unknown artist). Portrait of Sir Frederick Pollock, 1st Baronet (1783-1870) by Samuel William Reynolds.

Appointing the jury proved challenging. Several farmers asked the high sheriff of Glamorgan to remove their names from the jury list because they feared reprisals. They need not have worried as Pollock resisted having any farmers on the jury which was eventually drawn from gentlemen and tradesmen mostly from Cardiff and Merthyr Tydfil. In his address to the jury the Attorney General gave the prosecution's version of events at Pontarddulais. He drew the jury's attention to:

> ... the appearance of the mob, and to the manner in which they had provided themselves with arms and implements of destruction. It appeared that some of the mob were disguised, so as to give them the appearance of women - they were arrayed in female attire, they had their faces blackened, and many of them had arms. Shots were fired, and in one instance, where a gun had been taken, it would be shown that it was loaded, and then the marks of shots would be proved to them to have been visible on the toll-house. It would be also shown that the mob had implements of destruction of various kinds. Sledges, hammers and pickaxes were found upon them. With these weapons the work of destruction was commenced. All the windows were broken, and the endeavour was made to pull down the house. That work would have been

33

> *completed but for the interruption given to it by Captain Napier. There could be no doubt of the riotous character of this assembly.*

He then addressed the questions of what role Jac Ty-isha had played in the direct confrontation between him and Captain Napier and the controversial claim that Jac, on being taken to the tollhouse and searched, had been found to have incriminating items in his possession:

> *It was the object of Captain Napier, by wounding the horses, to prevent the flight of the parties. Captain Napier fired at the prisoner's horse, and the prisoner came down, and then came into personal conflict with Captain Napier, and in that conflict was wounded, as you see. A shot was fired by the mob, which was returned by a volley on the part of the police. There was much confusion, and the parties fought hand to hand. ... There were found upon him a quantity of gunpowder and two powder flasks, a shot belt, with shot in it, some copper caps and a paper, of which the following is a translation: "David Jones, come with your armour and covering and assist me on Wednesday next, or else you shall not have more or further notice," and signed "Becca.".*

Baron Gurney advised the jury that they should find Jac guilty of the charge against him regardless of whether it was he who fired the shot at Captain Napier:

> *It is not necessary to prove that the person charged was the very man who pulled the trigger; all who banded themselves together in such numbers with weapons, indicative of such purpose, are equally guilty. Had any of these shots taken fatal effect, they would have had to answer for the crime of murder; and this consideration should lead rash and unthinking people to some reflection as to the danger they incur by engaging in such enterprises, which may, and continually do, involve them in more atrocious crimes and more condign punishments than they had anticipate.*

David Williams (*The Rebecca Riots*) notes that the Attorney General 'conducted the case with great moderation' and even passed a note to Hill congratulating him on how well he had made the case for the defence (Hill had spoken at great length with a focus on mitigation of punishment). The note read: 'You have just delivered one of the most appropriate, eloquent, and feeling addresses I have ever heard. I dared not, could not, add a word.' Despite Hill's efforts, the jury found Jac guilty but recommended mercy on the grounds of his previously good character. This fell on the deaf years of the judge who sentenced him to twenty years' transportation. On the advice of their solicitor, John Hugh and David Jones then pleaded guilty and were each sentenced to seven years' transportation. The judge justified the greater severity of Jac's sentence partly on the grounds that 'He appeared to be one in a station of society far above the rest – one not likely

Figure 21. Matthew Davenport Hill.

to be misled by others, and yet upon the evidence proved to be a leader, if not the leader of this lawless multitude.'

Matthew Hill argued that John Hugh and David Jones should be given lenient sentences because of how the men had already suffered including through injuries. David Jones, as well as the sabre cuts to his head, had also been shot (Jac refers to David Jones having been wounded by 'slugs' in his first letter home from exile). The accounts of any serious injury suffered by John Hugh (including that, like Jac, he had been shot in the arm) are contradictory.

Conspiracy or confusion?

There was much sympathy for Jac over the harsh sentence he had been given regardless of his guilt or innocence of the specific charge on which he was convicted. The Welshman, in a powerful leading article, strongly criticised the judge for punishing Jac for, it claimed, the behaviour of others rather that his own actions:

> *What in the name of common sense and of common justice has the punishment of prisoners to do with the conduct of the country? Is it supposed that the conduct of a farmer's boy, a lad who can hardly write his own name [this was not true but no doubt was said for effect], can influence the conduct of the million men who inhabit the country called Wales.*

The article also addressed the issue of who fired the first shot:

> *But the general opinion is that the Glamorgan policemen and magistrates were the original aggressors, and that it was from them that the first act of violence proceeded. There doubtless was an onslaught on the flying peasants.*

There is at least an impression that the evidence against Jac might have been contrived. Why, for example, did Jac, as it was claimed, still have some of the incriminating evidence (including percussion caps) on him on being taken to Swansea gaol and searched by the governor – wouldn't these have been confiscated by the police when he was first taken into custody? Why did the police and the two magistrates (one of whom at least seems to have been particularly gung-ho carrying four pistols) delay confronting the Rebeccaites at the tollgate? Was it a strategy to catch the *Rebecca* and other leaders red-handed? Also, the identification of Jac by Captain Napier as the man who had shot at him was not fully convincing – he repeatedly used the qualifying term 'to the best of my belief'. As well as any deliberate intention to set-up Jac for a very serious charge, there was also the fog of battle and the scope for confused identity, particularly with John Hugh given the similarity of name, the fact that both men were accused of shooting at the police from horseback and both had their horses shot from under them.

 Another factor may have been Napier's social ambitions which had been dented a few months earlier at Cwm Cile farm, Llangyfelach. He and his men were on a mission to arrest two Rebeccaite brothers. At the farm they were set upon by the whole family with the mother and sisters to the fore – the mother with a poker from the fire and one of her daughters with a reaping hook with which she cut Napier's head. David Williams describes how Napier was ridiculed in the London papers for what one publication described as his fight 'with the old woman with the frying pan.' This would have been a huge blow to Napier's pride as a determined social climber. Capturing a true Rebecca red-handed, with the prospect of huge reputational and monetary gain, must have seemed an attractive way to get his career back on the right path.

All that said, the evidence given by several police officers was mostly consistent with Napier's version of events, and the able defence team for the three men on trial should have been able to expose any wilful collusion or manipulation of the evidence. The overall impression, however, is that the police and magistrates were determined to get a high-profile conviction of a *Rebecca* for as serious a charge as possible, both to send a powerful deterring message to others in the movement and to further their own reputation. The police and magistrates allowed a situation to develop that gave the best chance of that result and, whether pre-planned in advance or not, specifically targeted Jac Ty-isha. The evidence (for example the behaviour of at least one of the magistrates) suggests that they went in at Pontarddulais heavily armed and looking for a fight rather than to protect property and restore order. Judge Gurney's instruction to the jury that they should find Jac guilty as charged, whether or not they believed it was he who aimed and fired at Captain Napier, cemented their success.

Petitions, admiration and remorse

Jac swore an oath to his father, after his conviction, that he had not been armed with either a gun or pistol at Pontarddulais. This was before he was transported, and it may be that he was still hoping to influence the reception of the petitions for his sentence to be reduced. The harshness of the sentence rather than the jury's verdict was the main grievance. It is telling that the jury, in finding Jac guilty, had asked the judge to show mercy in his sentencing and ten members had followed this up with a petition to the Queen on his behalf. Other petitions for mercy were also submitted and, to help their cause, while in Cardiff jail the three convicted men issued an appeal to their friends, in Welsh and English, to keep the peace. (They realised that any reduction in their sentences depended on the good behaviour of the Rebeccaites.) Jac's mother wrote to Queen Victoria but did not receive a reply. A public meeting at Llannon also pleaded on his behalf. The family tradition is that Jac took the blame for another. If this is correct, John Hugh, to whom Jac may have related, seems the most likely and unintentional benefactor.

Jac and his two companions rejected inducements to turn informer against fellow rioters, which may have been a factor in the failure to gain reduced sentences. In stark contrast, Captain Napier, who may well have been at least partly responsible for the extent of the violence at Pontarddulais, was lavishly rewarded by the Prime Minister with the sum of £500 (Pollock's attempt to get a knighthood for John Dillwyn Llewellyn was turned down by the government). The three convicted men were taken by packet ship to Bristol on route to Millbank prison, London. By coincidence, the great industrialist, Sir John Guest, was on the same packet and was much impressed by Jac's dignity and lively intelligence. In her diaries, his wife, Lady Charlotte Guest, recorded that she had shed a tear for this 'free child of the mountain, with all his faults and all his gradiences and all his romance.'

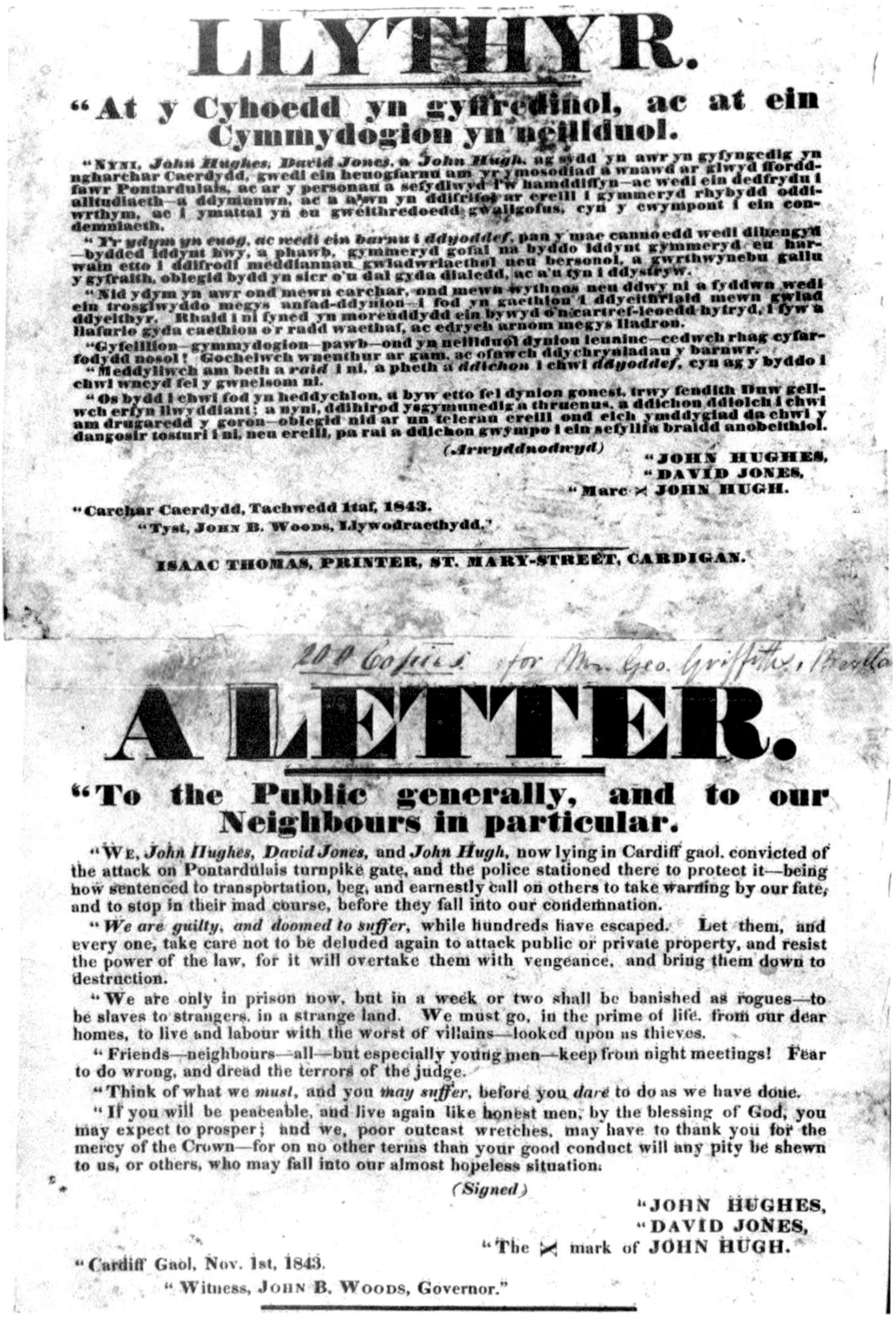

LLYTHYR.

"At y Cyhoedd yn gyffredinol, ac at ein Cymmydogion yn neillduol.

"NYNI, John Hughes, David Jones, a John Hugh, ag sydd yn awr yn gyfyngedig yn ngharchar Caerdydd, gwedi ein heuogfarnu am yr ymosodiad a wnawd ar glwyd ffordd-fawr Pontardulais, ac ar y personau a sefydlwyd i'w hamddiffyn—ac wedi ein dedfrydu i alltudiaeth—a ddymunwn, ac a bawn yn ddifrifol ar ereill i gymmeryd rhybydd oddi-wrthym, ac i ymattal yn eu gweithredoedd gwallgofus, cyn y cwympont i ein con-demniaeth.

"Ty ydym yn euog, ac wedi ein barnu i ddyoddef, pan y mae cannoedd wedi dihengyd—bydded iddynt hwy, a phawb, gymmeryd gofal na byddo iddynt gymmeryd eu har-wain etto i ddifrodi meddiannau gwladwriaethol neu bersonol, a gwrthwynebu gallu y gyfraith, oblegid bydd yn sicr o'u dal gyda dialedd, ac a'u tyn i ddystryw.

"Nid ydym yn awr ond mewn carchar, ond mewn wythnos neu ddwy ni a fyddwn wedi ein trosglwyddo megys anfad-ddynion—i fod yn gaethion i ddyeithriaid mewn gwlad ddyeithhr. Rhaid i ni fyned yn mhoreuddydd ein bywyd o'n cartref-lecedd hytryd, i fyw a llafurio gyda gaethion o'r radd waethaf, ac edrych arnom megys lladron.

"Gyfeillion—gymmydogion—pawb—ond yn neillduol dynion ieuninc—cedwch rhag cyfar-fodydd nosol! Gocheiwch wneuthur ar gam, ac ofnwch ddychrynladau y barnwr.

"Meddyliwch am beth a raid i ni, a pheth a ddichon i chwi ddyoddef, cyn ag y byddo i chwi wneyd fel y gwnelsom ni.

"Os bydd i chwi fod yn heddychlon, a byw etto fel dynion gonest, trwy fendith Duw gelli-wch erfyn llwyddiant; a nyni, ddihirod ysgymunedig a thruenus, a ddichon ddiolch i chwi am drugaredd y goron—oblegid nid ar un teleran ereill ond eich ymddygiad da chwi y dangosir tosturi i ni, neu ereill, pa rai a ddichon gwympo i ein sefyllfa braidd anobeithiol.

(Arwyddnodwyd)   "JOHN HUGHES,
                                           "DAVID JONES,
                                 "Marc ✕ JOHN HUGH.

"Carchar Caerdydd, Tachwedd 1taf, 1843.
       "Tyst, John B. Woods, Llywodraethydd.'

ISAAC THOMAS, PRINTER, ST. MARY-STREET, CARDIGAN.

200 Copies for Mr. Geo. Griffiths, Brallo

A LETTER.

"To the Public generally, and to our Neighbours in particular.

"WE, John Hughes, David Jones, and John Hugh, now lying in Cardiff gaol, convicted of the attack on Pontardulais turnpike gate, and the police stationed there to protect it—being now sentenced to transportation, beg, and earnestly call on others to take warning by our fate, and to stop in their mad course, before they fall into our condemnation.

"We are guilty, and doomed to suffer, while hundreds have escaped. Let them, and every one, take care not to be deluded again to attack public or private property, and resist the power of the law, for it will overtake them with vengeance, and bring them down to destruction.

"We are only in prison now, but in a week or two shall be banished as rogues—to be slaves to strangers, in a strange land. We must go, in the prime of life. from our dear homes, to live and labour with the worst of villains—looked upon as thieves.

"Friends—neighbours—all—but especially young men—keep from night meetings! Fear to do wrong, and dread the terrors of the judge.

"Think of what we must, and you may suffer, before you dare to do as we have done.

"If you will be peaceable, and live again like honest men, by the blessing of God, you may expect to prosper; and we, poor outcast wretches, may have to thank you for the mercy of the Crown—for on no other terms than your good conduct will any pity be shewn to us, or others, who may fall into our almost hopeless situation.

(Signed)   "JOHN HUGHES,
                                           "DAVID JONES,
                            "The ✕ mark of JOHN HUGH.

"Cardiff Gaol, Nov. 1st, 1843.
       "Witness, John B. Woods, Governor."

Figure 22. The confession of Jac Ty-isha (John Hughes), David Jones and John Hugh.

A new life in Tasmania

In March 1844, the three men embarked on the convict ship *London* arriving in Tasmania seventeen weeks later. A week after their arrival, on 17 July, David Jones died in Hobart. Jac Ty-isha and John Hugh were placed on probation on Maria Island (off the coast of Tasmania, or Van Diemen's Land as it was then known). The wounds he had received at Pontarddulais were a likely contributing factor, exacerbated by the gruelling voyage. John Hugh survived his seven-year sentence.

Convicts spent an initial period on *probation* - usually two years, in public works' gangs on stations outside of the main settlements – before being given a pass to work for wages within a set district. Jac did get in trouble while on probation for misconduct but was also commended for capturing a fellow prisoner who had escaped. He was given his *pass* on 18 July 1846 and indentured. Again, his behaviour was not perfect - he was given 14-days solitary confinement for purportedly feigning illness - but he obtained a *ticket of leave* on 22 February 1853. On 19 May 1857, aged 37, he was given a conditional pardon with over six years of his sentence still to be completed but, rather than return home to Wales (if that was an option), he became a timber cutter and employed workers. At the age of 45, he married and had two children. His wife - aged just 25 at the time of their marriage, an Irish Catholic and a 'free woman' - died young or possibly absconded (there is no record of her death in Tasmania). His daughter, Lydia, married a silver miner and had a large family. Her descendants visited Tumble several times.

In October 1867 Jac was accused of having stolen a bill of exchange valued £26 10s but was found not guilty by the jury at the Supreme Court of Tasmania. He was successful in business and made a large profit from the sale of land. He remained in exile for the rest of his life. It is questionable whether returning home was an option but, if it was, he may well have chosen not to do so because of the quality of life he was enjoying and a lingering, unjustified, sense of shame. More than 50% of convicts escaped from Tasmania to Victoria. Jac did not even attempt to do so, perhaps because of his determination to live within the law.

Jac's letters home to his family are reproduced by Phyllis Brazell in her article in the 1990 edition of the *Carmarthenshire Antiquary*. They show remorse for his involvement in the riots and particularly for the pain he had caused his parents. The first is his farewell letter to his father written shortly before his departure for Tasmania. At the time of writing, Jac was expecting to be sent to New South Wales. He claims, not convincingly given their injuries, that he and his two fellow prisoners were in good health and spirit. He had bought or been presented with books at Cardiff and was looking forward to buying a dictionary. He was also looking forward to a better life than he had enjoyed in Wales. On his involvement at Pontarddulais he asserted: 'I take my oath before God that I had neither gun nor pistol in my possession.'

Figure 23. Jac Ty-isha in Tasmania.

The next letter to his father and mother was written in October 1844 from Tasmania. He informs his parents that he had arrived safely in Obertown, Tasmania on 10 July 1844, and been transferred to Maria Island. He assures his parents that things had turned out better than he had expected, despite his not deserving it. He mentions the sad death of David Jones, 'by the wounds he received by the slugs.' He comments on the delightful scenery and how in winter the trees lost their bark rather than their leaves and he lists the birds and animals he had seen and could name. He asks his mother not to worry about him and undertakes never again to stray from the righteous path.

Twenty years later in April 1864, seven years after his conditional pardon, he wrote again to his father. He laments the sad loss of family members back in Wales. He explains that he is writing sitting in chair resting his leg – he had nearly severed his big toe which was being held on by a little bit of skin (an occupational hazard as timber cutter). Otherwise he claims to be perfectly well. He comments on others who had returned to Wales having served their period of exile only to return voluntarily to Tasmania because of the severity of the climate in their homeland. He says that his intention remains firm to return home and to be buried alongside his family and friends (it is doubtful that this would have been possible under the terms of his sentence). He mentions having met another Welshman at Stanley and having been 'rather agitated with the grog.' He concludes that he had heard nothing of John Hugh.

In 1890, aged 71, he wrote to his brother, Will Hughes. He describes his deep religious commitment and his concern to know whether his brother shares it.

He mentions that his daughter, Lydia, had married and that she and her husband lived about 90 miles away with their daughter. He shares with his brother his success in having bought land two years earlier and having sold part of it for £320. He mentions that his son, Willie, had a farm alongside his but goes on to admonish him for not living there and for being wild and 'the only bad boy in our family.' He adds that he is no longer fit for hard work and was planning to live with a former estate owner for whom he had worked as an overseer for 14 years. Having sold his horse, he had walked 16 miles one day and 10 miles the day before to worship.

He looks back on his life in exile – how he had made two small fortunes, kept a public house ('drinking and fighting and all sorts of wickedness'), before finding deep religion. He says that he does not envy his brother having to live in the cold climate of Wales and how the country he now lives in flourishes with farming and tin and mineral mining. He speculates on why he does not receive more letters from home and wonders whether this is because he had brought disgrace to the family.

Figure 24. Jac Ty-isha with his daughter Lydia and son William in Tasmania.

Shoni Scubor Fawr

The loyalty shown to his comrades by Jac was not exhibited by the notorious ruffian, and former prize-fighter, John Jones, known as Shoni Scubor Fawr. Shoni, for personal gain rather than a commitment to the cause, attached himself to the Rebecca movement. His closest accomplice was David Davies - Dai'r Cantwr (a poet, ballad singer and former preacher from Llancarafan who had settled in Pontyberem). Shoni and Dai's favourite haunt was the Stag and Pheasant pub down the valley in Five Roads, but Shoni met his fate in the inn at Tumble. This is how the London Times reported the arrest of Shoni:

> *The two men who I informed you the other day were taken into custody by the police for the outrage at Pontyberem, at the Gwendraeth works, have to-day undergone a long examination in the Governor's room at the county gaol, before Colonel Trevor, the Vice-Lieutenant of the county, and a bench of magistrates. Mr. Hugh Williams defended the prisoners. One of them, who is nicknamed "Shoni Scyber Fawr," a noted boxer from Merthyr, is a very lawless and desperate sort of fellow of great physical strength. He was apprehended at a public-house among the hills by ten of the London police, whilst sitting on the settle with his loaded gun beside him. The police walked in, quietly seized him, pinioned him, and put a pair of handcuffs on him in a moment, before he was aware what was their intention. He then, however, kicked furiously, and attempted to seize his gun with his shackled hands, but he was easily overpowered. He is known to have led many of the gate-breaking expeditions, though there is no evidence of it.*

Shoni had been engaged as a 'paid hard-man' by the leaders of the Rebecca rioters. He took part in the destruction of several turnpike gates but then extorted money from farmers by threating to reveal their Rebecca activities. David Williams describes him as being at the 'lunatic fringe' of the Rebecca movement and certainly not meriting the comparisons made between him and Robin Hood. In 1843 Shoni and his accomplices ran amok particularly in the Gwendraeth Valley. On the evening of the Mynydd Sylen meeting (25 August 1843), Shoni got drunk and was seen wondering around Pontyberem with a gun and wearing some sort of petticoat that had once been white. Ending up at the New Inn, he fired at a man named Walter Rees, sending shots through his hat.

There were further incidents, including an armed attack on the house of Mr Newman of the Gwendraeth Ironworks in Pontyberem who, as the Times reported on 5 October 1843, 'was threatened with vengeance if he would not discharge his managing clerk, who had given offence by his activity in endeavouring to discover the perpetrators of a recent robbery.' On 23 September Shoni, Dai'r Cantwr and others set out from the Stag and Pheasant in Five Roads to attack the home of the managing clerk, Mr Slocombe. When they arrived at the house in Pontyberem, Mr Slocombe was not home but they made a threat through his wife that if he did not leave the area within a week he would be a 'head shorter', adding that no Englishman should be a manager in Wales. They left firing their guns into the house.

Shoni and Dai's luck ran out when a miner from Trimsaran turned informer. A division of the Metropolitan Police, eighteen men led by Inspector Tierney, with a local guide were sent to scour the area in search of Shoni and his accomplices. They searched every public house and other possible haunt of the two accused men and at around midnight apprehended Dai'r Cantwr in a public house near Five Roads. The following day, at about eleven o'clock, Shoni Scubor Fawr was captured 'at a place in the mountains, called the Tumble.' Both the prisoners were taken to Carmarthen for examination.

Although there were numerous charges against Shoni, he was tried, at the Carmarthen Winter Assizes on 27 December 1843, for the New Inn incident only. Dai was tried for his role in destroying Spudders Bridge (between Trimsaran and Kidwelly). Both were found guilty and sentenced to transportation – Shoni for life and Dai for 20 years. They left the dock laughing - both continued to inform on their former associates. They were chained together for the journey to Millbank jail – Dai remained cheerful but Shoni, the 'hard man' who had taken on John Nash (the champion of Cyfarthfa) in a bare-fist fight, is said to have sobbed bitterly.

Dai travelled to Tasmania with Jac and other lighter class offenders on the *London*. Shoni was consigned to the *Blundell* with other worst class offenders. In Tasmania, Shoni was constantly in trouble for stealing, refusing to work and for being drunk and disorderly. He was sentenced to various periods of hard labour and solitary confinement. Unlike Jac, he did not make the most of the new opportunity Tasmania gave him.

Jac Ty-isha's legacy

The Rebecca Riots and Jac's sacrifice were not futile. They played an important part in persuading the government to call a Commission of Enquiry to explore the grievances of the Welsh farmers. Legislation in 1844, known as Lord Cawdor's Act, amended the turnpike trust laws in Wales and lessened the burden of the tollgate system. This was followed by further legislation which helped relieve the condition of peasant farmers in Wales.

The cause of the Rebecca rioters was undoubtedly just. Sir Thomas Frankland Lewis, who chaired the commission on the Rebecca Riots, and the subsequent commission that abolished the turnpike trusts, delivered in 1852 'an eulogium to the Rebecca rioters.' He acknowledged that the tollgate system had become an oppression leaving poor farmers seeing no alternative to taking the law into their own hands. He commented on the skill and fidelity with which the rising had been organised and concluded that the Rebecca Riots were 'a creditable portion of Welsh history.'

A letter sent by Jac's granddaughter, Gertrude Thorne aged 12, after his death to Ty-isha farm records a fitting epitaph from a Waratah newspaper: 'Mr Hughes was one of our earliest pioneers. He was a deeply religious man, ever ready to assist anyone who needed help ... He was always cheerful and smiling and his friends at Waratah will miss him.'

Jac Ty-isha was a reluctant hero – a leader in a just fight against poverty and oppression who nevertheless had the humility to regret his role in the violence. His statue, erected by the people of Tumble near his old home, is much deserved. As a young famer and ploughman from Tumble, Jac had faced the combined might of the county and national establishment. He had stood trial and been severely sentenced, not so much for the crimes he may have committed, but as the personification of the whole of the Rebecca movement.

Figure 25. Jac Ty-isha's statue near his old home in Tumble (author's collection).

3.Early Coal Mining

On the 6 June 1601 Rowland Lloyd of Gelligatrog, Meinciau signed a lease for 'the grant of mines and every vein of coal at Dynant.' This may well be the first reference to coalmining specifically in the neighbourhood of Tumble but the anthracite seams of the Gwendraeth Valley and Mynydd Mawr areas had been mined at least as far back as the 16th century. When John Leland, the Royal Antiquary, visited the area between 1536-39, he contrasted its 'stone coles' (anthracite) with the softer, bituminous coals of Llanelli, noting that the 'Port of Burry' was the main harbour in Carmarthenshire for the export of coal. Later, the surveyor of the Duchy of Lancaster Lordships in Wales (1609-13) recorded that local 'tenants' on the Mynydd Mawr common had a long tradition of coalmining primarily to fuel the production of lime for use as a fertiliser.

Before the huge changes that came with the Industrial Revolution, mining was mostly on a small scale exploiting readily worked outcrops, and often seasonal, with miners also working on the land as tenant farmers or labourers. Through the 19th century more intensified coalmining developed in the Gwendraeth Valley and on the Mynydd Mawr, possibly accelerated by the Enclosure Act of 1811. By 1833 'the Tumble Colliery' was sufficiently important to be referred to as part of the case for extending the Kidwelly and Llanelly Canal to Cwm-mawr. This growth culminated in the opening of the Mynydd Mawr Colliery to exploit, on a truly industrial scale, the rich legacy of the complex local geology.

The lie of the land

Tumble sits on the anthracite belt of the South West Wales coalfield where geology and time have produced the best anthracite in the world - dense and hard with a carbon content as high as 97% in the deepest, most compressed measures. West Wales anthracite is very different to the softer bituminous coals of the *Valleys* to the east. It burns with little flame and smoke and has a higher energy density than softer coals. The Gwendraeth Valley offered the opportunity to exploit vast deposits of top-grade anthracite, but new transport connections were needed. In July 1869, *The Welshman*, prompted by the completion of the first section of the railway from Burry Port to Cwm-mawr, eulogised on the extent of the largely unexploited wealth:

> *We hardly know how to convey an adequate notion of the thick and extensive seams of coal in the Gwendraeth ... If we take a section at Mynydd Mawr, the top of the Valley, we find ... thirteen seams, making a total thickness of thirty-nine feet ten inches. ... and at Tanybanc, four miles still lower, nearly opposite Pontyates, the seams give a total of 28ft. 2in. It should be borne in mind that these seams ... are spread between the sandstone and other rocks, with wonderful regularity. A fault occurs here and there, and the seams occasionally vary in quantity and quality,*

but they are not capricious like lodes of lead or copper ore. One can with these facts comprehend more perfectly the immense storage of coal in the valley ... let us look at the seams found in the Cross Hands Colliery, Mynydd Mawr, stating the thickness of each. There are altogether nine,— The Great Vein 9ft; Wyrdd 3ft; Stanllyd 6ft; Grace Uchaf 4ft; Grace Issaf 3ft; Brassllydd 3ft; Gwendraeth 3ft; Five Quarters 3ft 6in; Rhasfach 1ft 6in. These are all workable, making a total of thirty-six feet.

M.R.C.. Price, in his paper *The Coal Industry at Tumble* (*The Carmarthenshire Antiquary Transactions 2013*), describes the SW-NE lie of the Gwendraeth valley with the strata generally dipping to expose seams along the south-eastern side of the valley, and on the Mynydd Mawr above Pontyberem. This geology made the use of slants or drifts the most obvious method of mining, with shafts for ventilation. The more important faults, including the Tumble and Dynant Faults, broadly follow the dip of the strata, running roughly at right-angles to the outcrop of the coal seams. The *Geological Survey of the South Wales Coalfield* published in 1907 gives a detailed account of the Tumble area. It refers to the Tumble Fault as one of a series of faults cutting the coal measures roughly between Cross Hands and Pontyberem and explains how the alternation of hard and soft strata gives rise to the ridges and hollows between Cross Hands and Tumble with the cockshot-rock forming:

a striking feature at the top of the scarp east of Tumble ... exposed in some crags and quarries traceable from Pant-gwyn at Cross Hands as far as Tumble ... At Tumble the measures are cut by the Tumble Fault, a down-throw east of some 200 yards ranging southwards towards Llannon and northwards to the Carboniferous Limestone at Foel Castell.

The Tumble Fault, like others of its kind, causes severe distortion and overlap of the coal seams. The Great Mountain No.3 shaft (later part of the Cynheidre complex)) at Cwm Sinkings, just over a mile from Tumble along the railway towards Llanelli, encountered no fewer than eleven coal seams or veins. This complex geology presented commercial opportunities but also severe engineering and safety challenges as mining evolved from local people exploiting surface outcrops to later deep workings to exploit the highest-grade anthracite.

K.C Treharne (*Glofeydd Cwm Gwendraeth*) comments that the quality of Tumble coal was particularly high. With the added advantage of the Wyrdd and Fawr (Big Vein) seams running close to the surface, Tumble featured prominently in the early development of the coal industry in the Gwendraeth Valley. There were mines in Upper Tumble, at Llechyfedach and Llech-yr-Odyn, in the early 19th century, but the vicinities of Bethesda Road and Dynant (between Tumble and Pontyberem) became the main centres in the decades leading up to the opening of the Great Mountain Colliery.

Dynant area

In 1625 Ieuan Griffith acquired mineral rights at Dynant neighbouring the holdings of John Jones of Coalbrook and Glan Gwendraeth. The families of these two men were in the forefront of early coal mining in Tumble and Pontyberem. Three main seams were exploited - the Gras, the Fawr and the Wyrdd. K C Treharne refers to mining in the area early in the 19th century, along the length of the footpath that follows the Afon Goch between Bethesda Road and Dynant Fawr farm. (He mentions that some twenty men may have lost their lives in these early workings, but this is not substantiated.) For a period from the middle of the 19th century, mining operations in the area were supervised by Evan Treharne described in the 1851 census as a 'Colliery Agent' with 26 men working for him. (In 1855 he acquired rights from the Stepney estate to work coal in the Tumble area.)

This early mining culminated in about 1857/58 with the opening of Dynant Fawr colliery on Stepney estate land worked by Jones & Sons. It seems to have comprised one or two drifts and an airshaft down to the Gras vein. M.R.C. Price notes that the workings were shallow but still prone to flooding (not helped by being located close to the banks of the stream) and encountered faulting in a little more than 150 yards. The colliery is recorded in the government's *Lists of Mines* as Dynant Fawr in every year from 1857 to 1863. It then disappears from the listings until 1875 when it is recorded simply as Dynant and remains so until 1889. There is no official record of a colliery named Dynant Fawr after 1863.

There were several changes of ownership over this period and there may have been separate operations using the Dynant name at the same time. There are references to D.H. Harris & Co running the mine in 1875, and in 1877/78 the Dynant Colliery Co. was established. At that time, the Dynant mining operations were connected to the Burry Port & Gwendraeth Valley Railway near Pontyberem. In 1888 Dynant employed fewer than 80 men and was abandoned the following year. Wilf Timbrell states that the end was brought about by flooding and that an attempt made by divers called in to get the pumps going failed. He also reminiscences about how he and his friends would throw stones down the old pit and count until they struck the water. He may have been referring to the airshaft, but accounts of fatal accidents suggest that, as well as the drifts, there was also at least one mine shaft in the area. On 14 December 1849, *The Welshman* reported:

> *An inquest was held in Llannon parish on the 7th inst., before Wm. Bonville, Esq., coroner, upon the body of John Jones, son of William Jones, of Mount Pleasant, near Cross Hands, who was accidentally killed at the Dynant colliery by a quantity of coals failing out of a basket upon the head of the deceased while ascending a coal-pit from his day's work.*

30 years later, on 11 July 1879, the same newspaper reported on an inquest, held at Tyr Eithen, Llangendeirne, on the death of David Thomas, Caegarw-fach, coal miner killed at Dynant Colliery:

> *From the evidence it appeared that on Saturday, the 28th ult., deceased and a man named William Williams went down the shaft of the pit to their work, and remained down till about 6 o'clock, when the signal was given to haul up the cage. While being hauled up a jerk was felt, and the cage was found to be loose. Williams succeeded in taking hold of the "guide" or wire rope, but deceased and the cage were precipitated to the bottom of the shaft. Williams thereupon slid down the "guide" and found deceased lying at full length beside the cage, quite dead.*

Smaller workings in the Dynant area included Clos-y-Bedw and Pwll Jones. Both closed in about 1847 as thicker coal seams along Bethesda Road attracted more attention. Nantddu, an independent colliery mining the Fawr, was located close to Dynant Fach farm and closed in 1918.

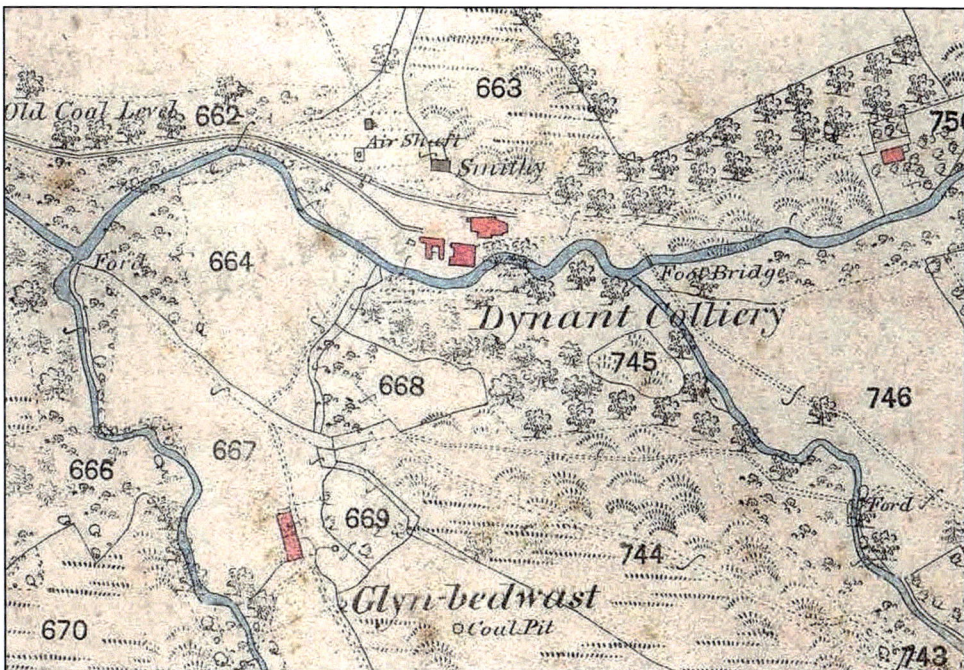

Figure 26. Dynant Colliery. OS map (25 inch), 1st Edition county series, surveyed 1878-79, published 1880. Features include the Air Shaft, Tramroad towards the canal/river and older coal workings. Courtesy of Phil Cullen.

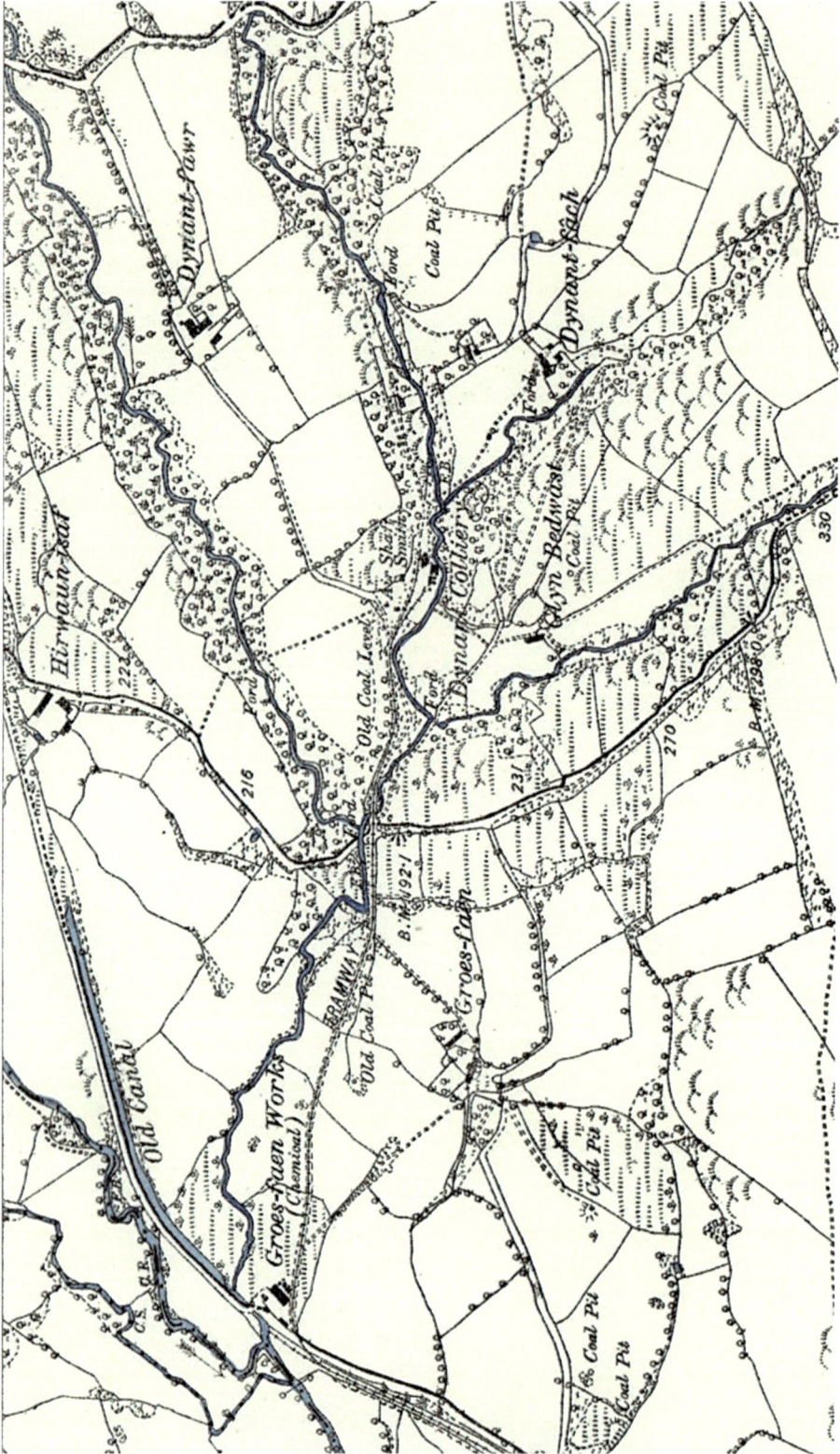

Figure 27. Wider view of Dynant area O.S. 1888. With permission of NLS.

Bethesda Road area

In the mid-19th century, the main colliery in this area was Dyffryn Araul. (Confusingly, early mines were sometimes individually or collectively also referred to as *Tumble colliery*.) The owner was Rev. David Parry Thomas of Cwm-mawr House who leased it to two other coal proprietors - Evan Evans of Coetcae, and his brother in law, Lewis Davies. This seems to have been a fraught relationship. There were issues with the payment of lease charges culminating in David Parry Thomas taking over the operation of the mine. On 22 May 1863 he was turned out by Evan Evans and his friends. A court case was brought against Evan Evans, Lewis Davies and Evan Lloyd (a collier) who were accused of having 'unlawfully and forcibly obtained possession of the Tumble colliery as situated at Llannon, the property of the Rev. David Parry Thomas.' The case was settled peacefully.

The 1841 and 1851 census records show that Dyffryn Araul was occupied by Archibald Skim, a collier, and his family. By 1851 Archibald Skim's two eldest sons were also colliers. Individual mine workings associated with Dyffryn Araul included: Pwll yr Engine (named after the engine that raised water from a stream near Guthrie House), Pwll y Balans (where coal was raised by balancing one bucket of coal with one bucket filled with water brought by a sluice from the other side of the road), Pwll Ladder and Pwll Walters.

Other mines in the area included: Pwll yr Odyn (a group of three mines), Pwll y Cooper (worked by a company from Llanelli who made barrels) and Pwll Blaen-gwawr which used fires to drive the ventilation. At Ty-isha colliery, on a site later incorporated within the garden of a house named Pistyll-gwyn, Morgan Hughes of Ty-isaf worked the slant with six men, two boys and two women. (KC Treharne gives other examples of women working the mines including in Pontyates in the 1840s.) One of the men, Issac y Llety, was paid one shilling and three pence a day. A small mine known as Tumble Colliery was opened in 1857 to the east of Bethesda Road with a drift into the Wyrdd. On 12 June 1863, the Welshman included this advertisement:

> ... to SELL BY AUCTION, without the slightest reserve, at the THOMAS ARMS HOTEL, LLANELLY, on THURSDAY, the 18th of JUNE, 1863, at Two o'clock, p.m., the whole of the valuable PLANT and MACHINERY, together with the LEASE (13 years of which are un- expired), of the TUMBLE COLLIERY, containing a surface area of about 300 acres, situate in the Parish of Llannon, in the county of Carmarthen. The Colliery is in present work, and abounds in well- known and valuable veins of Anthracite Coal and Iron-stone, and offers an eligible opportunity for investment.

Six years later, on 19 February 1869, the same newspaper reported the suicide of the part-owner of Tumble Colliery:

> *William Davies, aged 67, of Tumble Shop, Tyissa, in the above parish, committed suicide on the 12th inst., under very melancholy circumstances. The deceased, who was registrar of births, &c., for part of the Llanelly Union, was also part owner of the Tumble Colliery. It appears that the water had broken in [to the mine], and he got into difficulties. He seems to have been thoroughly upset by the pecuniary state of his affairs, and according to the evidence of his wife he lost his appetite, and could not rest at night. He seems to have kept his troubles, however, to himself; but on the 11th inst. he received a letter intimating that a writ would be served on him the following day, in respect of a bill for £100, which had been renewed more than once. This, it is supposed, quite unnerved him, and on the following morning be arose about 6 o'clock, and, going to an outhouse, hanged himself. The inquest has been held by James Rowlands, Esq., and a verdict that the deceased destroyed himself by hanging, while labouring under a fit of temporary insanity was returned.*

The colliery was closed by 1870 but there may have been some later re-working (some of the pits along the Bethesda Road were not filled in for many decades – as recently as the 1950s/60s the former factory in Bethesda Road burnt waste in an abandoned pit). As the sad fate of William Davies illustrates, flooding was an ever-present risk to mines in the area. In 1852, at the near-by Gwendraeth Colliery in Pontyberem, twenty-eight colliers were underground when water broke into the pit from old workings. Twenty-six men and boys lost their lives.

Figure 28. The incline at Pont Andrew forming part of the tramway (or 'horseway') leading from Tumble to connect with the former canal and later railway (author's collection).

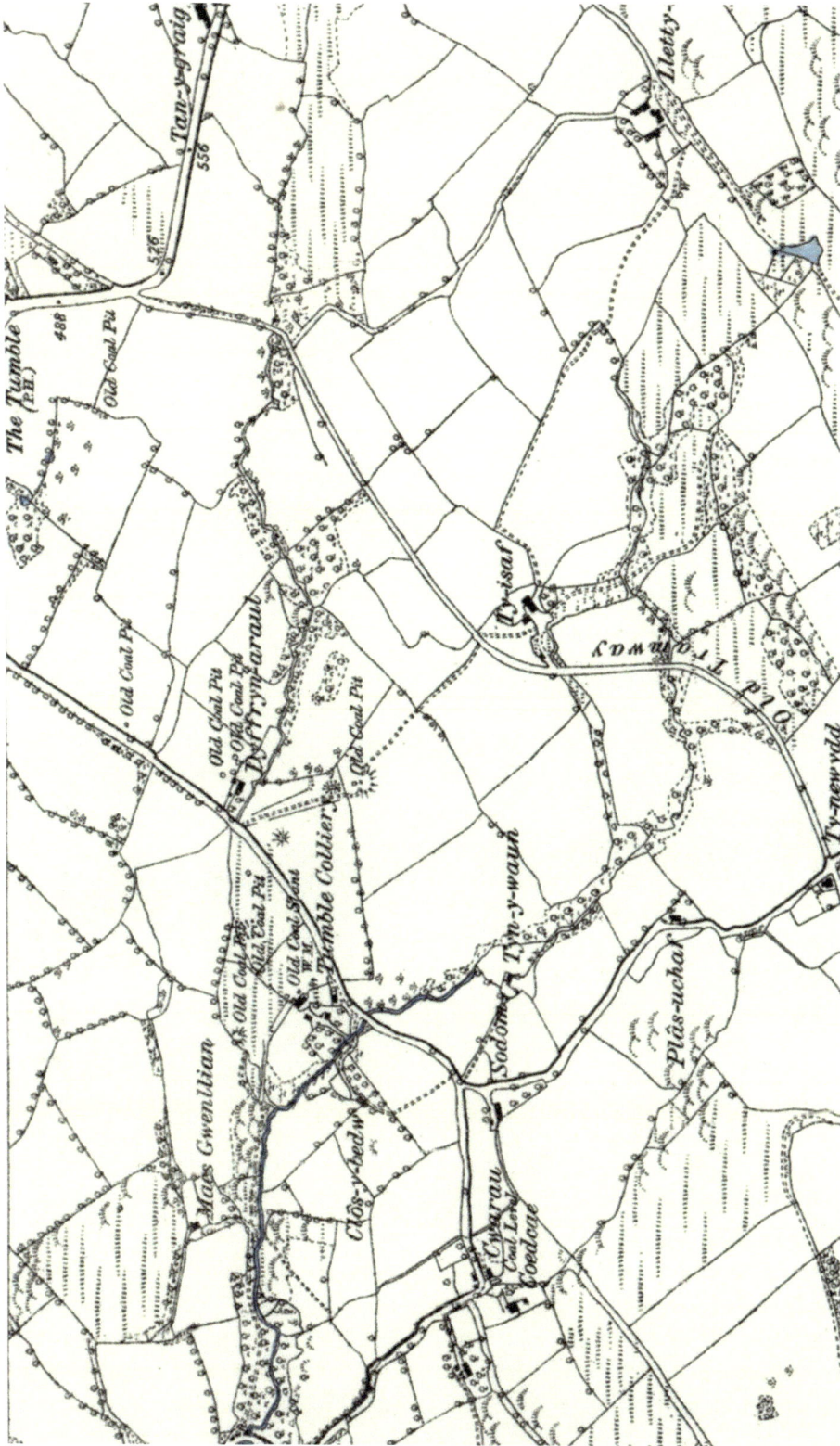

Figure 29. OS Map 1888. Bethesda Rd. area. With permission of NLS.

Transporting the coal

Some of the coal from the Bethesda Road and Dynant mines was taken by cart to Carmarthen or more locally to fuel limekilns and for household use. The value of coal in a cart was usually one shilling. At Porthyrhyd the carts met with others from Cwm-y-Glo (near Cross Hands). From the late 1830s transport by canal became another option. Small-scale working of outcrops and local marketing of coal continued. Ronald Rees (*The Black Mystery – Coal-mining in South-West Wales*) gives this example on the role played by a young Tumble girl:

> One of Anne Lewis's earliest childhood memories was waking to the thudding noise made by her father as he dug coal beneath the house. She was brought up on a farm between Tumble and Pontyberem, in the Gwendraeth Valley. Coal lay all around and, once or twice a week, around 1850, her father rose at 4:30am to dig coal from a roadside outcrop. Ann, who was then 10, arrived at 6:30 with a donkey, properly panniered, onto which she and her father loaded a hundredweight or more of coal. She then set off for Carmarthen, to meet, along with other donkey driving exporters and small colliery entrepreneurs, the Bristol boat at Carmarthen Quay. On the way, in response to requests from roadside cottages, she might have sold a few lumps of coal for a penny or two.

The 1851 census records Ann Lewis, aged 9, living in a small, 30-acre farm, Whitland, at the very lower end of Bethesda Road as it turns right towards Pont Andrew. Her father, Thomas Lewis, is shown as a farmer but Anne's three older brothers are all colliers.

The mining operations at Dynant were connected to the Kidwelly & Llanelly canal and then the Burry Port and Gwendraeth Valley railway that replaced it. Dynant Colliery itself was later also connected to the Llanelly & Mynydd Mawr railway by a rope-worked incline up which coal trucks were pulled from a winding house about 250 yards towards Tumble from the site of Cwm Sinkings. Wilf Timbrell recalls William Jones (Brynteg) telling him how he had been employed to drive the winding engine which he described as being located some distance beyond Pantyffynon farm. KC Treharne notes that there was probably a tramway (or *Horseway*), along the Afon Coch through Cwm-y-Dynant and past Pont Andrew (*Pont Hendro*), connecting the mines of Bethesda Road to the canal near Glynhebog (Pontyberem). This is now a foot path running from the far end of Bethesda Road – the possible passing places for trams were still evident at least up to the late 1960s.

It is difficult to estimate the number of men and women employed in coal mining in and around Tumble prior to the establishment of the larger collieries. The number of full-time miners was likely to be small relative to the number of farmers and farmworkers. But the distinction between miner and farmworker would not have been clear-cut as it was common for workers to be employed on both activities depending on the relative demand for labour (Ann Lewis' family at Whitland is just one example). It is, however, indicative of the growing mining community that by the time of the Rebecca Riots it was the colliers of Tumble, not the farmers, who in 1843 reportedly destroyed the tollgate in Upper Tumble. Wilf Timbrell, looking back at the early decades of the 19th century noted that many miners also owned or rented small farms and that other colliery workers and their families would help with the arduous task of haymaking.

4. Tramroad, Canal and Railways

In the 19th century major transport connections paved the way for the development of Tumble into one of the most important centres of coal production on the West Wales coalfield – the Carmarthenshire Railway or Tramroad, the completion of the Kidwelly and Llanelly Canal to Cwm-mawr and the railway that replaced it and, most importantly, the Llanelly & Mynydd Mawr Railway (L&MMR).

The Carmarthenshire Railway or Tramroad

On the 5th of November 1801, a meeting was held at the Kings Head Inn, Llannon. The outcome was a resolution to seek an Act of Parliament for the 'Intended Rail Road or tramway from the Flats near Llanelly to Castell-y-Garreg.' The Act enabling the construction of the Carmarthenshire Railway was passed on the 3 June 1802. It was only the second railway in Britain to obtain an Act of Parliament, and probably the first to become operational.

Figure 30. Alexander Raby.

Alexander Raby, the scheme's leading proponent, was a wealthy English entrepreneur who wanted to develop ironworks and collieries to exploit the mineral wealth in West Wales but was dogged by the supply and transport challenges. In the late 1700s he had invested in new dock facilities at Llanelli, later known as the Carmarthenshire Dock, with a tramroad serving it. M.R.C. Price (*The Llanelly & Mynydd Mawr Railway*) describes how the Mynydd Mawr and other hills inland offered an 'an El Dorado' for minerals, which Raby was determined to exploit. Canals from the river Loughor to Cross Hands had been proposed but ruled out because of the cost and engineering challenges.

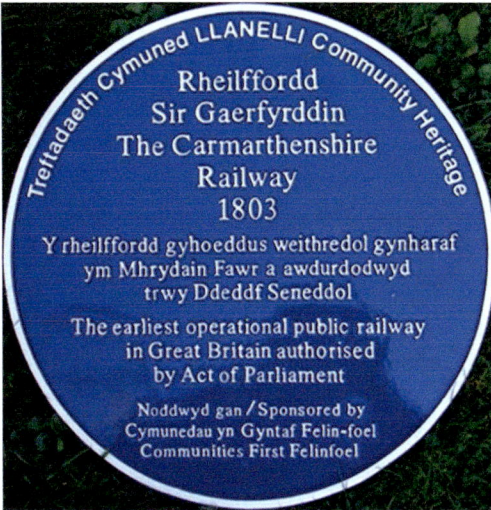

Figure 31. Plaque at Felin-foel.

Unlike most early railways which relied on local investment, the Carmarthenshire Railway had attracted outside capital (it had a London Committee). To help gain more local support, Raby undertook to use limestone exclusively from Castell-y-Garreg in his ironworks. By 1805 the line, running through Tumble, had reached Gorslas. The planned length to Castell-y-Garreg was never built - Raby ran into severe financial difficulties and was strongly criticised by shareholders for misusing Company funds to provide unauthorised branches to his own works.

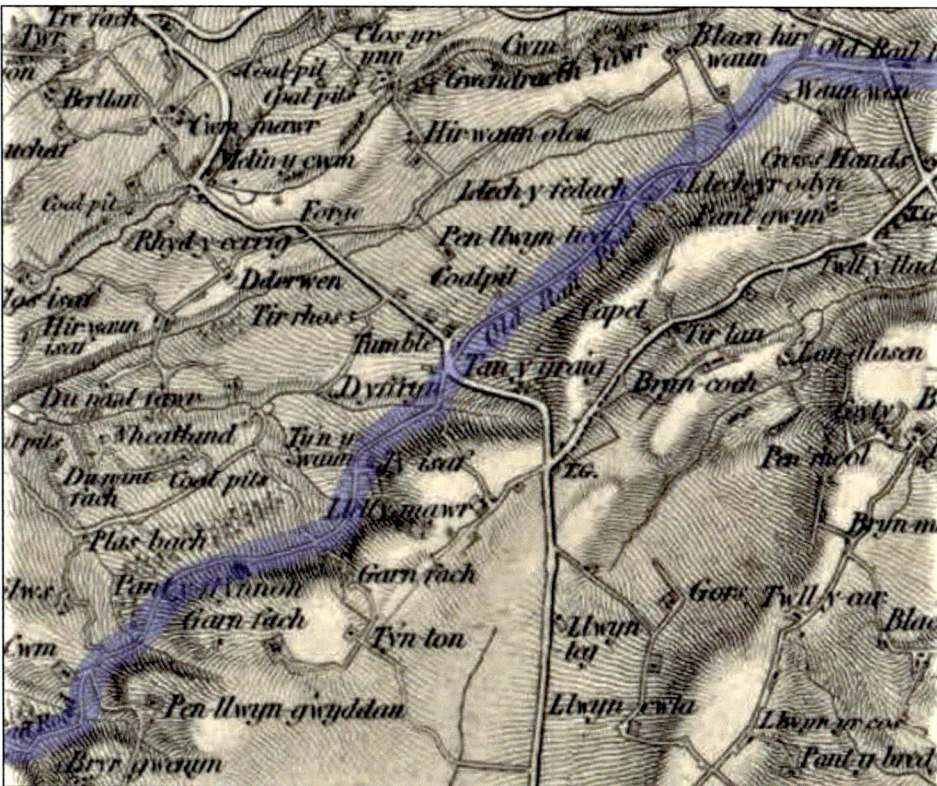

Figure 32. The route of the 'Old Rail Road' (Carmarthenshire Railway) through Tumble. Extract from 1831 Ordnance Survey map of Carmarthenshire.

During construction of the tramroad, four outcrops of anthracite were exposed near Cynheidre and exploited by the Brondini Colliery which was active until about 1827. In 1804 coal and culm were reaching the market via the Carmarthenshire Railway which was publicised as being far superior to any canal for regularity and value. From the start, however, the tramroad suffered operational challenges, including broken plates (iron rails attached to stones with 4ft. gauge) and regular derailments with horse-drawn waggons having to be unloaded before being put back on the tracks. A loaded waggon weighed 3 tons and was drawn by two horses. One journey between Llanelli and Gorslas could be made each day but farmers from the Cynheidre area who operated as carriers would sometimes break the journey about halfway so they could spend the night at home.

Figure 33. Commemorative plaque at Gorslas (author's collection).

In 1810 the Company advertised anthracite and ironstone collieries at Llech-yr-Odyn (Upper Tumble) and Hirwaun-ichaf. However, the upper reaches of the tramroad, towards Tumble and the Mynydd Mawr, were already in decline with smaller tonnages being carried each year. Traffic north of Cynheidre had probably ceased as early as 1816. In 1834, an application made to Parliament for a new Act to convert the tramroad into a 'railway for locomotive engines' stated that the tramroad was 'greatly out of repair.' In 1835 the stretch north of Felinfoel was described as 'broken up'. By the time of the Ordnance Survey map of 1830/31 (fig. 33), the tramroad was already being identified as the 'Old Rail

Road' and had become little more than a footpath to Llanelli. It did however set much of the route for the later L&MM railway.

Given its short life and operating difficulties, it seems unlikely that the tramroad had a big impact on the development of coal mining in Tumble but it did help bring attention to the importance of the coal and other mineral wealth of Tumble and the Mynydd Mawr, paving the way for the much more important L&MMR. The connection with ironstone and coal mines at Llechyfedach (Upper Tumble) is also interesting as these works have perhaps been overlooked with the later dominance of the Great Mountain Colliery in Lower Tumble. The discovery of coal outcrops near Cynheidre would impact on Tumble for the remainder of its coalmining history.

Figure 34. Sketch of the Carmarthenshire Railway by John Wynn Hopkins. Courtesy of the artist.

Kidwelly and Llanelly Canal

The next major transport development to impact Tumble was the completion of the Kidwelly and Llanelly Canal to neighbouring Cwm-mawr alongside the Gwendraeth Fawr river. In 1833, the canal company asked its engineer, James Green, to survey the route for extending the canal up the Gwendraeth Valley from Pontyates to Cwm-y-glo, near Cross Hands. He advised that:

> *The coal property above Cwm Mawr will have a ready and convenient access to the Canal at that place …. and as the Company have the power to lay down a branch Railroad from Cwm Mawr in the direction of Blaenhirwain which branch may be made to connect itself …… with the upper part of the Carmarthenshire Railway, near the Tumble Colliery. All the Coal district with which the upper part of the Carmarthenshire Railway communicates, will find its way to the head of your Canal, and hence to the new Harbour at Pembrey.*

A related proposal to re-build the Carmarthenshire Railway for locomotives obtained an Act of Parliament in 1834. The scheme did not go ahead but the plans for it may lie behind the reference in the report to connecting with the Carmarthenshire Railway near Tumble. The engineer's recommendation was accepted, and the canal was extended up the valley to Cwm-mawr via three inclined planes. R. E. Bowen (*The Burry Port & Gwendraeth Valley Railway and its Antecedent Canal*) describes the canal at Cwm-mawr and addresses the doubt raised as to whether the last incline was used:

> *The canal hit the Cwm-mawr/Tumble road where it was traversed by a classic hump-backed canal bridge. Immediately, the canal was on an aqueduct crossing the Gwendraeth Fawr river. The stonework on the aqueduct makes it an architectural gem. Once across, the canal immediately with a sharp turn eastward, entered the substantial terminal basin. This incline was completed. It seems ludicrous to suggest such a magnificent mass of engineering work did not carry a single barge.*

The construction of the canal from Capel Ifan (Pontyberem) to Cwm-mawr involved an incline at Hirwaun Isaf that raised the level by 84 Feet. The terminal basin at Cwm-mawr was 200 feet long and 45 feet wide. A huge reservoir (covering about 52 acres) to feed the canal was built at the steep-sided Cwm-y-glo (between Cefneithin and Cross Hands) to provide a continuous supply of water to work the inclines. There may have been a branch tramroad from the railway at Cross Hands towards the reservoir dam, but there is apparently no evidence of coal being transported from Cross Hands to the canal with any regularity.

The canal was opened to Cwm-mawr (or at least as far as Hirwaun Isaf) by about 1838. Whether coal was transported along the canal from Cwm-mawr is, according to Raymond E. Bowen, 'enshrouded in mystery' (by 1866 there may have been a narrow-gauge tramroad connecting Hirwaun Isaf to Cwm-mawr). There may also have been a connecting tramroad running for an unknown distance up the hill towards Tumble (the likely connection from Tumble through Cwm-y-Dynant is described in Chapter 3). The canal had a short working life. In under 30 years it fell victim to having been built as canals were losing their dominance to railways and steam locomotives. The complexity of operating the inclined planes and the threat of competition from other companies looking to build railways up the valley were likely further factors.

Figure 35. The canal aqueduct at Cwm-mawr. Courtesy of Travis Ratti.

The Burry Port and Gwendraeth Valley Railway

In the 1860s there were further attempts to rebuild, in various forms, at least part of the old Carmarthenshire Railway within more ambitious schemes. These came to nothing, but the threat of competition did prompt the Kidwelly and Llanelly Canal Co. to progress plans to convert the canal into a railway. The Welshman, on 28 October 1864, reported that a general meeting of the company had been held at which it was agreed to seek the necessary Act of Parliament (the meeting also resolved to seek funds to extend the railway from 'Cwm-Mawr

Bridge to the end of the great reservoir at Cross Hands'). The Act was passed in 1865, and the new Burry Port and Gwendraeth Valley Railway (BP&GVR) was opened for mineral traffic between Burry Port and Pontyberem in July 1869. The opening of the first section had been much anticipated by The Welshman (11 June 1869):

> It is now some nine months since the Burry Port canal was emptied and the first sod of this railway turned, amidst the liveliest demonstrations of rejoicing. At that time we gave a report of the interesting proceedings, and said a few words expressive of our faith in the success of the undertaking and confidence in those to whom the work was entrusted. Since then we have from time to time had much pleasure in reporting progress, and affirming our steadfast belief in the speedy completion of the railway, notwithstanding sundry prognostications to the contrary. The work has not been without its difficulty, but the engineer and contractors have been unwearied in their exertions and although the completion of the line has been delayed a few weeks beyond the date originally named, the public will we are sure be delighted to learn that the directors have now definitively fixed upon the opening day. On Wednesday, the 23rd instant, will be commemorated the completion of the first link in a line of railway that is intended some day to open this important valley from one end to the other, thus rendering its vast mineral wealth available to the enterprise of man. Everybody, we should imagine, would wish success to those engaged in a work of this description, and the directors and all connected with the Burry Port and Gwendraeth Valley Railway, are entitled to public gratitude for the step they have taken.

On 23 July 1869, the same newspaper gave this description of the new railway:

> Three railways once competed for the Gwendraeth mineral trade. The Old Carmarthenshire and the Kidwelly lines are not made. It is singular that the only one considered impracticable has been completed from Burry Port to Pontyberem, a distance of eleven miles. It is laid on the bed of the old canal which has been prepared for it by Mr Furniss, the contractor, who undertook the work about ten months since, and notwithstanding the heavy rains of last winter completed the first section within about a month of the specified time. We may here state that this is the first cheap railway made in South Wales, under a recent Act authorising the construction of light and inexpensive lines. The rails which weigh fifty pounds a yard are laid on massive rectangular sleepers of Baltic fir. The engines are limited to eight tons on a pair of wheels, but there is no reason why they should be less powerful than heavier locomotives, as the number of wheels can be multiplied. The line, which is substantially built, cost about £3,000 a mile, the contractor finding the capital. We went over it the other day to see for ourselves the condition in which it is left. The engine and trucks ran smoothly, the permanent way feeling as solid and

compact as any road in the country. At present no accommodation has been provided for passengers, the company judiciously attending first of all to the mineral traffic. The line begins at Burry Port, where arrangements are in progress for shipping many thousand tons a week. It then goes by a detour round the eastern shoulder of the Gwendraeth direct to Pontyberem.

The extension to Cwm-mawr was not completed until 1886. On 15 August 1878, the South Wales Daily News reported that:

The first cargo of coal from the celebrated Dynant colliery, which has only recently been connected with the Burry Port and Gwendraeth main line at Pontyberem, was shipped here on Wednesday, per "Europa" for Rochester.

In 1883 the Dynant Colliery Company sought permission to lay rails on the highway from the colliery to Cwm-mawr, but this was not granted. Passenger services were introduced up to Pontyberem in 1909, under a Light Railway Order. An extension to Cwm-mawr was put off because of the cost involved and the steep gradient, but in 1910 the company directors agreed to acquire additional land at Cwm-mawr for the provision of a station. Following substantial works, including realignment of the track, the passenger service was extended to Cwm-mawr on 19 January 1913. The public train service ended on 19 September 1953.

As collieries closed, including Cynheidre in 1989, the line went into a long period of decline. It finally closed, along with the Cwm-mawr opencast coal washery it had latterly served, in March 1996.

The Llanelly & Mynydd Mawr Railway

Alongside the development of the BP&GVR, further plans for a locomotive railway along the line of the old Carmarthenshire Railway (Tramroad) were prepared, culminating in 1875 with an Act 'authorising the building of the Carmarthenshire Mineral Railway from Llanelly to Mynydd Mawr.' The Act permitted the company to carry passengers and animals as well as goods and minerals. In 1876, the Directors of the Llanelly and Mynydd Mawr Railway (L&MMR) commissioned a survey of the mineral wealth to be won along the route of the proposed railway. The survey team, which included John Davies of Llannon Parish, recorded its findings in *Prospects for Minerals on the Mynydd Mawr*) in which it reported that on leaving the Mynydd Mawr towards Tumble:

... the next opening should be at or about Pantgwin which would be by a slant in the Big Vein and pits into the Pumpquart and lower veins. Such openings would win the Coal under Lord Crawford's farms of Pantgwin, 80 acres; Llanglasnant, 100 acres; and Bryncoch, 120 acres. Also under

Mrs Lloyd's farm of Tyrlan, 60 acres; Mr J.T. Jenkins' farm of Llechyfedach, 120 acres; and under Blanehirwain, 80 acres, the property of the late Mr. J. Lloyd Davies: Total area 725 acres. We estimate that this area contains workable Coal a quantity equal to 200 tons per day over 300 years.

Following along the course of the line towards Llanelly the next point of an opening is at the Tumble, which would be by pits, and would win the Coal under Lord Crawford's farms of Danygraig, about 130 acres; Tyryrbryn, about 20 acres; Tyissa, 120 acres; and Garnfach, about 30 acres; Mrs Lloyd's farm of Lletymawr, 90 acres; and other smaller properties about 20 acres; together making about 410 acres. At the rate of 200 tons per day, we estimate that the Coal under these properties will last upward of 230 years.

Despite the opportunity to exploit this mineral wealth, getting the work underway was far from straight forward – M.R.C. Price comments on the air of desperation that pervaded the boardroom by the autumn of 1879. On 31 October that year, shareholders voted to abandon the scheme. However, other interests lobbied in its support, including the Dynant Colliery Company who wrote in November to the L&MMR chairman stating:

In order to encourage the shareholders at their meeting to-day, perhaps you will kindly put the following before them. The Dynant Colliery Company, at the present time landing about 40 tons a day, and whose property reaches as far as the proposed line, which, if constructed, there is every probability that the greater portion of the output, which is gradually increasing, would find its way over this line.

The local support must have been welcome, but the main reason for this change of mind by the shareholders was the unexpected interest from John Waddell. A Scotsman, originally from Airdrie, John Waddell had successfully constructed railways in Scotland and England. His company, John Waddell and Sons, negotiated to build the line for payment of £60,000 - £25,000 in cash and £35,000 in shares. The Agreement was sealed on the 27 March 1880 to build a single line, with sidings and other smaller branch lines, mostly following the alignment of the old Carmarthenshire Railway. The challenges of the intersection between the railway and existing roads were considered by the Highway Board at its meeting on 16 September 1880. The report to the Board had this to say about the intersection at Llechyfedach, Upper Tumble:

At Llechyfedach I am given to understand that there is to be a level crossing. The old parish road at this place has been allowed to go out of repair, and it has for many years been taken into the fields, and all the banks taken down. The track of the old tramway has been used instead for about thirty years, and it has also been kept in repair by the Highway Board. If the railway company will lay down their rails at the back of the old tramway, a new road must be constructed for a distance of about 400 yards, through fields belonging to Llechyrodyn and Blaenhirwain, otherwise there will be no outlet at this place. The construction of the road will cost a considerable amount of money, but we have been in quiet possession of the existing road for thirty years, and have also kept it in repair during that time. Llechyrodyn farm is the property of Mrs Lloyd, Bronwydd, and Blaenhirwain of Mr Lloyd Davies.

John Waddell started work at the Llanelli (Sandy) end on 26 April 1880 and by December that year work was also underway at Cross Hands. There was concern that the railway had followed the line of the old Carmarthenshire Railway too closely and as a result was dogged by tight bends restricting the speed of travel to no more than 15mph in places. Nevertheless, on the 6 June 1881, perhaps as many as 1,000 passengers travelled by train through Tumble to Cross Hands for a picnic party and other entertainments (the return journey took well over two hours). This grand event marked the informal opening of the new railway. To get around the fact that Board of Trade consent had yet to be obtained, tickets were sold for the refreshments with travel on the train 'by courtesy of the contractors and officials of the Mynydd Mawr Railway.' The line was opened for public traffic on 1 January 1883 and connected to the Great Western Railway at Llanelli some weeks later. A goods depot and passing loop were provided at Tumble with a passing loop also at nearby Dynant. Minerals were the most important freight, but agricultural and other goods were carried to meet the needs of the small communities connected by the railway. The first non-mineral cargo carried by the L&MMR, ahead of formal opening, was a wagon load of flour for Mr Greville of Pontyberem.

Colliers had to pay to travel on the workmen's trains (until the GWR took over the line from Waddell & Sons, Tumble colliers had their fares deducted from their pay). M.R.C. Price records a conversation he had with William Davies of Cefneithin about the workmen's services in the early 1920s. The train was known to the colliers as the *spake,* suggesting that it more closely resembled the primitive railway that took men down mine drifts than a proper passenger train – 'The coaches were old and decrepit, with bare wood seats and no lights. The windows had no glass, and only sacking for cover.' There were 'stopping places' rather than proper stations and the terminus at Cross Hands was known as 'station fach'. Priority was always given to trains carrying coal, so the men often had a long wait for their train home. Unlike on the BP&GVR, passenger travel on the L&MMR was informal and limited (see Chapter 9).

The opening of the L&MMR marked the start of a new era in the history of the village. However, things did not get off to a good start. M.R.C. Price records that in 1883 the Company's finances were in a mess, it owed at least £6,000 to John Waddell & Sons, and traffic levels, with a depression in demand for anthracite being a factor, were not enough to generate the necessary income. On the positive side, it was announced that arrangements were being made to carry the output of the Dynant colliery which would provide 'a considerable increase in the revenue of the company.' These conditions gave John Waddell the opportunity to take a dominant position in the company. He was determined to make a success of the venture and invested a further £3,000 on a connection with the Dynant colliery by way of a rope-worked incline with a winding house at its head located about 250 yards from the future Cwm Sinkings shafts. Unfortunately, the colliery was soon to close because of flooding, but John Waddell's investment demonstrated his commitment to the Tumble and Mynydd Mawr area. Assured of dock improvements at Llanelli and determined to exploit it with the benefit of the new railway, John Waddell did not give up. If he had the history of Tumble could well have taken a different turn.

Post railway nationalisation, British Rail ran the former L&MM line until 1966 when it was effectively handed over to the National Coal Board. The line north of Tumble towards Cross Hands was dismantled in 1971. The line south of the village, towards Cwm Sinkings, remained, in an increasingly decayed, state for almost thirty years. This was the sad end to John Waddell's railway. In its relatively brief but highly productive life, it had transported the hard-won mineral wealth of Tumble and the Mynydd Mawr to the port at Llanelli and the world beyond. From the Great Mountain Colliery alone it had carried some 10 million tons of coal over 75 years.

Figure 36. The John Waddell locomotive was transferred from the L&MMR to the Great Mountain Colliery in 1919 and kept the name of the former colliery owner alive in Tumble for 40 years.

Figure 37. The first L&MMR bridge south of Tumble towards the former Cwm Colliery (author's collection).

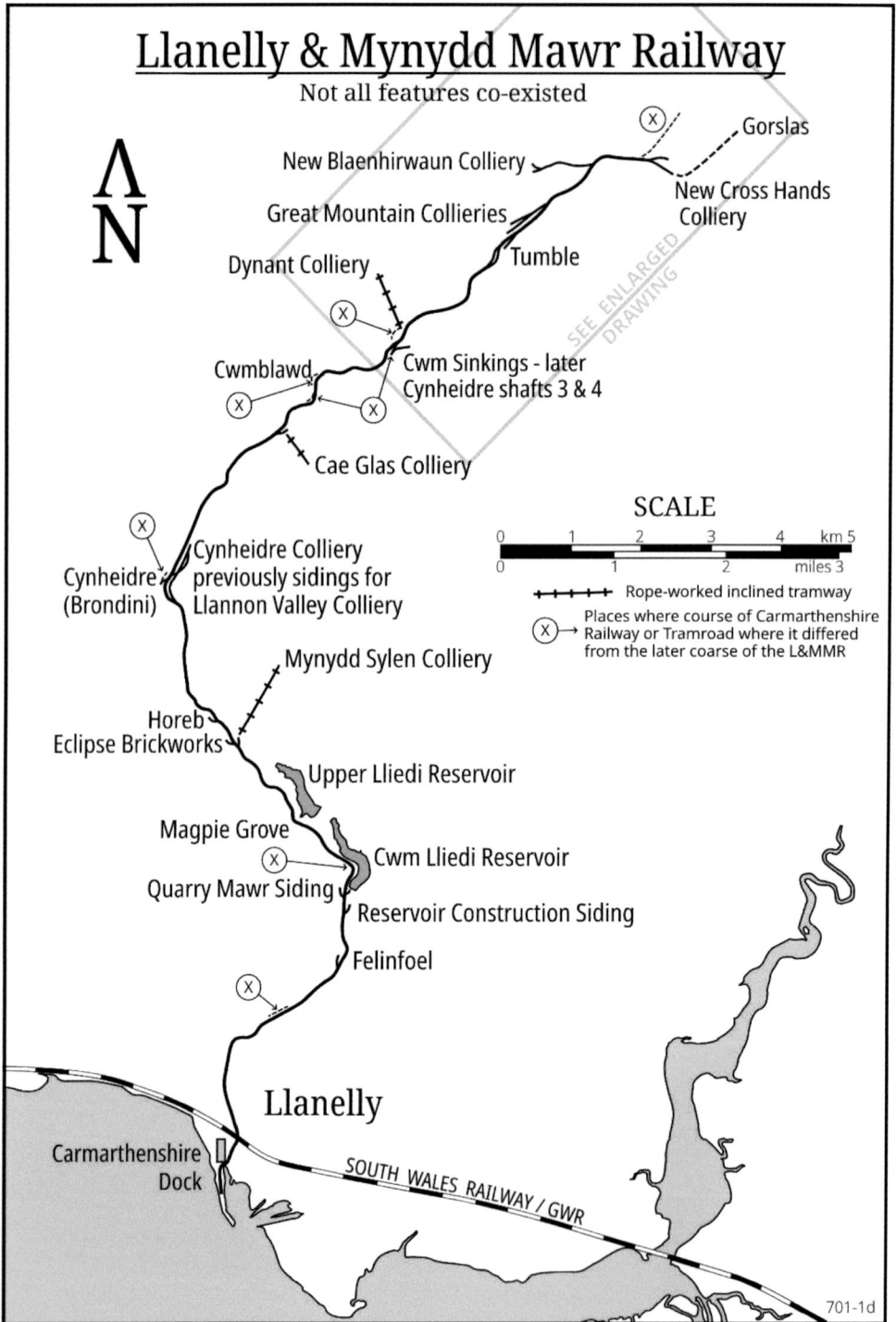

Figure 38. Llanelly & Mynydd Mawr Railway. Drawing by John de Havilland.

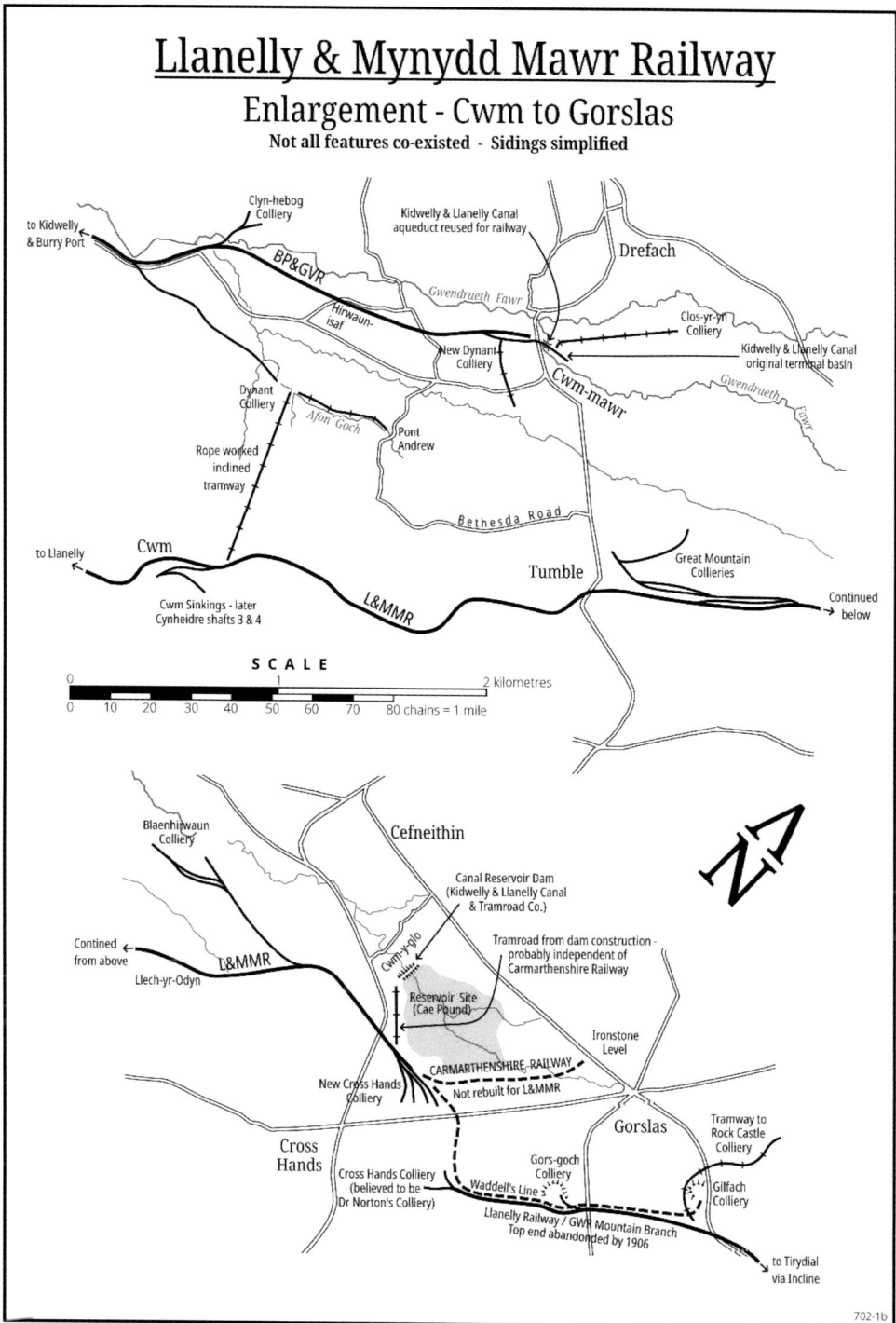

Llanelly & Mynydd Mawr Railway
Enlargement - Cwm to Gorslas
Not all features co-existed - Sidings simplified

Figure 39. Llanelly & Mynydd Mawr Railway, Cwm to Gorslas enlargement. Drawing by John de Havilland.

5.The Great Mountain Colliery

On 29 September 1886, John Waddell acquired 292 acres of land and mineral leases at Danygraig farm, Tumble. This was probably the most important event in the history of the village. His Great Mountain Anthracite Collieries Company soon began to drive what later became the Great Mountain No. 1 Slant. The company took advantage of an earlier excavation by a local man, John Davies, known as *Drift Archie* after the local contractor who had overseen the work. It is not clear whether these workings were operated commercially. (Wilf Timbrell suggests that they were but ran into financial difficulties and had to be abandoned.) There may have been an accompanying shaft, and the excavations were used by the Waddells to ventilate their No.1 Slant. It seems that John Davies had failed to reach the rich coal deposits later exploited by the Great Mountain Colliery, but he was to return as a highly popular colliery manager.

Figure 40. Miners at the opening of the colliery in 1887.

The Great Mountain colliery opened in 1887. By 1892, it employed some 700 men producing 400 tons of high-quality anthracite a day transported to the outside world along a siding to the L&MM railway. John Waddell did not live to see this growth – he died in Edinburgh on 1 January 1888, aged 59. M.R.C. Price describes him as 'a man of vision and dynamism in the great age of railway construction, his energy and experience were much missed.' He was succeeded in the business by his sons George (1855-1919), Robert (1864-1923) and John

(1865-1923). His grandson, also John Waddell, lived at Ravelston and became the company's President, Director and Engineer.

Figure 41. Great Mountain Colliery (c.1906). Names from left to right, back row: Danny Davies, Tom Hughes, Harry Brazell, Tom Collins, Harry Evans, Dai Brynteg, Dai Morris, Martin Rees, Wilf Timbrell. Bottom row: John Rees, Harry Challinder, W. Tanner, Johnny Mills, Dafydd Rees, Moses Rees (mechanic), John Rees (Smithy), Richard Rees (fitter), Alfred James (Mason). ©National Museum of Wales.

Two Collieries in one

Work started on the Great Mountain No. 2 Slant (*Slant Newydd*) in 1906 about 400 yards from No.1. Wilf Timbrell witnessed the cutting of the first sod - he had been sent with a message to John Davies who by then was the colliery manger. The ceremony was also attended by John Waddell Jnr. and Owen Howells, an old miner of High Street. High quality anthracite was found as the slant was driven through the Braslyd, Pumpquart and Stanllyd veins to the Fawr (Big Vein) near the Blaenhirwaun fault. Although part of the Great Mountain, No.2 Slant was effectively worked as a separate colliery. Both slants were served by the same small power station located between them which also provided electricity for village street lighting and, at a very basic level, for its homes. At 3,500 and 2,240 yards long, the two drift mines were among the longest in the Gwendraeth Valley, with workings in the Fawr extending as far as Llannon.

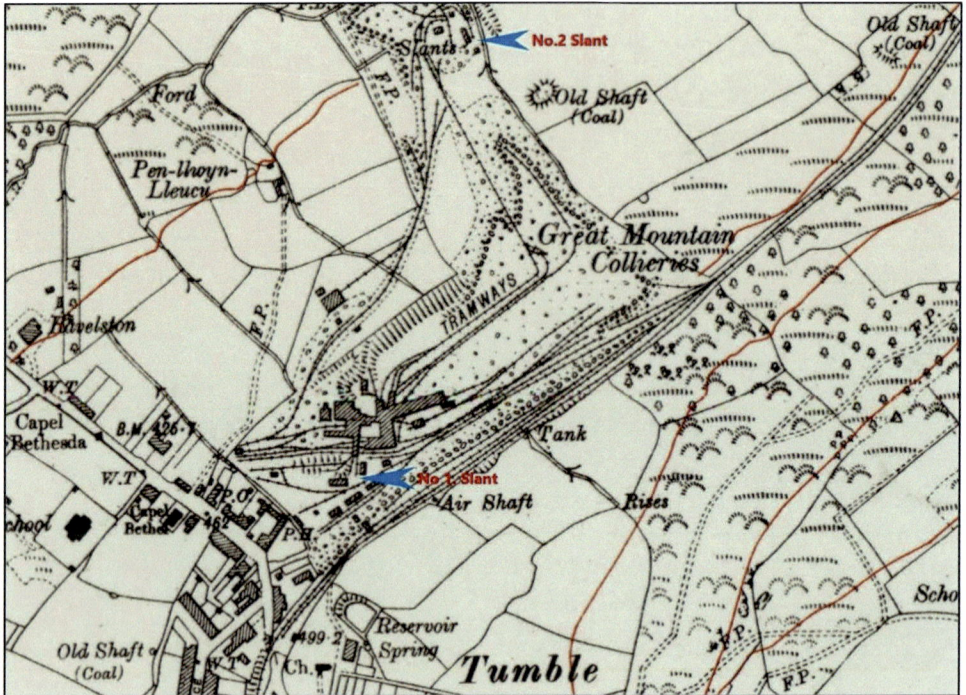

Figure 42. OS Map 1913, showing position of No.1 and No2. Slants. Other features include Pen-llwyn-Lleucu (Lleci) where the pithead baths were later built and Ravelston, home of the colliery owners. Map reproduced with the permission of the NLS.

Wilf Timbrell records an early incident involving a tip fire:

> *A serious slag tip fire happened at the colliery about 1898, which endangered the foundations of the main winding engine. This was inadvertently caused by the tipping of red hot ash from the steam boiler furnaces. The pipes from the supply pond were incapable of providing a sufficient quantity of water to extinguish it, and a horse drawn fire engine was called to assist. It was stationed on the pond embankment and water was pumped through canvas hoses to the scene of the fire. A deep, wide gully was made afterwards to ensure no such recurrence would take place, and larger pipes were laid from pond to colliery. This is the only remembered occasion of a horse-drawn fire engine coming to Tumble.*

Despite difficulties with the anthracite trade and industrial disputes, the Great Mountain saw considerable early growth. It was by far the most important customer of the L&MMR. In September 1887, 9,765 tons of coal were transported over the line with all but 295 tons coming from the Great Mountain. In 1906 extra siding capacity was provided on the railway north of Tumble. Mechanical coal cutters were introduced in part of No.1 Slant as early as 1909 but the colliery remained largely un-mechanised throughout its life achieving high levels of production un-hindered by unreliable machinery. By modern standards, there was an element of child exploitation, with children as young as 13 employed in un-skilled work for very low reward. This is how Wilf Timbrell describes his experience:

> *If a boy or girl passed the Labour examination at school, they were allowed to leave at 13 years of age. Having achieved this, my first job in 1904 was to pick stones from a moving belt before it discharged the crushed coal of the specified size into a railway truck below. Work commenced at 6:45 a.m. and terminated at 4:30 p.m. In the summer, work would continue to 5:00 p.m. for five days, for work to terminate at 2:00 p.m. on Saturday. Brief meal times were staggered with other boys so that production and crushing were continuous. Boys would be paid one shilling a day, and the man in charge of five or six boys would receive two shillings and nine pence each shift. As the boy moved to more important stations on the coal cleaning process he was given 2d a day increase. At 15 or 16 a youth would be put to expedite the movement of coal trams because of his higher mobility. The exploitation of youth was prevalent in all departments of the mine.*
>
> *Safety regulations were practically nil, with no guards to protect a person from moving machinery. One local boy, Howard James, met with the fatal accident because of an unprotected revolving shaft. He was the son of William James, then living in High Street. A short time before that Johnny Williams was killed underground. He was living with his parents in High Street.*

Turning to the older miners, Timbrell describes how on fine summer mornings they would congregate and sit near the pithead as early as 5:30 a.m.:

> *They would chat and diligently rub the glass and brass work of their Davy Lamps, on which their lives could depend, before descending the slant on board the 6:00 am spake. Colliery workers were paid fortnightly on alternate Saturdays. They would often have a long wait in queues for Mr Kidd, the head cashier and sales manager, to arrive by horse drawn cab from Llanelli. The workers were not slow to make their displeasure at being kept waiting apparent! Things got better with the opening of new colliery offices and branches of banks in the village. As though long shifts at the colliery were not enough, many miners also owned or rented small farms in the area and were helped by fellow colliery workers and their families with the arduous haymaking.*

Figure 43. Great Mountain Colliery ©National Museum of Wales

Figure 44. Great Mountain Colliery power station. Courtesy of National Archives and Carmarthenshire Libraries

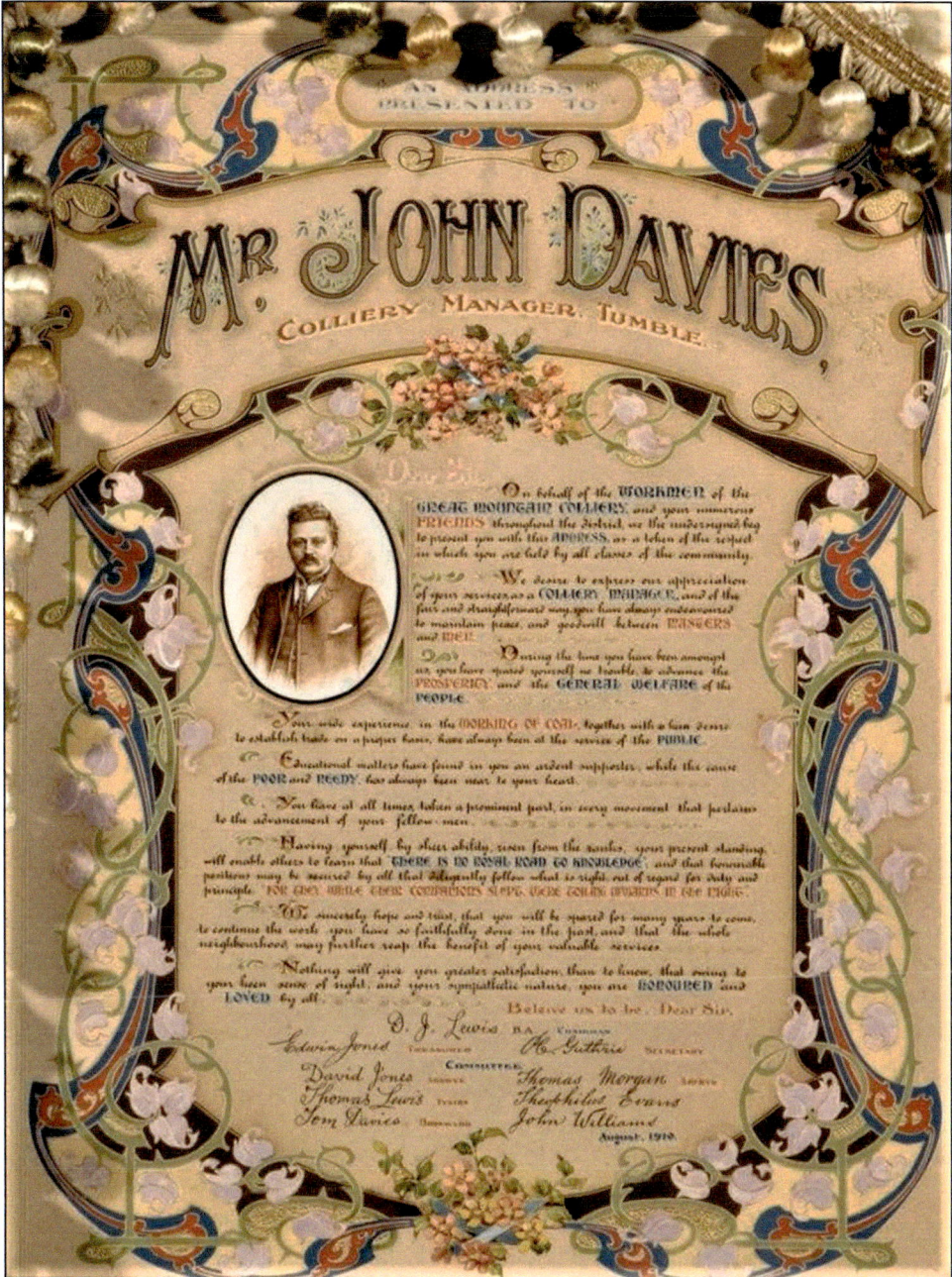

Figure 45. Illuminative address presented by the workmen of the Great Mountain Colliery to John Davies, the highly popular colliery manager, 1900-1908. A local man, John Davies had also been one of the first to survey the site of the colliery and undertook early excavations. Courtesy of National Museum of Wales.

Figure 46. Keystone from Slant 1, Great Mountain Colliery (at former entrance to the colliery). Author's collection.

Figure 47. The coalface at Great Mountain Colliery (1934) by Fred Roberts of Tumble.

Modernisation and change of ownership

During the First World War, the Great Mountain and other coal mines came under government control. Although nationalisation had been an option, after the War Lloyd George returned the mines to their former owners. In the 1920s further modernisation at the Great Mountain included a washery and later a new lamp room. Both slants were highly profitable but as early as 1921 the Waddells were looking to develop new mines in Cwmgwili or Pont Abraham to exploit reserves south of Cross Hands. These plans were overtaken by a period of intense industrial unrest.

Figure 48. A Great Mountain collier and his butty (abt. 1920). Identified by descendants as Tom Rees and his younger brother Sil (Sylvanius) Rees.

Most owners wanted to reduce wages below the levels paid during the War which led to the national miners' strike of 1921. The owners in the Welsh Anthracite district did however recognise that for future viability they could not just rely on cutting the wages of miners – they also needed to restructure. Although their colliery was doing well, in 1923 the Great Mountain Collieries Company became part of the new United Anthracite Collieries Ltd (UAC) which also included pits in Cwm-mawr, Pontyberem and near Ammanford. John Waddell joined the board of the new combine. The Great Mountain was one of the most productive collieries in the group. In the mid-1920s, around 1000 men, working below ground, produced 230,000 tons of anthracite year, 230 tons per man – the colliers hewing at the coal face would have been extracting far more per man but could not have done so without the support of all their colleagues across the colliery specialisms. A further 270 or so men worked on the surface.

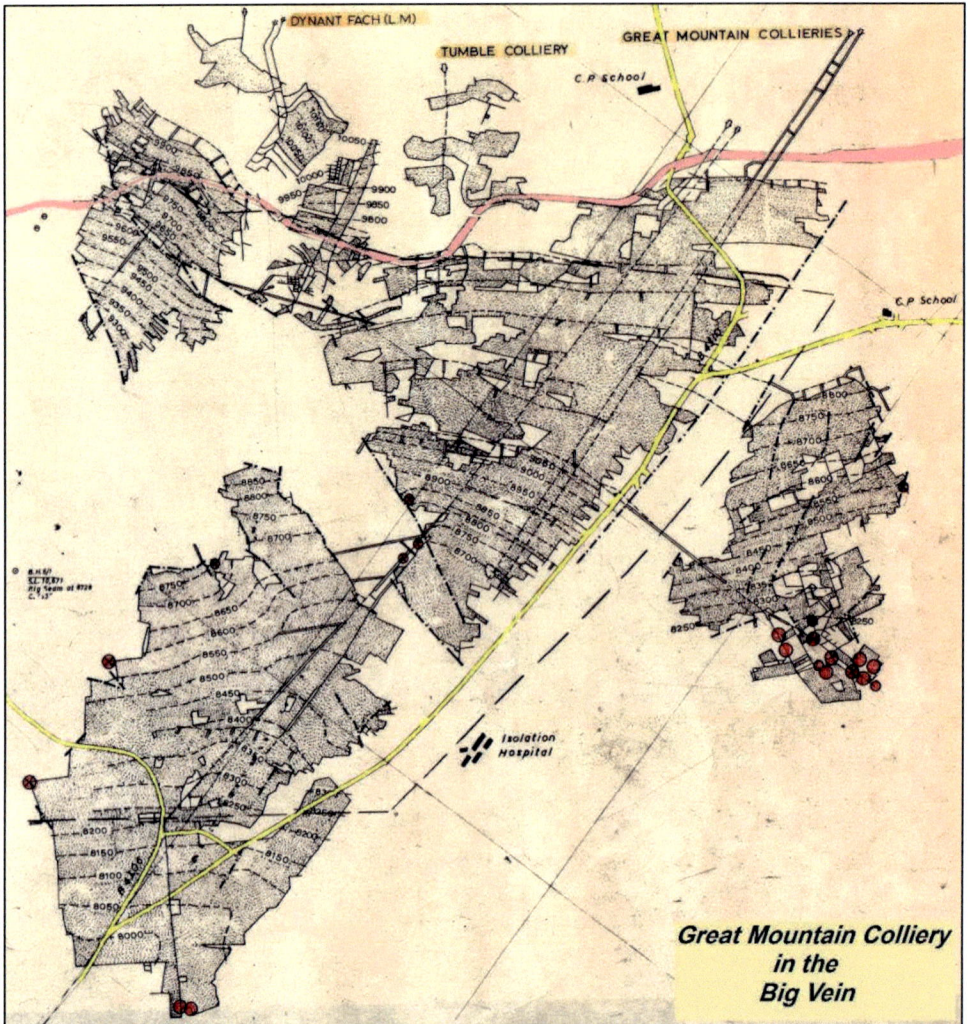

Figure 49. Drawing showing the extent of the GMC workings in the Fawr (Big Vein) extending to Llannon. The red dots indicate incidents of outbursts. Courtesy of Phil Cullen.

The General Strike of 1926

The move to larger colliery owning groups resulted in local owners being replaced by industrialists, and even politicians, with no feel for the Carmarthenshire mining communities. This lack of local knowledge and empathy contributed to the serious strike in 1925 which began in Ammanford when the UAC management ignored the established practice of *last in first out* when they laid off men. The miners were defeated but their militant mood carried through to the General Strike the following year. The miners held out longer than workers in other industries but after 6 months were forced back to work as the impact on their families became unbearable.

Glyn Anthony, in his semi-autobiographical *Coal Dust & Dogma*, gives an evocative account of what life was like for Tumble's miners and their families during the prolonged strike:

> People waited for the decisions of this union or that conference, but gradually it became evident that the lock-out was going to be a prolonged affair and the village seemed to settle down to its unaccustomed mode of living. There was no sound of hooters heralding the beginning of another day, no tramp of feet going down the High Street to the mine, no black-faced figures clad in clothes impregnated with coal dust, making their way home in the early afternoon. On the hearth there were no zinc baths full of hot water waiting for the men to wash the grime of the pit off their bodies. The whole tempo and appearance of the village changed. Every day came to life much more slowly, many colliers getting up late and making their way down to the soup kitchen, the first activity of the day. Many who kept pets or pigeons found the time most useful for repairing or improving or building new pigeon sheds or rabbit hutches, while most found time to tend their gardens more seriously and efficiently than ever before.

As the months went by feeding the family became more of a problem:

> The miners' strike committee decided that a soup kitchen must be opened to feed all those who had been locked out. Boilers for cooking were researched for and collected, a wood and coal supply built up, and trestle tables borrowed from the chapel halls and set up in the big Welfare Hall, which was used as a cinema at night. ... Not only farmers contributed to the two-meals-a-day fund, but local breweries, solicitors, school masters, jewellers and various other merchants as well. Most gave money but some gave help in kind e.g. eggs, half a sheep, loaves, vegetables etc. Dramas were performed in the Welfare Hall and in all the neighbouring villages. Any money collected was donated to the kitchen funds.

> About one o'clock there was a continuous stream of colliers passing our house in small groups. They were colliers of all ages, going down for their mid-day meal to the Welfare Hall at the bottom of the village not far from the colliery itself. Some of the young ones were beating their tin plates or mugs with a knife or fork, but the older ones were more discreet, having wrapped up their utensils and carrying them without such ostentatious abandon.

Glyn Anthony also describes how a group of Tumble miners formed a choir and drove to North Wales in a Ford car to give a series of fund-raising concerts. It seems that the tour was arranged by Tom Nefyn, the Ebenezer preacher who was from North Wales. If Anthony's account is correct, the tour was highly successful and raised £275 for the miners' fund.

Figure 50. GMC miners on strike in 1926.

Amalgamated Anthracite Collieries and the Canadian trade

George Waddell, whose father had founded the colliery, died in 1926. M.R.C. Price maintains that it is unlikely that he would have agreed to the UAC becoming part of Amalgamated Anthracite Collieries (AAC) which it did in 1927. The Great Mountain was valued at £3 million and its profits subsidised weaker parts of the AAC's empire. The company's chairman was Sir Alfred Mond – a major industrialist who had a reputation for caring for his workers but whose name in Tumble, and across south Wales, was more closely associated with *pele mond* - a mix of small coal and cement used as cheap household fuel.

Despite the technology being developed in Wales in the 19th century, in the upper Tawe valley, the use of anthracite in iron-making, and for locomotives and steam ships, had been far better exploited in the United States where the Pennsylvania coalfields, with a strong Welsh contribution, produced huge quantities of anthracite of very similar quality to that of South West Wales. The reluctance in the UK to use anthracite for industrial purposes increased the importance of export markets. Sir Alfred and the AAC's managing director, Sir Alfred Cope, gave the Great Mountain and their other anthracite collieries access to the Canadian market and the trade developed rapidly. When the St Lawrence River froze, the coal intended for the Canadian market had to be stored locally, and in Tumble much larger storage facilities were built adjoining the railway.

The facilities were introduced by the surface superintendent, Mr Walker, who had previously worked for the Waddell company on major projects including the Mersey Tunnel (he lived in 62 and 64 High Street which were joined together to give him a residence seen as appropriate to his position in the colliery). He worked alongside J. Moses Rees, the Head Mechanic, who was the first occupier of 1 Railway Terrace where he lived for the rest of his life. Wilf Timbrell gives this account:

> The huge Canadian market for anthracite coal was temporarily closed for the winter months by the freezing of the St Lawrence River. This hazard to the regular working of the colliery was overcome by Mr Walker by erecting a strong reinforced wall and converting the embankment space between the colliery and the main railway line into storage space for hundreds of thousands of tons of coal. When the thaw came in the spring and the St Lawrence opened to traffic, this proved to be an advantage for the owners to give a speedy turn round for ships at Llanelli and Swansea docks. Thousands of tons could be loaded simply by workmen manipulating lengths of corrugated sheeting to cause a stream of coal to flow into the trucks below. Trainloads would leave Tumble each day until the boat or boats were loaded. It was said of him [Mr Walker] that when on the construction of the Mersey tunnel he devised an arrangement for the excavated sand to return as concrete. He won the admiration of all in the village by being kind, modest and approachable.

In 1935, the Great Mountain produced a profit of almost £400,000 with other ARC collieries barely breaking even. M.R.C. Price describes how, despite the opening of the Canadian market, the Great Mountain then 'gradually slipped into the mediocrity of other anthracite mines' in part because of weaker management resulting from all the ownership changes. The decade did see an important advance with the opening in 1936 of the pithead baths, the first in the Gwendraeth Valley. Easter 1943 saw a near major disaster when one of the waste tips slipped, completely blocking No. 2 Slant (Slant Newydd). Buildings were damaged but fortunately there were very few men underground at the time and they all made it to safety.

Dusting the Coal

Should a miner be paid for all the coal he extracts or just pieces above a certain size? This question put the Great Mountain at the centre of a protracted court case in the 1930s. The South Wales Miners' Federation (with James Griffiths its president personally involved) had championed the cause of the Great Mountain miners in a dispute at the colliery. The owners were refusing to pay the miners for coal they extracted in pieces below a certain size. The case was considered by the courts and even went on appeal to the House of Lords. It took three years to settle what was effectively a test case with Stanley Matthews, a collier from

Cross Hands, making a claim on behalf of all his Great Mountain colleagues. The courts eventually ruled in 1936 in favour of the colliery owners. The miners responded with a novel form of working to rule – *dusting the coal* before putting it on the conveyor belt. This involved filling the trams by hand with large coal having *gobbed* or thrown to one side the small coal. The effect was greatly reduced output and colliery owners, who reputedly lost £50,000 in three weeks, capitulated.

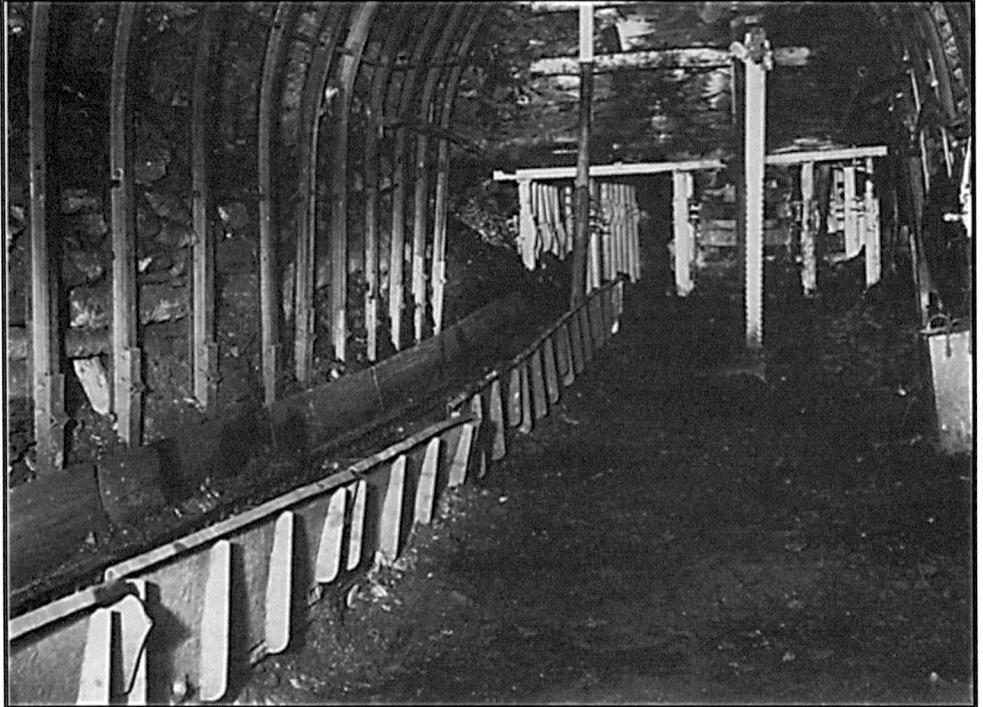

Figure 51. GMC - possibly the Pumquart seam in Slant 2 but not confirmed. Courtesy of National Archives.

Cwm Sinkings

In 1939 the AAC began work sinking a new shaft at Cwm Sinkings alongside the L&MMR over a mile south of Tumble towards Llanelli. The plan had been to link the shaft to the Great Mountain, but this was abandoned possibly because of a risk of flooding (a link was made to the Glynhebog drift). Nevertheless, the Cwm shaft, completed in 1941, was adopted as Great Mountain No.3. By the end of 1958 it was connected to the new Cynheidre *super-pit* but, ahead of the formal opening of Cynheidre, coal was wound up No.3 shaft. So, the Great Mountain can claim to have lifted the first coal taken from the *super-pit*!

Figure 52. Cwm Sinkings as left by Amalgamated Anthracite. Courtesy of Phil Cullen

The shaft became Cynheidre No.3 and in 1962 and was joined at Cwm by the Cynheidre No. 4 shaft. Cwm then formed part of the largest anthracite mine in western Europe. Phil Cullen gives this account of the colliery:

> *The history of this location is one of the strangest in the whole Valley, listed by the name Great Mountain No. 3, although it was never connected to Great Mountain in Tumble. I worked here after it became part of Cynheidre from 1977-1980 and never once did I hear anyone refer to this name! In 1936 Amalgamated Anthracite announced a major new project on this site, in close proximity to Cwm Farm. However, it was not until 1939 that shaft sinking was commenced. Between 1936-39 two headgear frames, a steam winder house, compressor house, boiler house, fan house and workshops were constructed at the site. It was claimed by the Company the venture would provide employment for 1500 men for 50 years! The Company clearly had major plans for this location and a washery and screens were to be constructed at a later date. The shaft (which in later years became Cynheidre Shaft 3), was commenced in June 1939. The shaft which was brick lined had a diameter of 18 feet and was sunk to the Pumpquart Seam at a depth of 598 yds. There were two cages installed and a BCC steam driven winder provided. Probably due to the outbreak of the War the second shaft was never sunk by the Company, (it was 1962 before Shaft 4 Cynheidre was sunk on this spot with a new headgear frame and winder house) and special permission sought to complete the single shaft in 1941. It looks as if the War curtailed this project. The shaft was linked up with Glynhebog Drift Mine and acted as a return airway.*

Figure 53. Cynheidre Shaft 3 at Cwm Sinkings (Pumpquart Dumpend) by Fred Roberts.

Figure 54. Construction of Headgear for Cynheidre Shaft 4 at Cwm Sinkings (author's father, Rhys Alexander, on the right). Author's collection.

Figure 55. The headgear of Cynheidre Shaft 3 at Cwm Sinkings. Courtesy of Phil Cullen.

Other local mines

The Great Mountain was by far the largest colliery in Tumble and its surrounding area, but there were other mines contemporary with it within a mile or so of the village. These included New Dynant colliery in Cwm-mawr, which opened in the early 1900s, and the nearby Clos-yr-yn. At its peak in the 1920s, New Dynant employed around 500 men (about half as many as the Great Mountain).

M.R.C. Price describes how in 1905 the owners of Closyryn entered into an agreement for a private siding to the colliery: 'extending beyond Cwm-mawr station through a somewhat restricted bridge beneath the road to Tumble. A private and steeply graded tramway was provided to convey coal from the mine down towards a loading point on this siding (fig. 57). The Clos-yr-yn slant was initially abandoned in 1925 but reopened by a local man, Thomas Griffiths, in 1930. Things did not go well - the handful of miners encountered an inrush of water from old workings which not only flooded Closyryn but also part of New Dynant. The flooding of New Dynant was cleared but Closyryn was finally abandoned later that year.

After its peak in the 1920s, New Dynant went into gradual decline and closed in 1952. Nine men lost their lives at the colliery - Phil Cullen, Gwendraeth Valley Coal Mines, records an accident in 1935 when a workman died having rolled down the tip and breaking his neck.

The nearby Cwm-mawr Colliery was redeveloped in the 1900s by the New Cwm-mawr Colliery Co. Following a takeover by Welsh Anthracite Collieries Ltd in 1921, it reached a peak in 1930 employing 134 men. In the face of difficult geology, the mine had to be abandoned just four years later in 1934. Other smaller mines in and around Cwm-mawr included the Glosuchaf Slant which re-opened in 1908 and employed no more than 33 men before closing in 1917. While in Tumble itself there was the short-lived Little Mountain mine which employed a maximum of 21 men and operated for just two years – 1902-1904. Nant-Ddu, a private mine close to Dynant Fach Farm, owned by John Davies of Pontyberem (Nant-Ddu Colliery Company Pontyberem), employed a maximum of 18 men between 1910 and 1918.

Nationalisation and Indian Summer

During the Second World War, coal mining became a reserved occupation, so miners were exempt from having to enlist. The increasing demand for coal to fuel the war effort led to young men, *Bevin Boys*, being brought in to work in the mines often with little experience of heavy manual labour let alone coal mining. Sadly, if understandably, these young men struggled to fit in, and apparently this was particularly the case in Tumble and other Carmarthenshire mining villages where Welsh was by far the dominant language. Perhaps because of this, relatively few *Bevin boys* were sent to work at the Great Mountain.

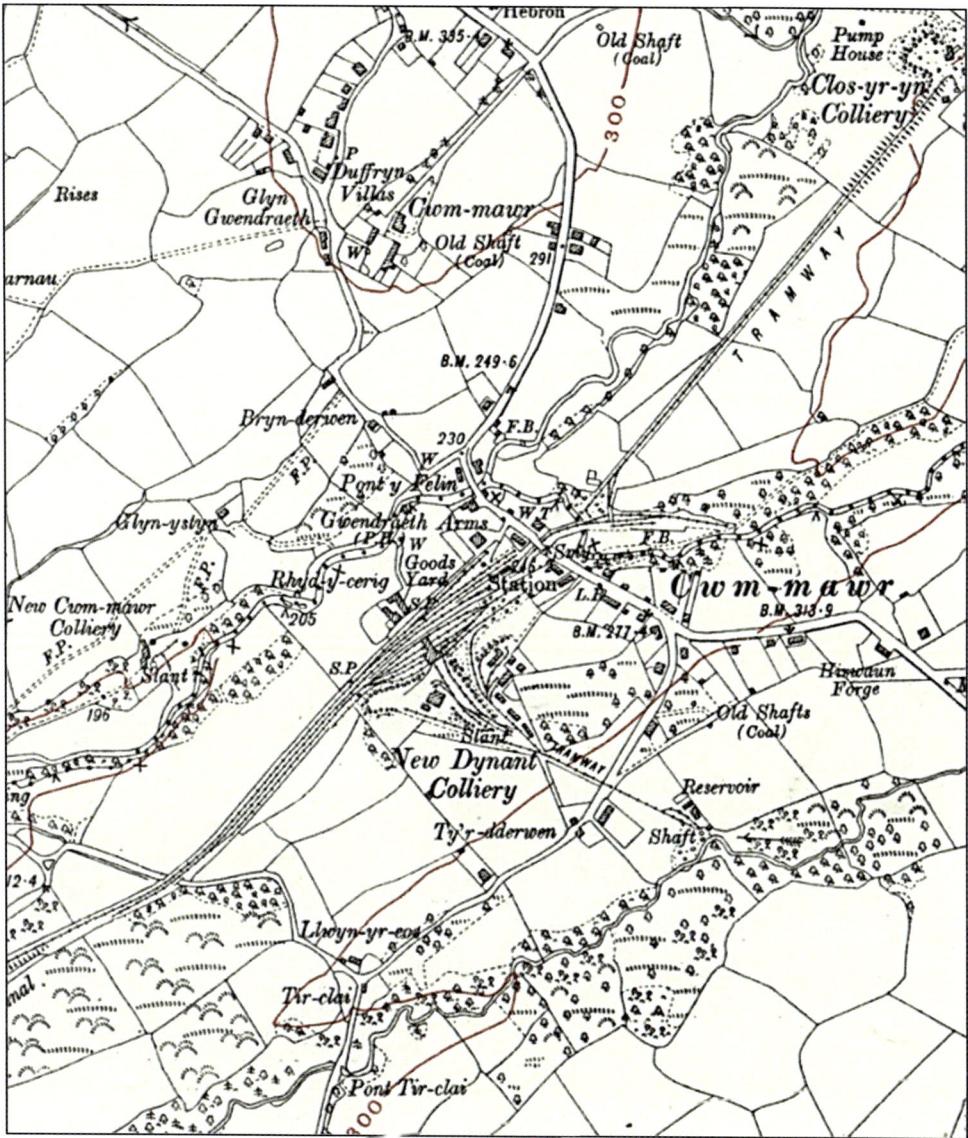

Figure 56. OS Map 1913. Features include - New Cwm-mawr colliery (lower left), New Dynant Colliery, Clos-yr-yn Colliery connected via tramway to sidings at Cwm-mawr. Map reproduced with the permission of the NLS.

Despite the demands of the War, from its high point of well over 1000 men, by 1946 the Great Mountain employed just over 500 men below ground and around

170 above ground. In that year, it was nationalised along with the rest of the coal industry. Nationalisation brought investment but the anthracite district was something of a backwater for technical developments – though the Great Mountain Colliery continued to be highly-productive. On 19 January 1948, the Western Mail reported the exploits of William King:

> THERE was much excitement in the Great Mountain Colliery, Tumble, near Llanelly, yesterday when it was officially announced that William King, of Tycroes, Pantyffynon, a 41-year-old married man, had produced 71 tons of anthracite in five days this week. A fortnight ago King produced 61 tons, which he cut and loaded by hand within the same period in the Braslyd seam.
>
> "The seam is only 2ft. thick and 'is underlayed with 6in. of rashings," the official statement pointed out. "This gives an overall height of only 2ft. 6in. for him to work in for the full shift, which means that he has to work on his knees for the whole of the period. The coal is most difficult to work as the inclination of the seam is 15in. per yard, and the man has to work on this gradient.
>
> King began his herculean achievements about five weeks ago when he produced 51 tons of coal in five days. Last year he cut a 5ft. section of unblemished coal from a Great Mountain seam to enable Mr. Barney Seale, the London sculptor, to carve from it the statue of a miner, which was exhibited in London's recent Miner Comes to Town exhibition.

William King was clearly an exceptional collier. On 17 June 1955, the Western Mail reported:

> A LIFE - SIZED bust of a miner, carved by Mr. Atri Brown, the sculptor. from a 4cwt. block of anthracite hewn by William King at Great Mountain Colliery, near Swansea. is to be shown in Paris. It is among works lent by the National Coal Board for the International Art Exhibition in Mining and Metallurgy which opens to-morrow. The sculptor spent six months on the bust after he had visited South Wales mines to study types of miners as models. It called for delicate handling from the time the anthracite block left the pit, in a specially-fitted lorry to the time it was finally smoothed off for exhibition. Mr. Brown could not use his sculptor's tools: he carved the head with penknife, woodcutting tools, and an electric polisher. Special precautions were taken for the safe transfer of the bust to France.

M.R.C. Price describes how, despite this massive change looming, the 1950s were something of an *Indian Summer* for the Great Mountain and indeed Tumble as a community. The Western Mail reported that on 16 December 1954 the colliery produced 1,041 tons of coal - the highest output for 25 years with No.1 Slant producing its highest ever output in a day - 808 tons. Coal cutting machines had been brought in and were in regular use by the early 1950s. In 1955, the Great Mountain employed about 900 men (compared with 700 in 1948) and produced 172,437 tons of anthracite. Attention was however increasingly being concentrated on developing a *super-pit* at Cynheidre, six miles down the Gwendraeth Valley.

The DVD, A *History of Coal Mining in the Gwendraeth Valley 1850-1989*, records interviews with Great Mountain Colliery miners reminiscing on the last three decades of the colliery's active life. They describe the training they received as boys of 14 or 15 at centres in New Dynant and Glynhebog before starting work at Tumble, often on the screens picking out the stones from the coal. From there they could begin to specialise in a range of colliery trades, above and below ground, including electrician, blacksmith, haulier and mechanic. Some would work as a *butty* before rising to assistant collier and full-blown collier hewing the coal and timbering at the coalface. Others would take on the highly responsible role of fireman (setting the explosions to blast through rock and to release the coal for the colliers to work).

The men interviewed concurred that the Great Mountain was a particularly difficult colliery to work compounded by the ever-present risk of an outburst (see Chapter 8). Though varying between the two slants and the districts and seams worked, the dust and heat were exceptional. In one area of No. 1 Slant, working the Fawr (Big Vein), the heat was so bad, 'like a hot oven', that it was known as the *Burma,* reflecting the conditions in which men were fighting in the tropical jungles in the Second Word War. The colliers themselves, and the boys and men supporting them, worked wearing just shorts, socks and boots. The sweat would pour from them even when standing still. Frequent blasting and poor, out-dated ventilation meant that the dust could limit visibility to a few feet and took far longer to clear than in better ventilated mines.

Throughout its time of operation, the Great Mountain was worked mostly by the *hand-got* method – that is, it was reliant on colliers extracting the coal (including by *under-cutting* the coal seam), supported by an assistant collier and a *butty* who would shovel the coal into horse or mechanically pulled drams or onto conveyor belts where these had been installed. The seams worked could vary from an almost unimaginable 2' 6" up to 8 or 9 feet in the Fawr (Big Vein). These seams did not run in consistent long lengths suited to the use of machinery - they lacked *conformity* by being frequently broken by faults adding to the challenge of winning the coal. Despite all these difficulties, and relative lack of mechanisation (one old miner felt that this was actually an advantage because men were more reliable than machines), the Great Mountain achieved high levels of production over many years generating profit for its owners, supporting the community and serving the needs of the country not least through two world wars. This is a huge achievement given that the working conditions and level of danger were amongst the worst, if not the worst, in the Gwendraeth Valley.

Figure 57. Alan Merchant, blacksmith at the Great Mountain Colliery.

Figure 58. Stan Williams, Fred Roberts and others on wagons at GMC, 1955. From the collections of the National Monuments Record of Wales: © Copyright: Vernon D. Emmanuel

Cynheidre and closure

Cynheidre opened in 1960 with underground connections to other local collieries. In 1961, with men having been transferred to Cynheidre, the Great Mountain was left with 229 men. It closed on 5 May 1961, but No. 1 Slant continued to provide pumping facilities for Cynheidre right up to 1986.

However, this was not an end to coal mining in Tumble. As M.R.C. Price notes, the mining history of the village came a full circle with the opening of the private Dynant Fach mine in the 1970s near the old Nantddu slant. Owned by K.V. Thomas in the 1970s, in 1988 it came under the newly formed Tumble Anthracite Company (also trading under the name of Thomas Bros.). In 1997 the company was replaced by the Dynant Fach Colliery Co., but this change was short-lived as the mine closed in 1998. Phil Cullen notes that the mine was the largest and most advanced private mine ever to work in the Gwendraeth Valley, post nationalisation, with four drifts (working the Fawr and the Gras), pithead baths and a coal preparation plant.

The era of open-cast mining, though no-doubt bringing much needed, if short-term, jobs saw the virtual obliteration of the physical remains of Tumble's coalmining heritage. The site of the Great Mountain and the neighbouring Blaenhirwain collieries, following the opencast operations, became the Mynydd Mawr Woodland Park. The Dynant area was also extensively covered by opencast operations.

Figure 59. The final night shift at the GMC descend the steep slant on the spake for the last time. Courtesy of Phil Cullen.

Figure 60. GMC Slant 1 (abt.1983). Courtesy of Phil Cullen.

Figure 61. Remains of drift at Tumble colliery, 1978. From the collections of the National Monuments Record of Wales: © Copyright: Vernon D. Emmanuel.

6.The Tumble Strike of 1893

In the early 1890s colliers across South Wales were facing the prospect of very substantial cuts in their pay rates. The sliding scale agreement, introduced in 1875, meant that the wages of miners varied depending on the selling price of coal. Between 1868 and 1891 the wages of South Wales miners had in fact risen substantially - by 50% in real terms. However, in 1893, faced with a 25% wage reduction, caused by a fall in the price of coal and the application of the sliding scale, they went on strike. John Davies (*A History of Wales*) describes how in that year 'there was bitter fighting in the Rhondda and in northern Monmouthshire, and a thousand soldiers were sent to the coal-mining valleys.'

This was the national backdrop, but the dispute and disturbances in Tumble in 1893 were particular to the Great Mountain Colliery. The Tumble miners were not alone however - they attracted considerable support from other West Wales coalfield Districts. This is not surprising given the depth of the cuts that the owners were seeking to introduce and the potential consequences for other collieries. The colliery owners proposed to cut a face-workers rate on the Fawr (Big Vein) from 1s 5d for 'Cutting and Filling Large Coal' to just 1s per ton, and for 'Timbering Double Levels and Inclines' from 2s 6d a pair to 1s 2d a pair. For miners on a day rate, they were seeking to demand 12 full drams (wagons) a day before they would pay the 4s 6d rate rather than the established practice of starting that rate at 7 drams.

The Company argued that these cuts were justified by improved working practices and conditions enabling miners to be more productive. It is possible that the matter could have been settled through considered negotiation and compromise, but there were two aggravating factors that became at least as important as the proposed cuts themselves and stood in the way of amicable resolution. The first was the decision of the Company to bring in what were known as *strangers* from Scotland and the North of England (primarily Durham) who were seen by the local miners, or *old workers*, as undermining their position. (These *strangers* should not be confused with the men brought in earlier, mostly from Scotland, because of the need for their expertise in opening up the colliery and who had been largely accepted by the locals.) The second factor was the Welsh blacklegs who were prepared to continue to work at the reduced rates being offered by the owners.

The spark that lit the tinderbox – 4 March 1893

The result was a highly volatile atmosphere surrounding relations between the Company and its workers which ignited on the first Saturday in March 1893. The owners and the unpopular Scottish manager, Robert Beith, apparently refused to meet a deputation of local miners to discuss their plans to cut wages. In response, the miners picked up their tools and went on strike encouraging others to join them in a bold attempt to bring work at the colliery completely to a halt.

At 7 o'clock that evening, Rennie, another Scotsman, was manning the engine that pumped water out of the mine. He was confronted by striking miners who tried to force him to stop the engine. At first, he resisted, expressing concern for the ponies stabled underground, but in the end had to give in to the pressure. This was clearly a step too far for the colliery manager who called in police reinforcements from Llanelli. By the time they arrived things had calmed down and they did not stay for long.

The great miners' leader, William Abraham - Member of Parliament for the Rhondda and better known by his bardic name of Mabon - associated himself closely with the cause of the Tumble miners and was to play a major role in the dispute. He was called in by the miners and met with Robert Beith on 22 March. The colliery manager attempted to deflect the argument about wages to focus on operational improvements that had been made (a shift from *Pillar and Stall* to the *Long Wall* system). But Mabon would have none of it bringing things back to the planned wage cuts and the unfairness of applying the same pay rate regardless of the differing working conditions from one coal seam to another.

Violence breaks out – 8 April 1893

The strike continued and on 8 April the miners organised a very large meeting to be followed by a procession with the objective of gaining further support for their cause. In a letter published in *Tarian Y Gweithiwr* on 20 April, David Roderick, locally elected representative of the miners (known as a checkweigher), gave an account of events on the evening of 8 April from the perspective of the striking workers. He described how the purpose of procession was to impress upon the blacklegs living in the village that they were betraying their colleagues. Workers from the Upper Division met near Cross Hands and at 5 o'clock, led by the brass bands of Cwm-mawr and Penygroes, they marched to meet colleagues from the Lower Division beyond Bethania chapel in Upper Tumble. The combined group then proceeded two-by-two with four of the workers carrying a white flag decorated with a black boar and bearing the words 'Where are my brothers?', aimed no doubt at the blacklegs.

Along Tumble Row, the procession found some of the blacklegs standing at their doors who, according to Roderick, were shamefully watching the procession pass by while others went into hiding. Roderick further maintained that while a stone may have been thrown through the widow of a blackleg's house, with all the people lining the street it was unclear as to whether one of the marchers had been responsible for the act. The procession, numbering about 1,500 people, then gathered on the top of *Tanygraig mountain* (Graig Llechyfedach) where

Roderick describes how they had one of the best meetings he had experienced. Chaired by John Jones (Holven) with main speakers from local collieries including Emlyn, Cross Hands and Glynhebog, the meeting determined that all blacklegs must leave the colliery, and that a further meeting should be held on Cae Pound, Cross Hands on Mabon's Day (1 May). The meeting was closed with a Welsh hymn sang to the tune Aberystwyth. The Upper and Lower Divisions then marched home led by their respective brass bands.

The intentions of the leaders were peaceful and lawful, but they could not be in full control of all involved. Reports suggest that some groups left the meeting to rampage along Tumble Row singling out the homes of blacklegs to throw stones at their windows. Roderick maintained that it was only a small number of people from the mass gathering who had caused the trouble. The South Wales Daily News of 10 April gave this account which, while more colourful, supports the view that the procession was mostly peaceful:

> *On Saturday last, early in the afternoon, the miners engaged at the Great Mountain Colliery, Tumble, all of whom have been subjected to enforced idleness for the last two months or so, formed themselves into a procession, numbering close upon 1,500 men, and, headed by two brass bands, marched through the village. Their object was to publicly manifest their indignation against the management of the colliery for what they consider to be the shameful manner in which they (the workmen) have been treated. Whilst passing some of the dwelling-houses belonging to the colliery company some of the processionists threw stones and smashed several of the windows of these houses. The manager, Mr Beith, was immediately informed of the occurrence, and he telephoned down to the head office at Llanelly requesting that a detachment of police should be sent up as soon as possible. About 8.30 on Saturday evening five police-officers journed to the Tumble, the distance to which, from Llanelly, is about eight miles, but upon arriving their found everything to be in a perfectly normal state, the processionists having dispersed without causing any further damage than the smashing of a few windows. It is a regrettable fact that the relations between the management and the employees are very strained at the present time, and unfortunately there are no immediate prospects of a re-start of the pit.*

The District Meeting of the Miners' Federation, chaired by John Jones of Pontyberem, decided to allocate £100 from the Federation's funds, supplemented by a levy of a shilling per head on members, to support the striking miners. The fund had reached just over £462 by the end of November - less than had been expected. Each striking miner was given 4 shillings a week out of the fund (a collier on day rate earned 4 shilling and 6 pence a day).

The Mabon's Day meeting and march – 1 May 1893

As agreed on 8 April, the Mabon's Day meeting went ahead on Cae Pound, Cross Hands (the site of the former feeder reservoir for the canal in Cwm-mawr), chaired by John Jones. The Western Mail gave a detailed account of the day:

> The labour dispute at Tumble, a mining village in the midst of the anthracite coalfield of Carmarthenshire, is apparently as far from being settled as ever. The Great Mountain Colliery - fortunately the only colliery affected so far - is practically at a standstill. Up to the present the men have shown stubborn resolution not to accede to the reduction, amounting, according to them, to 30 per cent, proposed by the masters. In this resolution they have the sympathy and support of the anthracite colliers in the district. This was very obvious on Monday, when some 3,000 colliers attended a demonstration to protest against the conduct of the masters and to show disapproval of the employment by the latter of "blacklegs." About mid-day colliers from within a radius of eight miles marched into the village of Cross Hands to the music of brass bands, &e., to near what is locally known as the "great Pound." A platform had been erected at the foot of a hill, and here a mass meeting was held. Mr. John Jones, Castell Holfen, Cross Hands, presided. The proceedings were conducted in Welsh and passed off in a very orderly manner.

The crowd then formed itself into a long procession:

> In the front there was a goat led by two youths. The demonstration consisted of about 3,000 persons, and, to the strains of five brass bands and the tootling of a fife, took a circuitous route around Bethania, and finally appeared at Tumble. Some half-dozen policemen and a sergeant were in the village to see that the peace was not broken, but as the demonstration passed through there was not even hooting. The women who appeared at the rear of the procession, many with babies in their arms, sang as they trudged through the village, a kind of requiem. After proceeding about a mile, the demonstration broke up at the Gwendraeth Arms, near Cwm-mawr.

This sounds like a carnival atmosphere, but violence broke out on the streets and at the Tumble Hotel. Robert Beith was reportedly struck in the face 'until blood flowed.' The names of the antagonists in the court cases that followed suggest that some of the clashes were between the Welsh colliers and non-striking English and Scottish workers and management.

At some point during the day the Western Mail reporter took the opportunity to interview Robert Beith who claimed that the owners had been expecting a counter proposal from the men that had not materialised. He maintained that the dispute affected only those men who worked the Big Vein (Fawr) where the company had introduced a new system of winning the coal, which offered 'great advantage to those men, both in respect of safety and ventilation, and the coal could be won a great deal easier.' The manager implied that it was unreasonable that, despite all the expense the company had incurred to make these improvements, the men still wanted the old pay of 1s 5d per ton rather than the shilling per ton offered by the colliery. He claimed to have ten men working underground and expected that he would have plenty of men doing so in a few days on the company's terms. According to Beith, only about 165 men were receiving strike pay as the others had gone to other collieries.

Figure 62. Mabon – 1895.

The miners' leaders, led with energy and influence by Mabon, continued to focus on the miners' genuine grievances. There were negotiations in June based on a four-point plan developed by the miners' leaders. However, during a relatively quiet period in June and July, men continued to be brought to Tumble including from the North of England suggesting a continuing lack of understanding by the owners and management of the importance of this factor as a deal blocker. It seems that some of these further *strangers* had been misled by an advertisement placed by the manager of the Lodging House looking to boost his income. An attempt by the colliery to evict 17 tenants in Tumble Row failed because of a technical fault in the paperwork but must have added to the feeling of unfair treatment held by the local miners.

A further meeting was held at Cae Pound in August. Mabon was one of the main speakers and the miners reaffirmed their confidence in his leadership. There was some optimism that that a resolution with the owners could soon be found but this turned out to misplaced.

Violence erupts again - 4 September 1893

Monday 4 September saw the worst violence of the disturbances. Looking back on the day the Evening Express commented:

The general tone of sullenness and discontent which has characterised the colliers on strike in the district of Tumble for some weeks past appears to have culminated on Monday evening in conduct subversive of all sort of law or discipline. For a time at least during that evening colliers and their friends indulged in flat rebellion. They triumphed over the small force of police matched against them, and in the course of not much more than one short hour spread devastation along the route they took. ...

There were 6 policemen on duty in Tumble that day. The two local men had been reinforced by Sergeant Bryant, Police Constables Sayers and Rees of Pontyberem, and Davies and Thomas of Llanelli. Starting with the confrontation at the colliery itself, they were to lose control of the day's events.

It all began with a large meeting of the men and a deputation sent to negotiate with George Waddell. The colliery owner was accompanied by Robert Beith who, as highlighted in a report in the South Wales Evening Post, was particularly disliked by the miners. The meeting, in the colliery manager's office, got nowhere and as the miners' leaders were leaving, they were met with growing agitation amongst 15 to 20 men assembled in the yard outside the office. One of the men in the crowd picked up an iron bar and, whatever his real intention, the policemen present thought that he was going to thrust it into the fan of one of the machines. They reacted by grabbing him and marching him to the office. This was seen by the miners as a provocative and unnecessary act.

Assault on the lodging house

Possibly intimidated by stones thrown at them by *strangers* (this was disputed), some of the crowd who had gathered for the earlier large meeting made their way to the Lodging House, home at the time to the *strangers*. Soon a crowd of between four and five hundred had gathered and there was nothing the six policemen at the scene could do to stop an assault on the building. Just after six o'clock the serious disturbance started. A number of the strikers were on the opposite side of the railway to the Lodging House and the mostly Scottish workers. The confrontation started with hooting and jeering and developed into stone throwing at the Lodging House. This escalated with, according to eyewitnesses, about 20-40 men in front of the crowd leading the way urged on by some 400 or 500 people. The windows at the back of the Lodging House, overlooking the line, were soon smashed by missiles of all shapes and sizes. The crowd then took position on a piece of ground owned by the colliery fronting the building and assaulted the rest of the windows and their sashes – up to twenty windows in all. The substantial mess-room (dining room) in the building (perhaps 40ft. long) was wrecked with the crockery that had been laid out on the tables smashed by stones and other missiles which were found piled up in the room. Some resident families were so afraid that they left to hide and did not return to the Lodging House until the morning.

Figure 63. A later photograph of the Lodging House in a dilapidated state. Its final use was as National Coal Board storehouse. Courtesy of National Museum of Wales.

'Rampage' along High Street and the assault on Bryngwili

Having taken out their anger on the Scottish workmen, at about 7 o'clock the strikers turned their attention to the Welsh blacklegs living along High Street (still Tumble Row at the time). The Evening Express described the scene:

> *Leading up the hill from this lodging-house are over a hundred small cottages belonging to the company, forming an irregular street, and tenanted by colliers and others. Up this street, after they had done their worst at the lodging-house, the mob went pell-mell, and, picking up all the stones they could find en route, they landed them through the windows of the cottages as they proceeded. A good deal of discrimination and selection was exercised in this bombardment. The attentions of the crowd were apparently extended only to their enemies. The cottages of turncoats and blacklegs unfailingly received these casual demonstrations of unpopularity, whilst the others escaped without injury. A very large number of windows were smashed in, and the crowd appeared to have things for the once all their own way, the six constables, of course, being quite ineffectual to cope with the rush.*

A telephone message was sent along the Mynydd Mawr railway to Captain Scott who was in charge of the Llanelli division of the county police. He, with Sergeants Hopkins and Evans and ten constables, travelled on a special train from Llanelli to Tumble. They set off at about 7.40pm, but made slow progress owing to notoriously difficult line with sharp inclines and bends and a struggling steam engine. The Evening Express commented that 'the police had upheld the reputation of their class by arriving - this time through no fault of their own - when the row is all over.' The reinforcements patrolled the village until about eleven o'clock and were considering returning to Llanelli when they received news from Mr Watson, the colliery's cashier, that a group of strikers had attacked Bryngwili near Cross Hands - the home of Robert Beith, the unpopular colliery manager.

The Evening Express described this as 'a particularly grievous outrage.' On receiving Mr Watson's message, the police immediately mounted a train that took them part of the way to Cross Hands. They then had to walk across fields to get to Bryngwili arriving too late to catch the men involved in the attack. They learnt that a group of about 15-20 men had proceeded to Cross Hands from Tumble and were buoyed by alcohol by the time they reached Bryngwili where they had expected to find the colliery manager at home.

The windows of the house had been smashed by stones taken from the garden rockery, and attempts had been made to burn the curtains inside the windows. Having done as much damage as they could from the outside, the men had then broken through the glass porch and solid front door. Once inside they had hurled more stones and smashed a grandfather clock, a sideboard and internal doors. The police found Mrs. Beith prostrate and hardly able recount what had happened. Had it not been for Mr Watson, who had just moved to the area and was staying in the house for a few days, she would have been alone with the young servant girl (her husband had yet to return home from Tumble). Mr. Watson and Mrs. Beith had both been struck by stones and had marks on their heads and faces to show for it. Mrs Beith had also been struck in the face by a brass stair-rod wielded by one of the men. The young servant girl, who had hidden in the kitchen, was not harmed.

Having failed to make any arrests at the scene, Captain Scott took some of his men to Cross Hands to continue the search but without success. Neither Mrs Beith nor Mr Watson could identify their attackers (there was speculation that the men may not have been from the area). On developments back in Tumble, the Evening Express reported that:

> During the whole of the succeeding evening Tumble was in a state of intense excitement. The police who returned from Cross Hands found that the Scotch miners and the Welshmen still employed at the pits had turned out in force to meet the rioters if they returned. They all bore formidable bludgeons, and it is probable that if they had returned there would have been still more serious proceedings. Everything, however, in the shape of violence was apparently over for the evening.

On 5 September, the Cross Hands Colliery Company requested that more policemen be sent to the area. The authorities in Llanelli decided to send as many as they could together with a detachment of the Inniskilling Dragoons from Swansea which arrived in Tumble the next day and camped near the colliery. Noel Gibbard records that altogether there were 62 policemen (44 from the County, 5 from the Borough and 13 from Swansea), and 24 soldiers. The police were housed in Bryngwili, Tumble Inn and the Lodging House. The Tumble Inn was ordered to close at twelve noon and all other public houses within a three-mile radius by four o'clock in the afternoon. Two magistrats were sent to the village to read the Riot Act should they consider it necessary.

Arrest and trial of Thomas Lewis, John Lewis and Caleb Morgan

Having been unsuccessful at Bryngwili, Captain Scott did arrest three of the men alleged to have been involved in the earlier riot at Tumble – the brothers Thomas and John Lewis residing at the Farmers' Arms, Cross Hands, and Caleb Morgan of Tabw/Tuber Villas, Cross Hands. The three had allegedly been identified by the police during the violence. They were taken to Llanelli and kept in custody at the county police station. They were tried at the Carmarthenshire Quarter Session on 20 October having been charged with attempted riot and tumultuous assembly. They were defended by Mr J Lloyd Morgan, MP and pleaded not guilty. Police Sergeant Bryant in his witness account of events outside the colliery manager's office described how 15 to 20 men had assembled:

> One of the men flung up his hat, and said to the men, "Come along," and they went through the yard, past the office, and on to a workshop. There one picked up an iron bar, swinging it about in the air, and called to the others to come on. Cursing, swearing, and singing were indulged in. They made for the fan. P.S. Saer caught hold of the man with the bar, and witness got between both, and tried to reason with the men. There was, however, a general struggle between Saer and the men. A dozen of them were endeavouring to strike witness and Saer. Witness backed and evaded the blows. Hundreds of other people now came on the scene, as did also two more constables. Witness eventually gave up the struggle. Seeing this, the mob rushed headlong crying, "Now boys, for the lodging-house."

Sergeant Bryant claimed that the Lewis brothers were among the first to enter the yard and that he had later seen John Lewis throwing stones at the Lodging House. He had asked Lewis to stop, but the latter had taken a 'fighting position' and given the reply 'You stand back, you - else I'll smash you.' Caleb Morgan, according to Bryant, had then thrown half a brick through one of the windows and had to be held back from 'thrashing' him. PC John Thomas, of Llanelli, said that he had heard a man shouting as he was heading for the lodging house, 'If you have any pluck in you now's the time to show it.' PC Thomas Rees, Pontyberem, claimed that a man had shouted, 'If you have any Welsh blood in your veins let us show it to-day.' There were contradictory accounts of whether the Scotsmen at the lodging house had thrown stones at the miners - Mrs Bryant, wife of PS Bryant, said that she had seen Scotsmen sitting on the embankment but not throwing stones.

The defence called character witnesses only. Despite the police evidence, the jury found the prisoners not guilty on the first count and the chairman of the court, Lord Emlyn, ruled that it would be futile to proceed with the other charge. The verdict was met with applause and the prisoners were 'feted' outside the court room.

The plight of the 'Strangers' – 8 September

On 8 September the Evening Express reported on the plight of the men from Scotland and the North of England who, unlike the Welsh blacklegs, were mostly seen as innocent victims of the disturbances who were simply trying to earn a living for themselves and their families:

> *A terrible fate hangs over Tumble, in consequence of the district miners on Wednesday having resolved to make a murderous attack upon the Scotch and North of England miners employed at the Great Mountain Colliery, near Llanelly, unless they had left the place within 24 hours of the holding of the mass meeting on Wednesday after noon. The unfortunate men are penniless, and the refusal of the district to pay their fares home has placed them in a sad plight. On Thursday afternoon a deputation waited upon Messrs. Waddell and Beith with a view of getting assistance from the proprietors, and they also refused to render any help, at the same time advising the men to return to work. All the Welshmen and those in a position to pay their own fares left on Thursday in fear of the dreadful threat made. However, the Scotchmen and others, numbering about 50, after consultation with each other, resolved, under the circumstances, to return to work until Monday week, when, unless the management demand notice, they will have had sufficient to leave the place. They expressed a desire to tramp it home, but, with wives and families, this was found to be impossible. Work will be resumed this (Friday) morning, unless the rioters will return prior to their going down the pit. ... Although penniless, and the masters having refused to pay them the money due for work, twelve Scotchmen started tramping from the Great Mountain Colliery, Llanelly, this morning, owing to the merciless threat of the Welsh colliers. Fully 60 of the Scotchmen and Englishmen who remain there through poverty went down the pit protected by a strong police force. These men have their wives and children there. Serious rioting is expected when darkness sets in this evening.*

The account anticipated that there would be a march that day on Tumble of 12,000 miners and that full preparations were being made for the expected serious conflict. However, the march did not take place and the military in Swansea determined that while the Inniskilling Dragoons on duty in the neighbourhood did not need reinforcing their withdrawal would spark renewed hostilities. Strike-breakers had enabled work to resume at the colliery, but Scottish workmen were passing through Llanelli on the way north and more, but not all, were expected to follow. An application had been made to the colliery management to assist the men returning home, but this had been refused. Meanwhile, a detachment of the Dragoons had, according to the South Wales Echo, 'made an extensive reconnoitre of the district via Cross Hands and Penygroes but found no indication of renewed disturbances.'

By 11 September, the Dragoon contingent had been strengthened to 32 men under the command of Lieutenant Hamilton and was expected to remain in the neighbourhood for some time. They were accommodated in the colliery yard where two large tents had been erected for sleeping and dining accommodation. (Wilf Timbrell refers to their campsite being in a large field of Penllwynlleuci Farm on which the pit-head baths were built in the 1930s.) The colliery continued to operate with some 30-40 men employed and the South Wales Echo reported that:

> ... the company were prepared to take on 200 men, and were willing to give the old hands the first chance, but if the old hands did not avail themselves of the opportunity offered, colliers from afar would be engaged to fill their place. Several of the English and Scotch hands have left absolutely penniless, with the prospect of a three hundred miles' walk home. They strongly repudiated the suggestion that they were working below the standard rate of wages. "That", said a Durham man to me, "would be the very last thing I should think of doing. The fact is, we refused to work until the standard rate was conceded, and we are not working below it. We get 4s 6d per day plus the sliding-scale arrangement, I am a member of the Miners' Federation of Great Britain and am a believer in Trades Unions".

Tumble's 'tyrannous and ignorant multitude'

True to form, on 8 September the Western Mail, the voice of the Welsh establishment, laid into the people of Tumble with this leading article under the title 'Expulsion of British subjects':

> If the latest news from Tumble is anything like true, it is clear the natives of that part of Carmarthenshire know nothing of the principles by which society is held together. It is always easy to understand blows and bruises given and caused and received by an excited crowd, and to understand and excuse, to some extent, mob violence to property under intense

irritation. That is frenzy altogether, without any root of premeditation or of enduring malice.

But the Tumble miners, reinforced by their allies, had a very different method of procedure on Wednesday. With them there was, in fact, a great deal more method than madness. They straightforwardly proposed that all the men from the North of England and Scotland employed at the Great Mountain Colliery should "leave the district that day," adding, with haughty tyranny, that if any of them were found in the neighbourhood at night no mercy would be shown them." Then the six thousand Welsh miners from Tumble and all the countryside between Ystalyfera. and Kidwelly proudly and calmly marched away in a long, brave procession, headed by five bands.

Surely the reporter who sent this startling news must have been dreaming or romancing. If he has only stated facts, where were the magistrates who had gone up to this remote mountain village armed with the Riot Act? Where were the police? Where were the Dragoons while this "heart- rending scene," as the reporter calls it, was going on, while honest men at honest work were jumping hedges and running for their lives over fields, and women and children weeping bitterly at the harshness of their treatment?

When we read, further, that "some of the Englishmen and Scotchmen left by train and others on foot," we seize the chance of believing that there is internal evidence here of there being something wrong with this report of what actually took place. The Englishmen and Scotchmen could not leave Tumble by train unless the officials of the Great Mountain Colliery surrendered to the mob, which we are not disposed to believe. They could not dream of doing that, for they had police and Dragoons to fall back upon, and, if they had failed, the whole resources of the Empire in case of need. To lend any countenance to such mob demands is to give up the strength of civilisation and sink into barbarism again. In fact, we find it difficult to believe that any Englishmen or Scotchmen would demean themselves by obeying such orders from a tyrannous and ignorant multitude. We should rather have expected them to die fighting in the last ditch if there were no other course open to them.

In a letter to the Western Mail published on 9 September, a Scotsman gave his views on how his countrymen had been treated:

I know something of the anthracite colliers between Seven Sisters and Pontyberem and, for many reasons, like them greatly. Blood, however, is thicker than water, and, in justice to the Scotch miners at Tumble, I feel bound to ask if the Caledonian Societies at Swansea, at Merthyr, and at Cardiff are not bound to take instant action to demand for Scotchmen in Wales from the Government the same absolute unfettered right to earn their living in peace and quietness in Wales as a Welshman is at liberty to do it in Scotland, if he can. If the Scotchman is not to be guaranteed this right in Wales, beyond all question, then, the Act of Union here is a bigger farce in its relation to Wales than ever it has been in Ireland. Besides, Scotchmen have gone all over the world for centuries, and held their own against all imaginable odds by the force of their own individuality. It is too late in the day to think Scotchmen are going to be beaten off the field by a crowd of misguided Welsh miners. The Caledonian Societies of South Wales owe a duty to the expelled miners of Tumble. Their persecution affects all Scotchmen. Let us unitedly demand protection for them from the Home Secretary. "He that touches us shall not depart with impunity." In any case, it is clear that if there is any reality about the Caledonian Societies of South Wales they cannot do less than see, in this cruel emergency, that their unfortunate countrymen at Tumble either have their fares paid for them back home or are cared for and protected so long as they remain here, as a matter of principle,—I am, &c., Cardiff Sept. 8. J. M.

Mabon account – 16 September

On 16 September Mabon gave an account of developments at Tumble published in the South Wales Echo two days later:

We regret very much having to report that this dispute is not yet settled. Also that the new feature thereof—the sentimental part of it—seems to us more difficult of amicable settlement than the real wage dispute with which it commenced. What blocks the way to settlement at present is not the wage question, but the fact that a body of strangers has been engaged at the colliery since the commencement of the wage dispute. There are, it should be remembered, strangers and strangers at present employed at the Tumble. The first batch of these were working there prior to the dispute. Against these the old workmen have no complaint nor grievance. With all these they were on very good terms. These at present are, like the others, working on terms that the old workmen were willing to accept, but which the company would not grant to them. Hence the existing feeling towards them. The second batch are those men who have been engaged since the wage dispute commenced. These the workmen believe to be simply tools in the hands of the company to defeat them on the wages question. These consist of a small number of Welshmen, a small number of Englishmen, and a larger number of Scotchmen, between 40 to 60 in all, we were told. Against all these there exists some feeling, but the feeling is much more bitter towards the small batch of Welsh transgressors than against the members of the other two nationalities. It is, therefore, not a question of nationality, the Welsh against the Scotch people, as some people seem to think. It is nothing of the kind. It is the

Welsh against all fresh hands that come to work to the place while there exists a dispute respecting the amount of work to be done and the wage to be paid.

Mabon went on to comment on the determination of both the employers and workmen not to give in on the issue of the *strangers.* The employers were prepared to take the *old workmen* (about 24) back, on preferential terms, in their old working-places and to relocate the *strangers* to another part of the colliery. They were also willing to settle the new and disputed price lists by arbitration. Mabon noted that at a general mass meeting held on the mountain on 6 September, the *strangers* had expressed their willingness to leave for home with their families if given funds to cover the cost of their journeys.

On the position of the *old workmen*, Mabon maintained that on no account would they work with the *strangers* as they believed that to do so would preserve a 'continual source of annoyance, danger, and disorder.' They, the *old workmen*, firmly believed that these men had been brought in to enable the company to reduce the price list and then defeat them. Mabon made a plea to Welsh colliers not to work as blacklegs. In his view, had it not been for the issue of the *strangers,* the pay dispute itself could have been easily settled. Indeed, had the management made the same pay offer some six months earlier he believed that there would probably not have been a day's stoppage at the colliery, no disturbances and no need for the military and police then surrounding the village. He hoped the local authorities would 'in their wise discretion withdraw the military from the locality of the colliery at once.'

Soldiers' sports day and reading room opened – 23 September

While the strike continued, an unusual event took place in Tumble on the Saturday 23 September suggesting that things were calming. The South Wales Daily News (28 September) reported that:

> *... the detachment of the 6th Inniskilling Dragoons, at present stationed at Tumble, under the command of Capt. C. H. Paynter, gave an enjoyable athletic meeting. Chief Constable Phillips, Mr R. Beith (manager of the Great Mountain Colliery), Capt. Scott, and other prominent local gentlemen kindly helped to make the affair a success.*

Following various races involving the soldiers, miners and local children two of the soldiers:

> *... attired in female costume and with a dodger in the tub—three shies a penny—took a considerable amount of money. After the sports the soldiers gave a concert, under the patronage of Captain C. E. Paynter, Captain Scott, Mr T. Thomas (magistrate, of Llandeilo), Mr Beith, &c., the occasion being the opening of a new reading room, built by the Great*

> *Mountain Colliery Company, for the benefit of the inhabitants. Captain Paynter consented to formally open the room. Staff Sergt. Farrier Fatten occupied the chair, and assisted by Sergeant Harewood, used the hammer manfully. The soldiers sustained the programme in capital style, and were loudly applauded by a crowded audience.*

Despite this happy and surprising scene, the tension had not gone away. Nearly a month later, on 21 October, the Cardiff Times reported an alleged incident involving Scottish and English workers being shot when travelling in the workmen's train. In fact, all that had happened was that some boys playing with a catapult had fired a missile into the compartment causing a very minor injury to one of the men.

The authorities count the cost and men return to work – October

On 26 October 1893, the Western Mail reported the meeting of the Carmarthenshire County Council at which a letter had been read from the Secretary of State saying that the expenses of military deployed at Tumble for feeding and billeting of the men would be paid by the War Office, but that all other expenses should be paid by the local authorities. The newspaper gloatingly reported that:

> *A special rate of ½d. in the £ is a pleasant reminder to the ratepayers of Carmarthenshire that luxuries have to paid for. The Tumble riots quickened sluggish temperaments in the neighbourhood: it was a brave sight to see the dragoons sweeping through the villages. The whole thing was invigoratingly novel, but now the day of reckoning has arrived, and the privileges are forgotten in the penalties.*

While these administrative matters were being dealt with, as late as 28 October the Western Mail was reporting fear of further disturbances at Tumble:

> *Matters are still in a very unsettled state at Tumble, and there is some fear lest the Welsh colliers, flushed by the acquittal of three of their number at the Carmarthenshire Quarter Sessions, should again make an attack on the Scotch workmen, and repeat the scenes which terrified the neighbourhood a little time back. It appears that an application has been made by the management to increase the police force already stationed in the villages of Llannon and Tumble, and which comprises some sixteen men.*

The South Wales Daily News on 2 November reported that men were returning to work and mentioned, in particular, some 30 to 40 men from Llanelli and Felinfoel and the prospect of the colliery being in full swing in a very short time. However, things were not as straight forward as that suggested. There was ill-feeling between the local *old hands* of Tumble and the men from Llanelli and

Felinfoel as is evident from this letter from a Tumble collier published in the same newspaper on 14 November:

> *In reply to the Collier of Felinfoel's letter, and who is working at the Great Mountain Colliery, I beg to inform him that he and his fellow-workmen from Felinfoel and Llanelly ought to be ashamed of themselves. Their unfaithful and unfair conduct working as blacklegs during the Tumble Colliery dispute throws a cloud of disgrace over the Llanelly and Felinfoel district generally. The Felinfoelians and L!anellyites cannot say the same as the Durham and Scotch miners, that they were led here by fraud, and wanted help to return back. Possibly they will find some other excuse. What do the public, generally think of them, as the old workmen who are standing up for their rights are obliged to depart with their large families, crossing that mountain to earn their daily bread, or leaving their wives and children to be thrown out into the road, while the Felinfoel and Llanelly men are coming to betray and undersell them? Reconsider your position, brethren, and repent. and seek for work where there is no dispute pending, and do to others as you wish others to do to you. – I am &c, AN OLD WORKMAN*

This version of events was hotly disputed by a representative of the Felinfoel workers who claimed that he had never undercut the *old workmen* in terms of hours worked or pay rate.

The end of the strike and Mabon's balanced view

The long-standing dispute finally came to end on 1 January 1894. That morning a well-attended meeting of the *old hands* formerly employed at the colliery was held at the Gwendraeth Arms in Cwm-mawr. After a lengthy discussion, a deputation was appointed to meet with Robert Beith with the aim of reaching a settlement. The men selected - John Treharne, David Roderick, Jonah Evans, William Powell, and David Morgan – having met the colliery manager at his office, returned with the news that an amicable settlement had been agreed. The men would return to work on the same terms as those offered on 4 September, the day of the worst disturbances - Is 4d per ton for cutting coal and a percentage according to the sliding-scale. This was something of a victory in that in March 1893 the company had proposed one shilling per ton. The colliery manager had granted one further concession - that the men should be at liberty to choose their own doctor. The South Wales Daily News reported on 2 January that the news of the settlement 'evoked universal satisfaction both at the village of Tumble and in the Llanelly district.'

The final word on the events in Tumble in 1893 should be left to Mabon himself. In a powerful article publish in the South Wales Echo on 15 September he had expressed his strong regret about the violence resorted to by miners in disputes across England and Wales (his opposition to violence led to criticism from more radical miners). He saw violence as counterproductive bringing the case of the workmen into disrepute. However, he was supportive of the Great Mountain miners and their quite distinct cause and was concerned that the disturbances at Tumble would bring disgrace upon the locality and alienate public sympathy for a just cause.

He was critical of the press, especially the London newspapers, for mistakenly mixing up the dispute at Tumble with the wider unrest and violence across the South Wales coalfield. He argued that at Tumble the employers, not the workmen, were the aggressors. He contrasted how the wider South Wales disputes had been about workers seeking an increase in wages whereas at Tumble it was a case of the employers wanting to cut wages by more than 30 per cent to levels far below those paid at the colliery and at other collieries in the district for working the same seam. The employers had been convinced that they could attract enough workers at the new rates they were offering and had placed glowing advertisements in the press to attract men from Scotland and North of England.

Mabon expressed extreme sorrow over how these deceived *strangers* had been treated. He maintained that these men had initially refused to work at prices that undercut the locals and had been ready to return home with their families but were too poor to pay for the journey and the company had refused to fund them. As a result, they had been left with no choice other than to carry on working at Tumble for a time at the reduced rates paid by the company so fuelling and prolonging the wage dispute and disruption.

While not in any way condoning the violence which he abhorred, Mabon put the blame for the circumstances that led to the attacks on the *strangers* firmly on the shoulders of the company. Commenting on the Tumble workmen, he said that he could not account for how 'these peaceful, but ill-treated men' had become a 'furious mob'.

Full circle

Some seventy years later, *Men from the North* came to the Gwendraeth Valley again. This time the miners, with their families, from the Durham coalfields followed in the footsteps of their grandparents' generation to live in Tumble but to work at the expanding Cynheidre Colliery. Being uprooted and moved to an area with a different culture and language cannot have been easy, but they did generally receive a far warmer welcome than their predecessors. New homes were built for them (in Tumble these were predominantly within the new Rhosyderi estate adjoining the more established Rhosnewydd and Maesgwern developments built in the 1950s also mainly to meet the needs of the National Coal Board's workforce).

In Tumble School, the children of Durham families were initially taught in separate, mixed-age classrooms before being fully assimilated with local children of their age (the language challenges are noted in the school log for 25 March 1964). Some families found the move too difficult and returned to their native Durham. Others, however, settled permanently in Tumble adding to the richness of village life with echoes of all those families who had come from near and far to build the village some eight decades earlier.

GREAT MOUNTAIN ANTHRACITE COLLIERIES COMPANY LIMITED

REVISED LIST OF PRICES

As arranged between said COMPANY and DAVID MORGAN, THOMAS LEWIS, WILLIAM LLOYD, JOHN TREHARNE, DAVID RODERICK, DAVID MORGAN (2), JONAH EVANS, as deputation of the Workmen of the aforesaid Collieries on the 1st day of January, 1894.

BIG VEIN

	s.	d.	
Cutting and filling of Large Coal	1	4	per ton.
Cutting and filling of Thro' Coal	0	10	per ton.
Cutting and filling of Small Coal	0	2	per tram
Narrow Places not over three yards wide	3	0	per yard.
Stalls between three and five yards wide	1	5	per yard.
Machines Incline between three and five yards wide ...	4	7	per yard.
Double Timbers (not notched) in Stalls and Airways ...	1	6	per pair.
Props and Posts in Upper and Lower Sides only ...		6	each.
Cogs in Upper Side of Roads	3	0	each.
Cogs in Lower Side and in Gob	2	0	each.

All Double Timbers in Levels to be put up by Company unless otherwise arranged.

Clod 1/- per inch per yard to be paid for Clod in narrow places up to and including five yards wide. A double measurement to be made or 2d. per inch per yard to be paid in places over five yards wide.

Measurements to be made from top of coal.

		s.	d.	
Topholes.	Up to a distance of six yards	1	4	per ton.
	From six to twelve yards	1	6	per ton.
	From 12 to 18 yards	1	7	per ton.
	and so on for every six yards		1	per ton.

Props in Topholes for the first six yards in job to be put up free by workman but any distance above or beyond to be paid for, unless the timber is taken up by the Company, every additional six yards accordingly, as required.

Cogs in Topholes. These to be paid for as in stalls, c.c., those full height, 3d., the others on rubbish, 2d., each. Crossings to be driven at the same prices to the distances of 20 yards if required.

	s.	d.	
Double Shift (narrow places)	1	0	per yard.
Double Shift (wide places)	2	0	per yard.
Collier's Day Work, 4s. 6d. per day for experienced and competent men.			
Repairs (competent men)	4	6	per day.
Trammers ... ... 2s. 9d., 3. 0d., and 3	4		per day.
Hauliers ... ... 3s. 4d. and 3	7		per day.

All the foregoing are Standard Rates are subject to the existing percentages, viz : Colliers, 15% Day Wage Men 17½% and to any future advances or reductions as to be made from time to time **as per the Sliding Scale arrangement.**

Signed :

On behalf of the Great Mountain Collieries Limited

ROBERT BEITH, *Manager.* RICHARD ABRAHAM.

On behalf of the Workmen

JONAH EVANS. JOHN TREHARNE. DAVID RODERICK.
THOMAS LEWIS. WILLIAM , LLOYD. DAVID MORGAN.

Figure 64. The terms that brought an end to the strike of 1893.

7.The 1906 Jail Break

The 16th of June 1906 began much as any Saturday in Tumble. Colliers had surfaced from the morning shift on a fine day, collected their pay and perhaps visited the Tumble Hotel before going home for their tea. Some, including David Howells and his twin brother Thomas, returned to the pub that evening. The events that followed gave the Western Mail another opportunity to admonish the people of Tumble in lofty tones as it had done during the 1893 disturbances:

> The mining village of Tumble, near Llanelly, which gained an unenviable notoriety some years ago by an outbreak of rioting, which required the importation of a military force to subdue, was the scene on Saturday night of another wild orgy of lawlessness.

Wilf Timbrell provides the general context for the behaviour:

> On pay nights the Tumble hotel would be crowded to the porch, and the Workmen's club would be also well patronised. Fights would take place outside both buildings. That was the mode of life throughout the mining areas. Miners settled their personal disputes in bare fist fights ... These men were hard and tough, a quality acquired by the nature of their toil. Most of them had received a meagre education, paid for by taking pennies to the schoolmaster each week. In spite of their limited education, they were experts at the coalface and in the techniques of timbering etc.

That Saturday evening there was a send-off party for John Tomas, a member of the Greenhill family, who was leaving to live in Scotland, his wife's native country. Miners from the Great Mountain and Cross Hands collieries were drinking in the front bar of the Tumble Hotel. Just across the road was the house of Police Sergeant Lewis and his family which, from 1896 to 1909, also served as an informal police station (it was one of two houses built by Buckley's Brewery around the same time as they invested in the nearby Workingmen's Club). Timbrell sets the scene by explaining how he witnessed the events from the entrance to the colliery. In writing his account, he collaborated with his friend Edgar Jones – a tailor by profession and 10 years his senior. Jones' vantage point had been the front window of his brother's house on the other side of the road next door to the police house.

There was clearly heavy drinking and the Western Mail (rarely too concerned about balance in its coverage of events in Tumble) reported that a nasty quarrel had broken out between two men - Griff Evans and John Henry - causing Sergeant Lewis to intervene:

> Knowing the men he had to deal with, the sergeant, who is a most tactful officer, endeavoured to restore peace, but his appeal was lost on inflamed passions, and at last he ejected the most unruly of the crowd —a man

named David Howells. A well-known character in the district then turned the quarrel on to the sergeant, and his language was so foul and his demeanour so violent that he had to be turned out. In a few minutes Sergeant Lewis left the hotel, and, getting outside, found Howells waiting for him.

The officer again played the role of peace maker, his reward being a smashing blow between the eyes, which blackened both those organs and cut his nose very severely. This, of course, could not be tolerated, and Sergeant Lewis tackled his assailant and had him on the ground in no time. Then, however, Tom Howells, a brother, came along, and dealt the sergeant a cowardly blow on the back of his head, which stunned him for the moment. The officer, who is a fine specimen of manhood, standing 6ft. high, had by this time to tackle not only the two brothers, but a hostile crowd. He did not shrink from his duty, and in the emergency received the assistance of Mr. Williams, the well-known Llandeilo auctioneer, who, however, was laid out by a violent blow on the head. Police Constable Jenkins was also doing his best and was both struck and kicked.

This is Timbrell's different take on things:

This (the party) may have reached a noisy stage, but not uncontrollable. It may have been over-zealousness on his part, for no request for his assistance had been made, when the Sergeant entered the hotel. He often behaved in an overlordly manner and interfered with the liberties of the villagers. One particular customer had resented being ordered out by the sergeant for there were others there in a more drunken state. The sergeant was a tall powerfully built man, and the man also was tall and a fine athlete. It was after both had left the building that aggressiveness developed by the insistence of the sergeant to bungle the man [David Howells] homewards. The struggle followed and the truncheon drawn and the man was forced to the ground. The twin brother [Thomas Howells] was informed of what was happening outside and he ran and took the sergeant off by force. By this time the constable had arrived on the scene and both policemen took the first brother that had been involved to the police station nearby [at about 8.15 pm], and the other followed voluntarily and was also put under arrest.

The Howells twins were well-known Tumble characters and this, along with the drinking and party atmosphere, no doubt contributed to how the crowd of villagers reacted to these events. The perceived over-bearing attitude of Sergeant Lewis, a man highly respected in the force, will not have helped matters.

The siege of the Police House

After a quiet spell, it all came to a head again at closing time. A crowd of about 200-300 surrounded the sergeant's house. Lewis tried to get help from the police station at Pontyberem, three miles away, but the crowd would not let anyone leave the house and there was no telephone (the nearest telephone was at Cross Hands post office, and the private line of the colliery company did not operate on weekends). The Western Mail reported that the two policemen were:

> *... entirely cut off, and were at the mercy of the mob of roughs. Meanwhile the crowd shouted peremptorily for the release of the brothers Howells, and to enforce their demand they began a fusillade of stones at the doors and windows. In a few minutes there was hardly a whole pane of glass left in the building, and huge stones came crashing into the rooms, smashing the furniture to pieces, and one stone, bigger than a man's head, struck the sergeant just below the groin.*

A wooden gate was thrown through a sash window and an attempt was made by a section of the crowd to climb over the wall to get to the back of the building and into the kitchen which had been turned into a prison cell. The Sergeant's wife decided to take on the crowd, Mrs Lewis:

> *... pluckily made her appearance at the front door and remonstrated with the rioters. Her sex did not save her from rough handling, and, fortunately for Mrs. Lewis, her husband rushed out and carried her within doors again. By this time all the rooms in the house were strewn with stones, and hardly a wall or a door did not bear marks of the violence of the crowd.*

Without consulting his father, one of Sergeant Lewis' young sons also intervened. Grabbing a police cutlass, he went out onto to the street to defend the Sergeant who was remonstrating with the crowd. At the trial that followed, PC Jenkins described how, at his request, one of the Howells had gone to the window and urged the crowd to stop the stone throwing and to be quiet. The crowd had refused, and when Sergeant Lewis repeated the request the crowd had rushed at him. Having got the brother back into the house and closed the door, stones came crashing in including the one that hit the sergeant a no doubt painful blow. The police officers claimed that they had seen three of the ringleaders approaching the house each carrying a very large stone which they hurled through the window. These missiles were substantial coping stones from the walls and weighed between 15lbs and 20lbs each. The court heard that 16 stones had later been found in the front bedroom and 12 in the parlour, and that 15 panes of glass were broken. The total cost of the cost of the damage came to £5 9s 6d.

Sergeant Lewis described in court how on hearing stones coming through the back windows he could take no more and released the brothers. In court he said he had done so because he thought the house would otherwise have been demolished and that his and his family's lives were at risk. As the brothers left through the front door at dusk, they were met by a 'wild yell of exultation' and they were escorted home in triumph. Timbrell's account is consistent with this description of events but adds local colour:

> The proprietor of the little fair in the field where the Midland Bank now stands did not open for the evening and no paraffin flare lamps were lit, nor the oil lamp in its compartment at the entrance to the colliery. ... I felt sorry for the sergeant's wife and four young sons for whom it must have been a night of terror. The boys were well liked by the other boys of the village and continued to be so in later years, as can be shown as follows, seven years later Johnny, the eldest, was a member of the village rugby team and was instrumental in gaining victory in the 1912/13 semi-final on Stradey Park for the Carmarthenshire Challenge Cup which the team later won one by defeating Ammanford on Stradey Park.

This 'notoriously lawless district'

When the Western Mail reporter visited Tumble on the Monday all was quiet, but he reported that Sergeant Lewis' house had:

> ... an extraordinary appearance, and the sergeant is now in possession of a big stock of stones. It is a serious reflection on the county council that a district which has so much developed during the last decade should be policed by only two men. Especially stupid is the absence from the police-station of cell accommodation and telephonic communication. One shudders to think what would have happened had Sergeant Lewis decided to keep the two men in custody at all costs. Deplorable as were these happenings, they will serve one useful purpose, in demonstrating to the authorities the urgent need of making adequate provision in the matter of police supervision for this notoriously lawless district.

Summonses and counter summonses

A series of summonses resulted from the disturbances:

- The police summoned the following for their part in 'riotously disturbing the public peace' in the attack on the police house: John Henry (22) collier; Thomas Lewis (25) labourer; Henry L. Evans (21) blacksmith; Thomas James (29) collier; Benjamin Perkins, William Brazell, Richard Lloyd (all of Tumble Row); David Morgan, 10 Railway Terrace; John Jones and William Jones, Llettymawr; Rees Davies, Lodging House; David Williams, Treview.

- David Howells and his brother Thomas, both of 87 Tumble Row, summoned Sergeant Lewis and Mrs Lewis for assaulting David Howells.

- Sergeant Lewis summoned David Howells for being drunk and disorderly in Tumble Row on the 16 June and, along with his brother Thomas, for assaulting and beating him while in the execution of his duty on the same date.

The summons brought by the Howells against Sergeant Lewis and his wife for assault and the counter summons brought by the police against the brothers were heard at Llanelli magistrates court on 28 June. There was great interest in the proceedings and Tumble miners crowded the court (the atmosphere was highly charged - allegations were made that the witnesses against the Howells had been intimidated). The case against the Sergeant and his wife was heard first.

In opening, Mr. Ludford, representing the brothers, argued that the events had been 'provoked by the indiscreet and brutal conduct of the officer. He had acted with great indiscretion and behaved in a way that any policeman should be ashamed of.' David Howells then gave his version of the events starting with the row inside the Tumble Hotel between Griff Evans and John Henry. David Howells maintained that he had not been involved in that row but when Sergeant Lewis had intervened and ordered Henry out of the pub he had protested saying 'If he is to go out the two ought to go out.' The sergeant had then also ordered Howells to get out and as he was leaving, he claimed that the sergeant tripped him up and, while he was on the ground, put his knees on his chest to pin him down. He also claimed that Mrs. Lewis had thrown stones at him.

Mr. Richards, representing the Lewises, put it to David Howells that he and his brother had given the sergeant a 'fearful beating' resulting in two black eyes. Howells denied this suggesting that perhaps he had been struck by one of the stones thrown by his wife. He made the counterclaim that while inside the police station he had been struck twice in the face by the officer. This version of events was corroborated by another miner, Thomas Roberts, who brought with him a 'formidable piece of drainpipe' which he alleged was thrown by Mrs. Lewis at Howells. Roberts and Richards had this exchange:

> *Mr. Richards: Do you say that Howells was lying quietly on his back and the sergeant choking him? —Yes. And I suppose the crowd was waiting for him to draw his last breath? (Laughter.)— Yes. Do you seriously suggest that a Tumble crowd would allow a policeman to choke a man in that way? -I saw him doing it.*

Despite the evidence of Thomas Roberts, the charges against Sergeant Lewis and his wife were dismissed. The Howells brothers were each fined £5 and costs. This was not their finest hour, but they were skilled men who represented the colliery in timbering competitions which were the main field events at Eisteddfodau. They were also pioneering in bringing innovations to the village such as the motorcar. Their popularity, and the dislike of Sergeant Lewis' attitude, may well explain why such a large group of villagers reacted in the way they did on that Saturday evening.

Alleged ringleaders put on trial

The alleged ringleaders of the assault on the police house were put on trial on 14 November at the West Wales Assizes in Carmarthen. John Henry, Thomas Lewis, Henry L. Evans, and Thomas James were all charged with rioting and damaging the police station at Tumble on the 16 June. Mr. Denman Benson and Mr. A. Clive Lawrence appeared for the prosecution, and Mr. J Lloyd Morgan, K.C., M.P., and Mr. David Rhys for the defence. The case hung on whether there was convincing evidence that the men on trial had been ringleaders or had been picked on by the police to ensure that someone paid the price for the *rioting*. The defence team submitted that it would be extremely dangerous to convict upon the evidence of Sergeant Lewis.

Mr. Benson, for the prosecution, contended that the evidence of identification was complete, but this was challenged during the trial in relation to at least one witness for the prosecution - David Davies, an ex-constable of Glamorganshire. John Thomas, a colliery fireman living at 3 Railway Terrace, declared that he had seen Davies outside the shop of a Mr Daniel at the time of the events he claimed to have witnessed and so he could not possibly have seen the rioting and damage. Maggie Lewis of Tumble Row gave evidence that she had seen the gate being thrown at the sergeant's house by someone but not by one of the four prisoners. It seems that the people of Tumble, including Rev. Rowe Williams their Baptist minister and champion, closed ranks around the defendants.

In his summing-up, Mr. Justice Walton clearly felt the need to impress upon the jurors that they should do their duty. He was concerned about the difficulty in getting juries to convict in cases of disputed identification without the clearest evidence, especially where there was 'popular feeling' involved. He said, rather patronisingly: 'Juries, on the whole, may be trusted to do their duty. It is very rarely that a jury finds a verdict which is really unsatisfactory.' While recognising that it was the duty of the jury to be cautious so as not to convict the wrong men, he said that they should be 'conscientious, honest, upright, and courageous in returning a verdict of guilty if they thought they ought to.' The Judge seemed to struggle with Sergeant Lewis' decision to release the two prisoners. He recognised that he had done so to prevent further violence from the 'mob' but felt bound to say that it was an 'astonishing thing for a policeman to be compelled to release two prisoners by an outrageous mob threatening his property and, perhaps, his life.' He contended that most of the people in Tumble had participated in the riot and had been on the side of the rioters, and against law and order:

> ... It was obvious that most of the people knew perfectly well who were the ringleaders in this attack, and if it turned out that for want of evidence it was impossible to secure a conviction in this case it would be plain that the people of Tumble were on the side of the rioters and had no respect for law, order, and peace. It was perfectly ridiculous that, having regard to what happened, the people of Tumble should have called a public meeting and passed a. resolution protesting against a certain newspaper ("the Western Mail") describing the place as lawless. Evidence of this kind must not be treated lightly, as it was in the interest of everybody to prevent outrageous outbreaks of this kind and to preserve law and order.

Despite this clear lead from the judge, the foreman of jury, after an hour and a half's deliberation, announced:

> We have agreed that the four defendants were present at the time of the riot, but, owing to insufficiency of evidence, we cannot satisfy ourselves that they took part in the riot. Therefore, we give them the benefit of the doubt.

The Judge asked whether that meant a verdict of not guilty. The Foreman's reply of 'Yes' was met by 'suppressed applause'.

On 10 July 1906, the Chief Constable of Carmarthenshire, William Philipps, reported to a committee of the County Council and gave his support for the actions taken by Sergeant Lewis. He also recommended the erection of a proper police-station in Tumble. A committee member, Mr. Dudley W. Drummond, in moving the adoption of the chief constable's report, said that:

> He knew from personal observation what an unruly and dangerous neighbourhood this [Tumble] was, and he should certainly suggest that the surveyor should be asked to draw out the necessary plans for a new police-station without further delay.

Mr. Drummond expressed concern that there was no 'lock-up' in a district with several thousand colliers (the nearest were in Llanelli and Llandeilo). The Chief Constable's recommendation was unanimously adopted, and the County Surveyor was instructed to prepare plans for a police station in Tumble as a matter of urgency. The Surveyor later produced three different plans (one included a magistrate's room) with costs ranging from £1,160 to £2,200. There were concerns that the plans were too elaborate and placing unnecessary burden on the rate payer. The police station was however provided in Upper Tumble.

The aftermath – 'all the scum of the earth went to Tumble'

With the *jailbreak* disturbances following on from the 1893 riots, Tumble gained a reputation for lawlessness fuelled by the Western Mail and its strong pro-establishment stance. Rev. Rowe Williams again championed the people of Tumble. In June 1906 he wrote to the Western Mail protesting against claims that Tumble was a lawless district. He asserted that the village would 'compare favourably with any other place in Wales or England of its age and population for peace and tranquillity' and that improvement of its shortcomings would not be brought about by running the place down.

The following May, the Rev. Williams returned to the charge on behalf of the village. The issue was over the potential relocation of a workhouse girl from Pembrokeshire to Tumble. At a meeting of the Haverfordwest Board of Guardians at which the matter had been discussed, The Rev. J. J. Evans (vicar of Walton, Pembrokeshire) had described Tumble 'as a most dreadful place' adding that 'all the scum of the earth went to Tumble.' Following this he had been inundated with letters of protest from residents of Tumble. These included one from the Rev. Williams in which he gave his assurance that the workhouse girl would have a good home at Tumble. The Clerk to the Board of Guardians read out the letter in part at the Board's meeting in May 1907. His reluctance to read out a personal reference it contained to the Rev. Evans was met with laughter. When one member insisted on it being read out the Clerk again refused, to further laughter, suggesting that the Rev Williams had used down-to-earth Tumble language in describing his counterpart.

The guardians decided to allow the orphan girl to go to her sister in Cardiff in preference to Tumble. They declined Rev. Williams' invitation to visit every home in Tumble to see for themselves what the people of the village were really like. On 19 May the Pembrokeshire Herald gave a satirical account of the exchanges between the two reverend gentlemen:

> *A gem of Welsh humour, which will appeal especially to the Rev. J. J. Evans, flies as a spark from the anvil of "The dreadful village of Tumble." At a recent meeting of the Haverfordwest Board of Guardians the reverend gentleman oracularly asserted that "All the scum of the earth go to Tumble." The retort of the Tumble worm turning 'neath the heel of the oppressor' is unconsciously virile. "You come and stay at Tumble." From the vivid verbal description of "Dreadful Tumble" as a conglomeration of the scum of the earth the Rev. J. J. Evans must naturally look upon the invitation as an attempt to secure his presence in the infernal regions. But why the rev. gentleman's candid opinion of Tumble or any other place should demand the penance of his going the way of "All the scum of the earth" no man knoweth.*
>
> *Methodists, Baptists, and Congregationalists are already at Tumble, and only await the advent of the Rev. J. J. Evans, who is offered free hospitality*

by the Tumble resident who challenged his statement, if he will condescend to visit every house in the place, and after satisfying himself of their real character make a public withdrawal of "his slanderous statements." Tumble hospitality is a trifle overstrained. The idea of the rev. gentleman visiting three hundred happy Tumble homes and being interrogated by sturdy miners, and their even more verbally demonstrative better halves, as to why he designated them "All the scum of the earth," would possibly prove even more brim-full of interest than the door to door progress of an unpopular candidate for Parliament. That is, of course, unless the rev. gentleman speedily announced his complete conversion and full retraction of his former heresy. Then, awful fate, the Tumble people might keep him.

If not a statue like Jac Ty-isha, the Rev. Rowe Williams certainly deserves recognition for his staunch championing of the people of Tumble when they were under fire from all quarters.

The final word goes to Mrs James of Tumble Row

A few months later on 24 August, the drinking capacity of a Tumble man was challenged in court at Llanelli. Thomas James of Tumble Row had been charged with drunkenness but claimed that he had only had six pints and that it would take at least twelve to make him drunk. Mrs. James gave evidence asserting that her husband was 'neither drunk nor sober.' With this resounding support from his wife, James was fined 10 shillings.

8. 'The Price of Coal'

The men of Tumble, and their families, paid a heavy price for the profits generated by the Great Mountain Colliery. In 1913 an outburst (a combination of coal dust and methane) occurred in No. 1 Slant in the Fawr (Big Vein). This was the first outburst recorded in the Gwendraeth Valley – fortunately, there were no casualties. Outbursts, also known as blowers, involved an enormous quantity of fine dust being blown through small holes in the coal face by the power of the gas behind it. The warning was a *rap-rap-rap* like a motorbike starting – the signal for the miners to run for their lives. Phil Cullen (*Outbursts*) notes that the 1913 outburst was followed by a second one six weeks later and that over the next twenty years there were a further six with both slants affected.

With outbursts and other accidents, the colliery had the worst safety record in the Gwendraeth Valley with 61 men losing their lives – despite it fortunately escaping a major disaster. At least by 1936 the miners at Great Mountain could wash off the dust in the pithead baths before going home. Conditions underground were difficult, particularly in No. 1 Slant. The inadequate ventilation meant that men had to work in extreme conditions of dust and heat (far worse than in more modern pits). These are just a few examples of the type of accidents underground over five decades. They do not do justice to either the number of accidents or the range of dangers the men faced every day.

Tuesday 11 June 1918

Accidents underground involving the deaths or maiming of individual miners were common with a range of causes from roof-falls to incidents involving machinery or the drams that carried the coal to the surface. This is a particularly poignant example. William Owen John (in his twenties) of Park View, Tumble had been on active service in the Dardanelles (Gallipoli) and on the Western Front for 4 years before being temporarily discharged from the army because he had been wounded and gassed. He was deemed fit enough to go back underground as a rider on the drams. He was killed in No. 1 Slant, in a spot where the height of the road was only four foot. Some reports indicated that he was the victim of a roof-fall but at the inquest there was a suggestion that the accident involved one of the drams or a connecting rope – he had been found with a deep cut across his throat. He had started work at the colliery just the day before.

Monday 27 April 1925 - Gas

Morgan Daniels, fireman on duty at the Great Mountain, went down the No. 1 Slant early in the morning, accompanied by Mills, a boy of 18. Their job was to make the routine inspection before the morning shift started work at 6 o'clock.

When they reached the third stall in the incline, Daniels instructed Mills to stay put and he pushed further ahead with an electric lamp. A little while later Mills heard groans from his colleague and rushed forward immediately to find him collapsed. On feeling the gas overcoming him, Mills ran back for help and met night-shift men on the spake ready to make their way to the surface.

William Howells, another fireman, was a member of this party. Without waiting for a gasmask and guided my Mills, Howells raced back to find Daniels. On reaching him, despite the deadly accumulation of gas, he rushed forward and tried to drag his college out. However, Howells was also overcome by the fumes and collapsed on top of Daniels. Rees Morgan, the colliery manager, arrived at the scene ahead of the properly equipped rescue party. He insisted on trying to reach the men but in the process was himself overcome by the gas. Fortunately, the men with him had tied a rope around him and were able to drag him back to relative safety undoubtedly saving his life.

The two firemen were taken back to the main slant, unconscious but still alive. Dr Evans (the Tumble GP) and Mr J.R. Davies, the colliery first-aid man, gave them artificial respiration for over an hour underground. Still unconscious, at about nine o'clock, the men were brought to the surface and taken to the colliery ambulance room where further attempts were made to resuscitate them, but both died. There were touching scenes at the pithead when the bodies were removed to their homes. Both men had worked at the colliery for many years. Morgan Daniels (43) was married with five children, living at Gwynian House, Upper Tumble. William Howells (50) was also married, with nine children, living in Cwm-mawr. William Howells' bravery was recognised by the Carnegie Heroes Foundation Trust who also gave support to his wife and children.

Thursday 30 May 1935 - Outburst

Edgar Collins (fireman, aged 47 of Singleton Road) and Llewelyn Evans (collier, aged 33 of Railway Terrace) were driving an airway in the coalface. They were working in an opening of about three and a half feet high cutting the coal with mandrills. Collins, as fireman, was in charge of the operations. A third man, Samuel Roberts, a 'colliery repairer' of Pontyberem, had been assisting the work but had been ordered by Collins to work at another spot. Hearing an unusual sound from where the two men were working, Roberts returned to the airway shouting for his colleagues but without response. He then picked up a spare oil lamp and tried to force a way into the airway. He could see Evans lying in the coal dust between two posts. He tried to reach him but was beaten back by the volume of gas - his safety light was extinguished. The men had cut into a pocket of gas releasing a blower, as a result of which Evans had become wedged between two posts and Collins was buried in the coal dust underneath him. Dan Thomas of Heol y Neuadd, who had worked at the colliery for seven years when the outburst occurred, gave this account to Phil Cullen:

The men had tried to get out of the heading by crawling backwards out of the place, they had no room or time to turn around. The first man down the roadway had got a post stuck between his legs and due to the presence of the second man who was partly buried by the dust ... was unable to move forward to free himself and therefore the two were unable to get free.

Meredith Collins, brother of one of the trapped men, and William J. Rees of Drefach, with electric lamps, attempted to enter the gas-filled area, but were also forced back by the volume of gas. Rescue efforts were then taken up by the official rescuers who had to remove the posts between which Evans was wedged before he and Collins could be released. As in the 1925 accident, Dr Evans had descended the mine and under his direction ambulance men attempted to resuscitate the men for some hours without success. The cause of death was asphyxiation by gas. At the inquest, the efforts to rescue the men were described as heroic. Phil Cullen provides a more detail account including of the questions left unanswered by the inquest and later apportionment of blame. Over the next ten years outbursts continued occur - there were no fewer than thirteen between 1945 and 1958. In one incident in 1956 in No. 2 Slant, 450 tons of material erupted from the face filling the roadway to within two feet of the roof – the fireman who had set the charge in the new roadway had run for his life and survived.

Wednesday 4 November 1936 – roof fall

The Western mail reported: 'Well-known Half-back Killed in Pitfall. Ivor Matthews, aged 32, of Cefneithin, Cross Hands, near Llanelly, the well-known Rugby player, was killed by a fall of roof while following his employment as a collier at the Great Mountain Colliery, Tumble, on Wednesday. Matthews, who has played half-back for Swansea, Llanelly, Carmarthen, and Llandebie, was a single man.'

Friday 25 February 1958 - Outburst

Men working at the Fawr (Big Vein) in No. 2 Slant on the afternoon shift heard a rumbling noise – it was a blower. One man at the scene, Malcolm Donoghue of Ponthenry, described how on hearing a noise like thunder he and his butty (Glyn Jones) started running towards the top of the face, but someone (identified later as Bill Picton) shouted 'no, the other way'. The two men then ran to the bottom away from the blower and got clear but men behind them were caught by a fall of coal. Mike Gibbons, also of Ponthenry, described how:

There were eight men working at the face. There was no warning at all. We were working at the face where the roof was only four feet six inches high when a blower of gas came quickly. The area filled quickly with the fall but luckily for me some of the boys were near at hand and quickly extricated me.

A rescue team of volunteers rushed back to the face entrance and on clearing some of the dust found something buried which turned out to be the head of Bill Picton. They removed the dust from his face which enabled him to breathe and dragged him free. Having given the warning call to Malcolm Donoghue, Bill Picton had become stuck and buried by the dust erupting from the coal face. Mike Gibbons, who had been completely buried in the dust, was also rescued. Three men were less fortunate and lost their lives: Glyn Jones (27) of Heol-y-Neuadd; Ieuan Lewis (33) married, of Brodynys, Llandeilo Road, Cross Hands; and Mel Jenkins (33) married, with nine children, of Llanddarog. Phil Cullen gives this account of reflections made by Dan Thomas (Dan the Roadman), of Heol Y Neuadd, on his neighbour Glyn Jones (known in the village as Spadge):

Glyn had left his food box at home that afternoon and had returned to fetch it. His mother, who felt that it was unlucky to do so, pleaded with the son not to return to the mine and not to go underground that afternoon; however, Glyn was not of a superstitious nature and picked up the box, reassured his mother that he would see her later, and returned to the mine. She never saw him alive again.

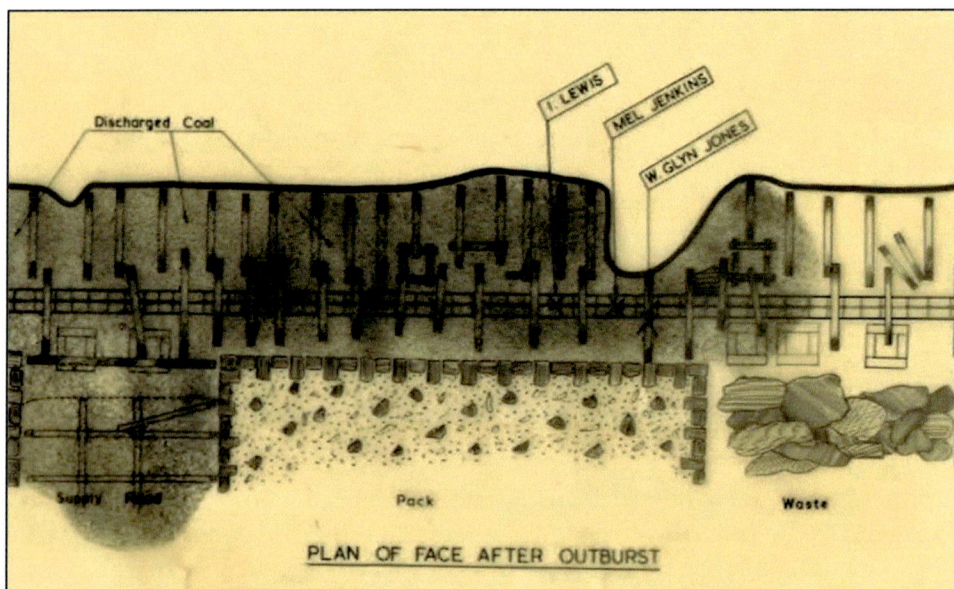

Figure 65. Extract of drawing partially showing the coal dust discharged by the outburst and the positions of the men who died. Courtesy of Phil Cullen.

Phil Cullen, in a more detailed account of this incident, describes how Malcolm Donoghue, who had escaped by squeezing himself through a narrow gap between the conveyor and the low roof, would for the next couple of years 'be woken during the night with dreams of running for his life out of the Gate Road and up the gradient to safety.'

Figure 66. The casualties are brought to the surface at GMC. Western Mail 26 February 1958

Phyllis M. Jones recalls the accident in her book, *They Gave Me A Lamp – Reminiscences of a Colliery Nursing Officer.* She had come to Tumble from Cornwall in the late 1950s to work at the Great Mountain Colliery as a Nursing Officer for the National Coal Board. This was her first serious incident. It led to her meeting two young local doctors – Dr G. Sheehan and Dr J. Hopkins. The two doctors were preparing to go underground to tend to the victims of the accident. She recalls them asking, 'as if it were their last request', whether they could telephone their wives first. On arriving at the scene of the accident the two doctors could do little more than to declare the three victims as dead. This was not Dr Sheehan's first experience of going underground in response to a major incident – a few years earlier, in 1955, he had gone down the shaft at nearby Blaenhirwaun Colliery following a massive gas explosion ignited by a spark from a stone lodged in a ventilation fan. He had tended the 6 men killed or fatally injured and others suffering severe burns.

Figure 67. The young doctors with Nurse Phyllis Jones.

The MP for Carmarthen, Lady Megan Lloyd George, raised the tragedy the following day in the House of Commons. On behalf of her colleague Jim Griffiths MP for Llanelli who could not be there, she asked the Conservative government to make a statement to the House on the tragedy. The government's response was to say that they had attended to certain financial matters regarding the families of the deceased and that there would be investigations by the Mines Inspectors into the outburst. Jim Griffiths MP pressed for a full inquiry. The government was not prepared to go that far but did announce a review of precautions taken at the Great Mountain Colliery to prevent such accidents happening again. The inquest was held at the Elim Chapel, Tumble on 6 March 1958, with the jury returning verdicts of accidental death.

In 1960, the National Coal Board opened an outburst research centre at the Great Mountain Colliery to undertake long-overdue research into the ever-present danger. When the colliery officially closed in 1962, the centre remained until being relocated to Cynheidre Shaft 3 at Cwm Colliery in 1970.

Dust - 'The Greatest Enemy'

An outburst was a dramatic event, but the big disabler and killer was the dust filling the men's lungs each shift leading to a condition known as pneumoconiosis. Wilf Timbrell considered himself and two of his friends from boyhood, all three octogenarians, to have been living proof of the impact of the dust of which all three had been spared by being employed in the mechanical department for most of their working lives. Sadly, he reflects on how 'many friends of our generation passed away as much as three or four decades ago from the scourge of pneumoconiosis.' Timbrell also notes that in the early days

126

the condition was not a recognised disease and was known in Welsh as *mogfa* (suffocation). Pneumoconiosis was a particular problem in the Gwendraeth Valley and especially at Tumble and neighbouring Glynhebog. Owners, out of ignorance or concern about compensation claims, were slow to recognise the life-shortening effects of this occupational hazard.

Mechanised coal-cutting made the dust more rather than less of a problem until long-overdue safety measures were introduced. The miners' unions campaigned strongly for compensation (Glyn Cox, the union secretary at the Great Mountain, wrote a pamphlet, *Martyrs to Dust*) but the miners of Tumble and elsewhere had to wait until after nationalisation of the coal industry and the passing in 1947 of the Mines & Industrial Injuries Act to receive compensation and even then getting deserved compensation was an arduous process with an apparent reluctance of the medical profession to put a man's disability down to the occupational disease.

Lung disease was the major contributory factor to the high level of unemployment in Tumble in the years following the Second World War. Official unemployment figures published in March 1946 (as reported in the Western Mail) disclosed that of the 650 unemployed registered at Tumble, four out of every five were disabled men. The management of the Llanelli Employment exchange commented on the difficulty of finding suitable work for those with pneumoconiosis and plans were developed to provide two special factories in the Gwendraeth Valley for disabled persons. A survey conducted by the National Union of Mineworkers (NUM) between 1948 and 1961 found that 40% of the underground workers suffered with some degree of pneumoconiosis.

By July 1950, the number of unemployed men in Tumble was still high at 339. The meeting of Britain's mineworkers' delegates at Llandudno was told all these men were victims of the dreaded mining disease pneumoconiosis, and that Tumble was a black spot for the disease in the coalfield with the highest incidence in the country (in 1951 of the 299 unemployed in Tumble, 247 suffered from pneumoconiosis). The NUM were tasked with urging the government to implement the *Grenfel* scheme – factories specifically for disabled miners. Construction of the factories was initially delayed by the post-War shortage of steel. By 1950 the factory in Tumble had been built but remained empty eventually to open in 1952. By 1956 the factory in Bethesda Road, on the site of an old colliery and former rugby pitch, was in full swing, employing 100 people making folding doors for portioning rooms and *Venetian* blinds *for brighter homes*.

Phyllis Jones, in a chapter headed *The Greatest Enemy is Dust,* described how the health and quality of life of a man inflicted by pneumoconiosis would deteriorate. She had observed that the first symptoms would be breathlessness walking up slopes which at first men would put down to advancing years. There would then be bouts of coughing and an increasing tightness in the chest, tiredness and the man's strength would start to drain. The symptoms would increase in intensity and quite often caused heart failure. She describes how a typical sufferer, aged about 45, would notice that he had to take 'spells' when walking and would soon have to stop work. In the next stage he would try bravely to keep in touch with the community by sitting on public seats, provided by the council, to chat with fellow sufferers. He would try to make it to the Welfare Hall or Rugby Club but eventually would be forced to remain in his house. He would then become demoralised and his bed would have to be brought down to the living room: 'The sick miner became a prisoner in his own home and suffered all the humiliation and depression which accompanied this state.'

There was still room for dark humour. Phyllis Jones retells a story of a group of miners during the war who were training with the Home Guard. One well-known character, WA Richards, remarked that, 'We'd be fine troops for any army, no guts to advance and no breath to retreat.' Another old miner on reaching the surface after his shift cleared his throat and said: 'I've coughed enough today to keep my Raeburn going for a week.'

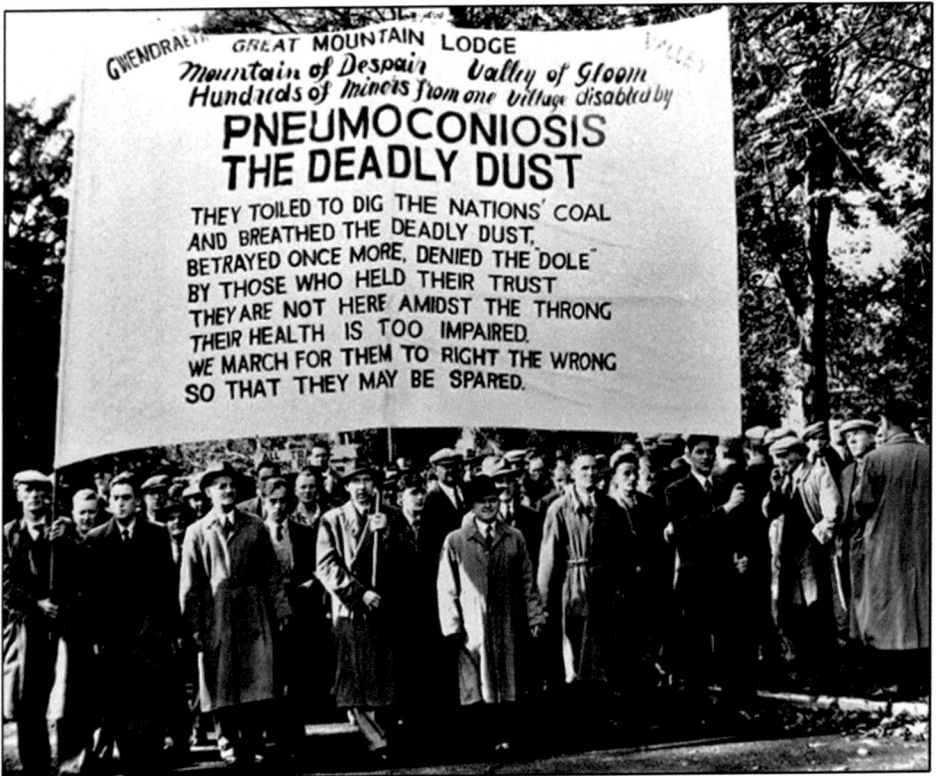

Figure 68. Great Mountain miners in the 1950s protesting against the attitude of the authorities to pneumoconiosis. Courtesy of National Museum of Wales.

With the closure of the Great Mountain Colliery, Phyllis Jones went on to work at the Cynheidre *super-pit*. She recalls her experiences there including a serious incident, an outburst, on 6 April 1971. Six men died including Luther Davies (56) an overman from Railway Terrace, Tumble. She describes Haydn Mills, a well-known Tumble character who fractured a pelvis in the incident, as an 'unsung hero' who 'played an important part in many rescues underground, because he was small enough and brave enough to crawl through a small space.' She also praises the colliery's First Aid Attendants and singles out David John Jones (Dai Coed-y-Bryn) who had spent a lifetime in coal mining. When the phone rang in the medical centre at Tumble, she would leave Dai to answer as, unlike her, he could speak to the men reporting an accident in their own first language.

Figure 69. Monument to the miners of GMC located in Tumble. (author's collection)

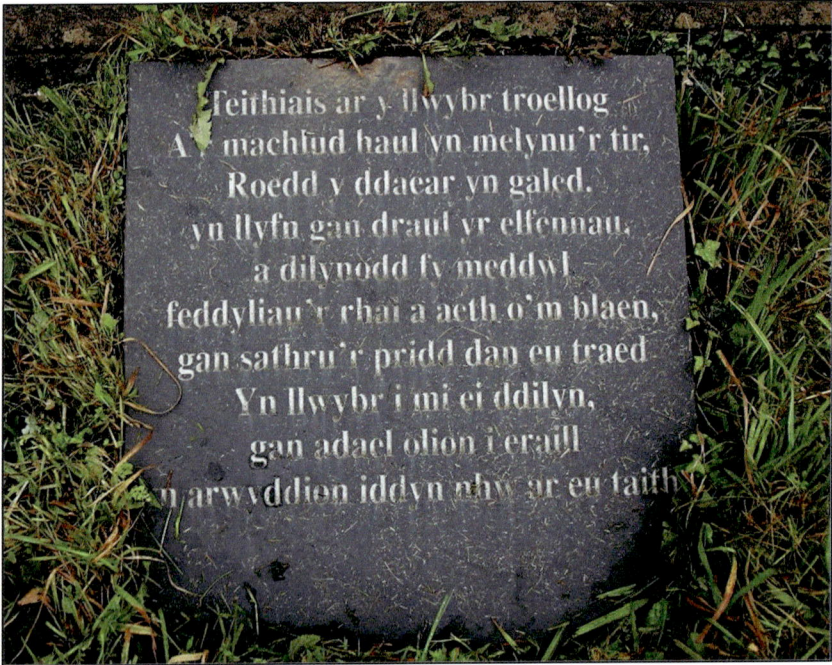

Figure 70. Poem in honour of the miners of GMC accompanying the monument (author's collection)

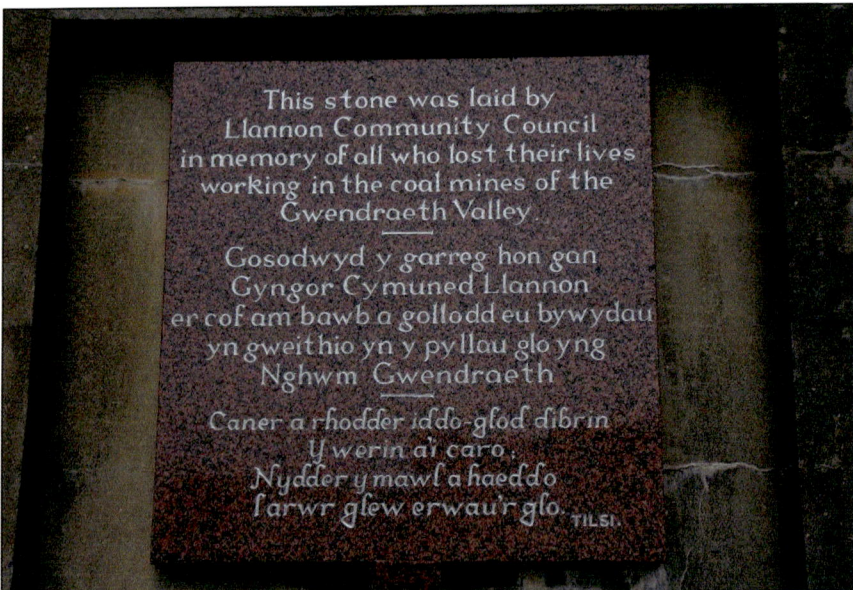

Figure 71. Memorial stone at former entrance to the GMC (author's collection)

9.Conditions Above Ground

Tumble's rapid industrial growth through the 1880s and early 1900s was not matched by the provision of basic infrastructure for the essentially new village. Amenities such as a good water supply, sewage, waste disposal and health-care provision were left wanting; and social, welfare and education provision took decades to catch up with the need. The colliery owners had made the investment in housing, if of a very basic standard, to attract the workers they needed but, along with the county and local authorities, had not invested in the welfare of the workers and their families. Indeed, in the early 1900s they took away the long-established right of miners to concessionary house coal – it took 30 years and court proceedings to win back this right (fortunately, Tom Jones of Rose Cottage, Greenhill, had kept his pay dockets which provided proof of 'custom and practice' in favour of the miners). There was also a period in the early 1900s when the colliery was seen to treat its tenants very unfairly including in ways that discouraged them from improving their own homes in Tumble Row/High Street. This physical neglect, and for a period seemingly uncaring attitude, may have contributed to earlier disturbances. There can be little doubt about the severe impact on the health of the village in the summer of 1917.

The typhoid epidemic of 1917

By the summer of 1917 there were some 40-50 cases of typhoid in the village with whole families affected and 8 deaths (this was not the first serious outbreak of typhoid in the village – between June and December 1892 there had been 14 cases). The cause of the outbreak was hotly disputed. The Llanelly Rural District Council, responsible for public health, claimed the source to be infected milk from one or more farms in Carmarthenshire but outside the district. The miners' representatives, led by S. O. Davies, a checkweigher at the Great Mountain Colliery, pointed the finger of blame firmly at the colliery owners and their neglect of the company-owned housing resulting in highly insanitary conditions – perfect for the typhoid bacterium to flourish.

In July 1917, Davies wrote two letters to the Carmarthen Journal drawing attention to the seriousness of the outbreak and making a detailed case as to the cause. He expressed angry disappointment with the response of the local authority including over its failure to respond to the miners' request for a temporary isolation hospital to be erected. At that time the workmen of the Great Mountain Colliery were subscribing weekly towards the building of a Public Hall in the village and had asked the District Council to convert the hall into an isolation hospital unless they were able to provide a purpose-built one. The miners' representatives were also disappointed with the support from colliery owners – they felt that John Waddell jnr. had been slow to intervene.

A deputation appointed by the miners had met with the District Council, but the discussions had gone badly (not helped by the Council questioning the credential of the deputation). Davies described the 'indifference or obduracy' of the District Council' which had compelled the miners to take the position that should the Council 'persist in its refusal to deal seriously and effectively with the typhoid, they, the workmen, for their own protection and that of many others, would be obliged to refuse work at the colliery.' Davies emphasised that the Great Mountain was one of the largest collieries in the anthracite district, and that at least half of its workmen lived outside Tumble (including Llanelli, Felinfoel, Cross Hands, Cefneithin and Drefach). He warned about the risk that these workmen would carry the disease to their villages and called for public opinion to be roused to get the District Council to act. He demanded the isolation of those stricken by typhoid: 'We have had no less than three families with every one of its members down with the fever!'

 To provide some respite, the villagers had themselves paid for ten convalescent patients to spend a few weeks by the seaside at Pendine (one had been called back home after just a day to look after his wife who had become ill with typhoid). Yet, to the consternation of the miners, the District Council and its Medical Officer of Health maintained the position that an isolation hospital was unnecessary. Davies challenged the Council's claim that the cause of the outbreak of typhoid was contaminated milk from certain farms which he described as 'an insult to the intelligence of the people who know this locality.' He argued that the outbreak was the consequence of overcrowding and described the village as:

> *... devoid of even the most primitive forms of sanitation, with its clogged superficial drains and culverts, the absence of a refuse receptacle, or means of its removal, its numerous cesspools and its hundred evil-smelling spots. Add to this at least a hundred company houses unfit for human habitation, with their open bedrooms, and one closet for two houses, which often means four families. Physical health is not easily attainable under condition that make common decency almost impossible. ... Frankly, we are fed up with both Mr. Waddell, the local representative owner of above-mentioned "company" houses, and the Medical Officer of Health, within whose area such disgracefully unhealthy conditions have enjoyed an undisturbed tenure for such a long time. We are tired of hearing those comfortable people talking interminably of infected milk, wells, typhoid carriers, etc all outside their own neglected area, while people are stricken, unto death in this fever- ridden village.*

A week later Mr E.R.R. Lewis had a letter published in the Carmarthen Journal in which he maintained that 'wicked attempts' had been made to 'conceal the truth regarding the ravages of this outbreak, and the scandalous conditions locally which were responsible for it.' He dismissed as 'far-fetched theories' claims, made 'by certain doctors', that the disease had been 'imported from the trenches' of the Western Front or, as the Medial Officer of Health maintained, from infected milk (the finger of blame had been pointed at Llwynybrai and Llwynifan farms, both conveniently outside the MOH's district). Lewis dismissed these claims as attempts to deflect attention from the insanitary conditions in Tumble, the true cause of the outbreak:

> *It may be stated that the drainage is quite primitive and seriously defective in many places and utterly incapable of fulfilling the demands of a congested village such as Tumble. Drains leave the premises of dwelling-houses and the water remains standing on the roads and ditches Some of these ditches are highly offensive and form hotbeds of disease. The unavoidable use of much soapy water by colliers at home makes these open ditches stink abominably during warm and dry weather. Many culverts also are inefficient; during wet weather they are of great inconvenience, causing floods, and during dry weather give off offensive smells from the stagnant waters.*

He also described how the Duffryn Brook, once a source of drinking water, had been polluted and how some years earlier had been the source of typhoid infection from which a whole family of ten had died – nothing had been done since to remove that danger. Turning to the condition of the colliery-owned housing he remarked that:

> *The houses of High-street, Tumble, have now almost become proverbial for their unwholesomeness. Here we find a long, ugly row of company houses, knocked up in order to herd together the workers who help to make the wealth of the colliery owners. Here are open bedrooms and bedrooms so small as to render physical health and moral decency almost impossible. The overcrowding is serious. The local representative owner of these houses admitted some few weeks ago that prior to the outbreak of war no less than "22 people lived in one of the company houses".*

He added that the 100 houses in High Street would 'stand condemned in the light of the most elementary laws of hygiene' and described conditions in Bethesda road as 'notorious'. S.O. Davies was dismissive of the report of the Local Government Board's Sanitary Inspector who had undertaken an inspection in the village accompanied by John Waddell and the district's Medical Officer of Health and demanded a full public inquiry.

At its meeting on 25 July, the Carmarthenshire County Council considered the provision of a temporary isolation hospital. It ruled out the option of using the public hall because it was 'not suited for the proper division of the sexes.' The Council did however give permission for the use of the new school as a temporary isolation hospital during the summer holiday. On 29 July, the Carmarthen Rural District Council, whose area included the farms identified as possible sources of the typhoid infection, received a letter from the Local Government Board's inspector reporting that he had found 'extremely insanitary conditions' at both farms. Whatever the original source of the typhoid, conditions in Tumble had provided it with a perfect breeding place. Responsibility lay with both the local authorities and the colliery owners who had allowed the condition of the houses they owned to fall well below the acceptable standards even of the time.

By November 1917 there was also concern over an influenza outbreak. Mrs Lewis of Caldy View, Tumble who, along with her husband Sergeant Lewis, had featured in the disturbances of 1906, was one of the casualties (Sergeant Lewis had died suddenly in 1914). Tumble had to wait until 1936 for its isolation hospital. The Carmarthenshire County Isolation Hospital was opened in February that year on an eight-and-a-half-acre site in Upper Tumble, initially with accommodation for 44 patients. It included a diphtheria block, a scarlet fever block and a mortuary. The total cost of the scheme was £21,000.

Figure 72. High Street around 1910.

Water supply

The quality of the village water supply had been a longstanding issue and had been linked to outbreaks of disease – in 1893 one of the Inniskilling Dragoons stationed in the village fell victim of typhoid and this was blamed on the poor quality of the water. The Llanelly Mercury on 26 May 1910 published this letter from a villager:

Sir,—May I, through the medium of the "Mercury," draw the attention of the Llanelly Rural District Council to the inadequate water supply in Tumble? New houses are being constantly built, two families live in the same house in many instances, and in almost every house there are two or three lodgers. New pits and drifts are being sunk, works are expanding, population is increasing; but the water supply remains stationary. It is futile to talk of reforming the working- classes, and to teach them the gospel that cleanliness comes next to godliness, if the means and wherewithal of cleanliness is kept from them. Does the District Council realise that we have an absolute right to a plentiful supply of water'? Yes, as much right as we have to the air we breathe; but perchance they think that the Almighty intended the rich to have a monopoly of the water, as they have of the land, etc. I feel positive that if Tumble had been inhabited exclusively by rich people, and that instead of workmen's cottages we had villas and palaces, we would, incidentally have a plentiful supply of water; nay, more, we would have a model railway system, and we would have sanitary arrangements worthy of the name. But, still, the workers, the producers of all wealth, are deprived of the very necessaries of life, to enable the few to scour the country in their motor cars, etc. How long, 0 God, how long? Thanking you in anticipation, —I am, etc., JOSEPH WILLIAMS. 36 Railway Terrace, Tumble.

Wilf Timbrell, reflecting on the early 1900s, described the water supply (adding some natural history notes):

This water came from a spring in a field near the lane to the Gweunydd Cochion and the pipes leading from it can be seen from the main road. A cistern is also to be seen at the bottom of the field opposite Abbey View, Heol-y-Bryn, from which pipes were connected to the roadside taps in High Street, and the overflow went to the colliery pond. On the left side of the main road near the spring was a narrow plantation of coniferous trees, extending parallel with the road for approximately 100 yards, and was known as Cwm-y-Ferren. We children had great fun during the summer months watching pretty red squirrels there springing from tree to tree. Unfortunately they are now extinct in the area. During dry weather periods it was a problem to maintain household and colliery supplies and the pond's level would get exceedingly low. Most families had water butts for rainwater storage. Careful watch was kept by a colliery employee to ensure all channels leading to the ponds were kept free of any restrictions. This patrol extended also to a spring at Graig-y-Lletty; its fine drinking water was discharged from a pipe into the pond.

The Carmarthen Journal reported on a special meeting of the Llannon Parish Council held in August 1918 at Llechyfedach School. The Council had been pressing the Rural District Council to improve water supply in the area and, while welcoming the work that had started on the extension of water mains to Cwm-mawr and Pontyberem, made clear its dissatisfaction with the District

Council over the position in Tumble where the water tap on the 'main road' had yet to be opened and water supply to Bethesda Road had also been delayed.

Figure 73. Heol y Neuadd. Possibly showing a roadside tap at bottom right.

Sanitary conditions

Wilf Timbrell commented on the 'appalling sanitary conditions' noting that the closets of High Street were shared by two families: 'A man was employed to empty the buckets into cesspits situated on open land some distance from the garden walls. Earth was thrown over the contents, if he felt disposed to do so, or if indeed he was sober! Who could blame him for being drunk!' The cesspits were removed after the typhoid outbreak and the night soil was carried away in carts. This method of disposal continued until 1930 when houses in High Street were provided with flushing toilets.

The condition of the Company-owned housing had not improved by the time the young preacher, Tom Nefyn, arrived in Tumble in the mid-1920s. Glyn Anthony in *Coal Dust & Dogma* describes the energetic campaign Nefyn mounted to get improvements. He personally undertook a survey of most, possibly all, houses in High Street and recorded all the faults in a report he presented to the Company. He was shocked by the state of the houses and outside shared toilets, often with missing doors, and the primitive arrangement for collecting the 'soil' from them. In a personal aside, Anthony recounts:

I remember seeing this tank going by once, when I was a boy. It was such a revolting and nauseating sight that I couldn't get the picture out of my mind for days, nor could I cease reflecting on the disgusting task of the two men working in the interests of village hygiene. This spectacle so frightened one of the women in the street that she shouted out, "Close your doors everybody, or else you will get typhoid".

Through Tom Nefyn's persistence and powers of persuasion, in a matter of months 'the street was echoing to the sound of hammers, the scraping of ladders and the clanking of buckets. The whole street was not only repaired, but given a face-lift as well, its drab façade enlivened with a light grey covering of plaster.' Glyn Anthony concluded his account with a further personal observation:

As a sequel, some years later the Company sold the houses cheaply to the occupants, and I have been filled with surprise and admiration at the beautiful alterations, replanning and tasteful decorations that have been made by their new owners, who are now rightly proud of their homes.

Street lighting and power supply

Street lighting was originally by oil lamps in glass-panelled compartments on top of eight-foot cast iron pillars (see example at fig. 74). On 15 December 1910, The Llanelly Mercury published this letter from Tumble's lamplighter in response to criticism of the village's street lighting:

Sir,—In reply to your correspondent at Tumble, I think if he gave more of his time to finding out facts than looking after other people's affairs he would not be so liable to make mistakes, as the street lamps have nothing whatever to do with the District Council, but they belong to the inhabitants of the village, who pay for them by subscription. (He must be backward with his subscription, and the committee had better look him up for it.) If he thinks he can give better light to the lamps than he can to the subject, he is invited to give them a trial for a week, by making arrangements with the lamplighter. — I am, etc., THE LAMPLIGHTER.

Later, the colliery power station, located between the two slants, provided electricity for village street lighting and, at a very basic level, for its homes. In November 1919, the Parish Council asked the colliery company 'for terms per annum for 50 Candlepower lamps for the areas suggested by them.' In July 1922, the Council 'Passed unanimously to ask Great Mountain Co. to push on as much as possible with the lighting of Tumble Street, as Cross Hands Co. has got everything ready and the light tested and provided satisfactory.'

Throughout this time, with lack of basic amenities and large families (as well as lodgers in many cases), the life of women was at least equally as hard as that of the men. Water had to be carried from one of a small number of public taps to be heated on the fire for cooking, bathing and washing. With miners coming home 6-days a week filthy with coal dust and sweat, working clothes had to be washed and dried ready for the next morning. During the First World War, many young women from the village worked in appalling and dangerous conditions in the munition factories including at Pembrey.

Getting about

The state of the roads serving Tumble was something of a scandal in the Edwardian era. This very sad account, published in the Amman Valley and East Carmarthen News on 9 December 1908 highlights the particularly poor condition of the road from Tumble to Llanelli:

> *The deplorable condition of Carmarthenshire roads has claimed another victim. The tragedy occurred on the Llannon Road, near Tumble, on Monday evening. It was on that particular stretch of road concerning which one of our County Councillors valiantly offered to bet £20 (it is not clear whether any odds were offered!) that it was the most disgraceful piece of road in Carmarthenshire. Our courageous Councillor can now with confidence increase the stakes at least to £100 (and also increase the odds), because, in addition to the frequent somersaults indulged in by the G.W.R. motor on the road in question, the occurrence of last Monday night has more than justified his attempt of impoverishing by £20 one of his guileless fellow-Councillors. The tragedy was the absolute refusal of a horse attached to a Llanelly mineral-water cart to attempt negotiating further the hopeless pitfalls and quagmires that characterise this muddy streak connecting Tumble and Llanelly. The poor animal laid down broken-hearted and breathed his last in despair. We are told that the driver transferred the poor creature from the road to the neighbouring field, and mounted guard over the heroic animal's remains until dawn revealed them to sympathetic workers wending their way to the colliery. We wonder will this touch the hearts of our callous County Councillors?*

Noel Gibbard describes the circuitous and difficult journey from Pontyberem to Tumble in the middle of the 19th century long before the construction of the main road that now connects the near neighbours. Wilf Timbrell describes how people travelled in the early 1900s:

> *The means of conveyance at that time calls for some comment, for everything was horse drawn. There were closed carriages for weddings and funerals etc, long four wheeled brakes for seaside trips, very often to Swansea or Llanstephan. Also for the rugby team when playing away, or teams to timbering competitions. Many business people owned a pony and trap, some of which could be hired by the public. Heavy loads were conveyed by carts or four wheeled drays or "gambos". There was only one "penny farthing" cycle seen in Tumble, owned by a workman to travel to*

and fro to Carmarthen at weekends. ... Progress was also taking place in the development of the internal combustion engine for road transport, resulting in the introduction of the motorcycle and motor car. Young men of the village who could afford to do so would visit the first motor shows at the Olympia, London, to see the various makes. As usual the twin brothers Tom and David Howells were always the "Pioneers". The village doctors were the first to change to new means of transport with the local business people following. But the first priority must go to the Waddell brothers and Robertson Grant, their brother in law. He held the motor car speed record from Land's End to John O'Groats in Scotland. The First World War greatly delayed the introduction in the form of buses and charabanc for public service. The Western Welsh and Jones [Brynteg] Brothers were the first in this field, between Llanelli and Cross Hands. The fair, one shilling and a penny return.

The Carmarthen Journal announced on 28 March 1913 that 'A road motor service between Cross Hands and Llanelly is shortly to be inaugurated. A trial run was made recently, and it was quite successful. The service will be a great boon to Cross Hands, Tumble and Llannon.' However, until the coming of a regular motorised bus service to Llanelli and Ammanford, Tumble remained a remote village (as shown by the difficulty the early rugby teams had in getting to away matches).

Figure 74. Brinley Jones ('Bryn y barbwr') on a charabanc trip to Aberystwyth with his grandmother, Margaret Jones (Tumble Hotel), about 1912. Courtesy of Lynette Griffiths

Passenger rail travel directly from Tumble was limited. Local tradition has it that in the early days a passenger wishing to travel from Tumble station on the Llanelly & Mynydd Mawr line could ride with the guard on the coal train to Llanelli (Sandy) and back. This extract of a poem by Emyr Wyn Thomas, published in *Y Tymbl Ddoe a Heddiw,* describes how Elisabeth Mary Aitken (1896-1990) remembered such trips around a coal stove, with bones shaking over the old points, and getting back in good time to catch train home:

I fynd I dre Llanelli o'r Tymbl, - rhaid dal y tren,

A sigai y sgerbydau pawb wrth groesi'r pwyntiau hen.

Yn fan y gard y stof lo, o'i chwmpas ar y llawr

Saif pawb 'no gyda'i gilydd, ar lein y Mynydd Mawr.

Dod bant wrth bond y Sandy, a dianc mewn I'r dre;

Rhaid dod nol erbyn amser I ddal y tren sha thre!

Wilf Timbrell mentions a popular Saturday afternoon passenger service to Llanelli 'with three or four long coaches with seats along the full length on each side, which were ideal for shopping expeditions.' The evidence is not clear, but these coaches were possibly last used to take Reservists and Territorials to war in 1914 (the service may have been discontinued because of the concerns of local shop keepers who were losing trade).

 In 1906 there had been a move to introduce a more formal passenger service ahead of the rival BP&GVR. This got nowhere probably because it would have required significant investment in the track (with its tight bends and inclines) and signalling. Also, the BP&GVR had the big advantage that most people lived down in the valley rather than on the hillside route of the L&MMR and it offered connections to the Great Western Railway at Burry Port. Timbrell described the service as 'a boon to the whole valley. It was a blessing to Tumble, even though it incurred a walk to and fro from Cwm-mawr. Churches and chapels were able to organise their Sunday school trips irrespective of distance. This remained the only rail passenger service till after the Second World War and was discontinued due to motorbus competition.'

Figure 75. Cwm-mawr Station.

10.Village Life

Tumble historically fell within the Parish of Llannon. St Non's Church dates to the 13th or 14th centuries and, by 1833, it was the parish church in the patronage of Rees Goring Thomas (the *Squire* of Llannon). As the population of Tumble and other Gwendraeth Valley mining villages grew, both the Nonconformist and Anglican churches responded.

Worship - Chapel

Noel Gibbard (*Hanes Plwyf Llan-non*) records that that the origins of Nonconformist chapels in the area can be traced back to the early 17th century with Baptist centres in the Parish of Llannon at Gelli-ciew and Allt-fawr. The early Calvinistic Methodist leaders in the first half of the 18th century, Howel Harris, William Williams Pantycelin and Daniel Roland, preached in the vicinity. Howel Harris preached in Llannon on 21 December 1742. The following year he walked with Williams Pantycelin (the writer of rousing hymns including the words of *Guide me, O thou Great Jehovah*) from Capel Ifan in Pontyberem to Llannon.

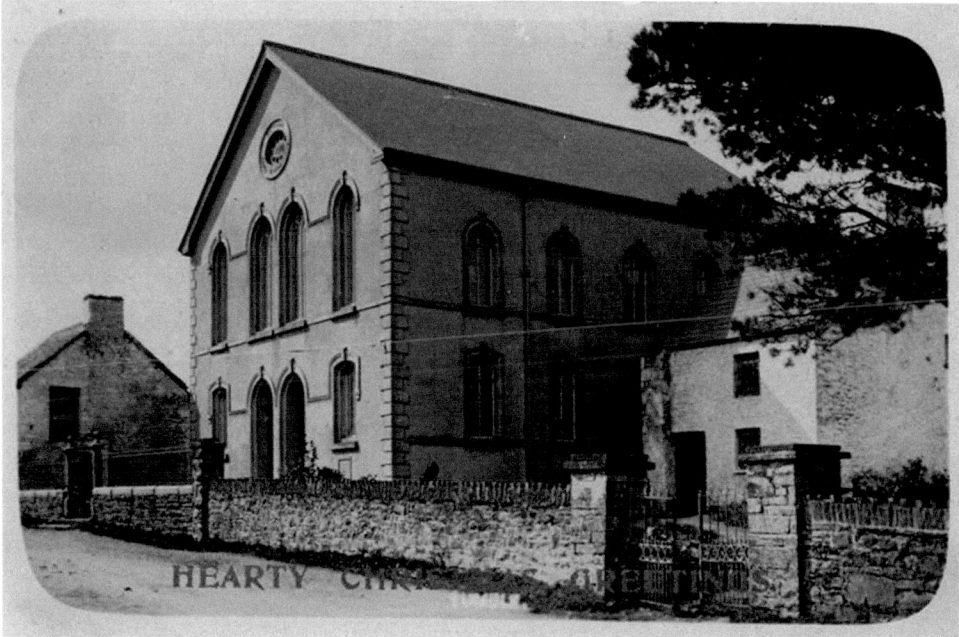

Figure 76. Bethania Chapel, Upper Tumble. Established in 1800, enlarged in 1835 and rebuilt/extended in 1854 and again in 1896 (author's collection).

Capel Seion (Independent) in Drefach, less than two miles from Tumble, was established in 1712 and, following a theological disagreement, members left to establish Bethania in Upper Tumble in 1800 (one of the early leaders was Evan Evans of Cil-carw near Pontyberem). Bethania did not get its own minister until Henry Davies in 1842, and it was during his time, in 1854, that the chapel was rebuilt. Bethania's minister from 1875 to 1912 was E.H. Davies. He was a strong Liberal and grandfather of the actor Rupert Davies who is perhaps best remembered for his iconic role as Maigret in the highly popular 1960s BBC television series. Chapels of other denominations followed Bethania mostly in the late 1800s matching the growth of the village.

D. Huw Owen (*A History of the Gwendraeth Valley*) comments that the Revival of 1904-5 had a considerable influence on the Gwendraeth Fawr valley. He describes how in 1905 'evangelical groups marched from Penygroes through Cross Hands on their way to Tumble and prayer meetings were held at the Cross Hands square and colliery.' Five members of Bethania Chapel were so fired by the Revival that they were expelled and formed the Gospel Hall in Cross Hands. As noted by Myrddin Jones in his history of Tumble Rugby Club (Chapter 12), the Revival even halted the playing of rugby in the village! Wilf Timbrell also commented on this period:

> *During the years 1904/5, Tumble like most of the villages in Wales, felt the surge of the wave of religious fervour that swept through Wales, under the inspiration of the young evangelist, Evan Roberts. This was a great influence to change many aspects in the life of the village for the better. Previously it was common occurrence to see drunken men staggering and behaving foolishly on their way home. The seeds had already been sown for reform in this sphere some years previously, by the formation of the band of hope and Rechabites societies. ... Eventually the revivalist movement faded and disintegrated, with two separate factions, Elim and Carmel still at Tumble.*

Nonconformity was influential in shaping the social as well as the religious development of mining communities like Tumble. It played to the long-established religious devotion of the rural valleys with the dangers of small-scale mining and the hard toil, and often poverty, of farming made more bearable by a philosophy that there were better things to come. This established order was challenged by the incoming surge of people to work at the Great Mountain – many from rural Carmarthenshire but others from further afield with differing social and religious backgrounds. The incomers included many young men separated from their family roots and the discipline that imposed – it is noticeable how many of the men involved in the violence of 1893 and 1906 were in their early twenties. The inevitable misbehaviour, often fuelled by too much to drink after a long shift underground breathing coal dust, was at odds with the highly respectable nonconformist roots of the community. In the late 19th and early 20th centuries it is as if two competing sets of social behaviour were uncomfortably rubbing shoulders with tensions across the community and no doubt even within individual families.

The chapels helped to build and maintain a strong and supportive community rising above the tensions that had erupted from time-to-time and given Tumble a poor reputation in some quarters. The role played by ministers such as the Bethel's Rev. Rowe Williams and later Ebenezer's Tom Nefyn, suggests that the nonconformist community leaders were not slow to roll up their sleeves and get stuck in on behalf of Tumble miners and their families – these two ministers, and no doubt others, saw the role of the chapel extending beyond religious well-being to supporting pressing work and social causes. Women played an important and influential role in chapel life and this will have further strengthened community cohesion and self-discipline. The chapels were far more than just a place for Sunday worship. With choirs, orchestras, societies and evening classes, they were a key part of life every day of the week. The richness of this activity is far better captured in the excellent photographic collection *Y Tymbl Ddoe a Heddiw*.

Bethesda Independent Chapel gave its name to the road in which it was built and, like Bethania, can trace its roots back to Capel Seion. The original chapel, built in 1888, was converted in 1905 for use as a schoolroom (it was extended in 1961 with the construction of a large hall to the rear). The nearby present chapel was built in 1905. Both Bethesda and the Bethel (Baptist) were designed by William Griffiths of Llanelli.

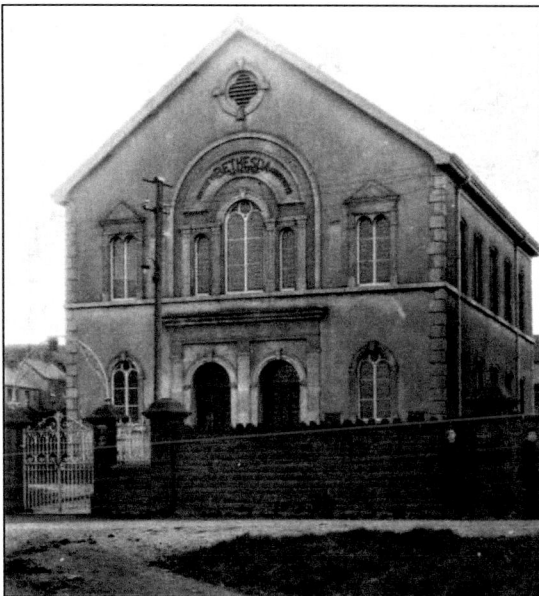

Figure 77. Bethesda

Bethel's mother church was Tabor in Cross Hands. First built in 1890, the original building became the vestry/Sunday School when the new chapel was constructed in 1904 at a cost of £1,820. Before the chapel was built, the Baptist minister, D. Morgan (Mathryfardd), led services near the railway bridge, followed by Sunday School in open fields and prayer meetings in the *long room* of the Tumble Inn.

The Rev. Rowe Williams was minister at Bethel from 1898 to 1909 - a period when Tumble had a poor reputation in some quarters. On fine summer days he would hold open-air services on Pen-llwyn-Lleucu (or *Llici*) Field, where the pit-head baths were later built, which attracted large congregations. Wilf Timbrell

143

recalls that before the opening of the new Bethel chapel in 1904, baptisms by total immersion were solemnised by the Rev. Rowe Williams in a pool especially made for the purpose by damming the stream 100 yards or so beyond Ty-isha Farm.

The Rev. Rowe Williams also sought to commercialise the holy well known as Ffynnon Josi located between Llannon church and Tumble. It was possibly the only well in South Carmarthenshire where such an attempt was made to exploit its attraction. The sulphurous waters were said to be of considerable repute, possessing similar qualities to those of Llanwrtyd Wells, and attracted votaries (persons bound by solemn religious vows) in horse-drawn vehicles. Having acquired the well (or at least rights to it), the Rev Rowe Williams enlarged it but his plans for commercialisation were it seems foiled by other waters seeping in and destroying the healing properties. The well deteriorated into mud and marsh - its location is marked on the old OS map of Carmarthenshire published in 1907 and clearly identified as *Ffynnon Josi (Sulphur)*.

Figure 78. Bethel.

The Calvinistic Methodist (Presbyterian) Ebenezer was built in 1892/93 in Ty-isha Road (its construction was delayed by the 1893 strike). Previously members of the congregation had met in 74 High Street made available by the colliery owners (a Sunday School had been held in 2 High Street). The first purpose-built chapel was formed from corrugated zinc sheeting - Wilf Timbrell notes that it was often called *Ty Cwrdd Sink*. It was located to the rear of the chapel that replaced it in 1901 (now only the graveyard remains). In 1907, the Waddells gave permission for English services to be held in the Reading Room. The expulsion

Figure 79. Ebenezer

in the 1920s of over 200 members of Ebenezer led to the establishment of the Llain-y-delyn meeting house a little further along Ty-isha Road (see Chapter 11).

Inspired by the religious revival of 1904/05, members of the Pentecostal church met originally in Cwm-mawr in the house of Jacob Skym. In 1910 they were given permission to use the Reading Room in Tumble before moving to Upper Tumble in 1919 where, in 1925, the present Elim Chapel was built. Carmel was first built at the bottom of Railway Place in Lower Tumble in 1918 and rebuilt in 1968. Unlike Elim, it is not part of the Apostolic movement.

Figure 80. The original Apostolic mission hall, Carmel, built in 1918.

Figure 81. Elim (Pentecostal) was erected in Upper Tumble in 1925.

Worship – Church

Although nonconformity dominated, particularly amongst the Welsh-speaking

Figure 82. The Rev D.J. Morgan blessing the ground before works starts on building St David's. The building in the background is the Lodging House.

majority with local roots, Eglwys Dewi Sant (St David's), located at the bottom High Street overlooking the colliery, was also a vibrant part of the community with services and Sunday school in Welsh as well as English. The original church (or more correctly chapel of ease), St Sulien's, was built by Rhys Peregrine, a local contractor, for around £178 (Wilf Timbrell comments that 'the bell was of beautiful design and tone.'). St Sulien's opened on 21 March 1889 to serve the increasing population, including newcomers from outside Wales attracted by the colliery. Noel Gibbard records that it was built on a burial ground that covered just over an acre and that there had been an earlier *vicarage* on the site (possibly accommodation for the poor) which had been endowed by the Earl of Crawford and Balcarres in 1869.

The present church was built, alongside St Sulien's, by miners during the General Strike of 1926 and was opened in 1927. St Sulien's then became the vestry and home to the Sunday school. Like Bethesda and Bethel, the new church was designed by William Griffiths of Llanelli. It is described by Coflein (National Monuments Record of Wales) as being:

> ... *constructed of coursed, rock-faced brown local stone with late Gothic detail in pinkish terracotta, of some refinement. The church comprises nave and chancel, south porch, transept-like vestries (north vestry and south organ chamber) and big five-light end windows. Stained glass includes works by Celtic Studios (1947-80), which includes one of the earliest works by Howard Martin (1947), and David Jenkins (1988).*

Wilf Timbrell commented on the contribution to the village made by the Rev. Eynon Hughes, the Church Curate in the 1900s:

> *There was great poverty then, more so amongst the old and sick people. The few shillings a week they received from the Parish distributing officer at Llannon were a meagre pittance to live on, and he worked untiringly on their behalf. It would be impossible to do him justice in words for he worked so efficiently and silently.*

Figure 83. Workmen building St David's with the Church Curate, R.M. Rosser. St Sulien's is in the background.

Figure 84. St David's Church under construction.

Education

Ty-isha farm, Tumble, hosted one of Gruffydd Jones' circulating schools in 1763-64 attended by 45 learners. The main purpose of this innovative education programme was to teach people how to read the Bible in their own language. Llannon National School was established with the support of Rees Goring Thomas, the *Squire* of Llannon, in 1841 (a few years later, in 1847, the notorious *Blue Books* enquiry into the state of education in Wales was published with its damning view of the impact of the Welsh language and nonconformity). For the next 30 years the National School was the main educational establishment in the parish. Noel Gibbard refers to Daniel Jenkins, Bryn-coch, carrying children to the school in his *gambo*.

Bryn-du school opened on 18 April 1875 as a Board school under the Elementary Education Act 1870. It was located between Tumble and Llannon on land provided by Bryn-du farm with places for 150 children. Nearly a thousand people attended the opening Most of the children were purely Welsh speakers and had to be taught English through the medium of Welsh - they were made to memorise and recite passages in English at the start of the school day. Absenteeism was a problem with children needed to work on their family farms. The teacher, a strict disciplinarian from London, kept a diary. Noel Gibbard, in his history of the parish, included this extract from February 1878: 'John Hughes (2), David Hughes, William Roblin, and Th. Morgan punished for absenting themselves from school. Found out that they had been at the Ploughing Match.'

Figure 85. Bryn-du school around 1905.

148

Llechyfedach Board school followed in 1895 and, on its first day (27 August), admitted 130 children. The first headmaster was Mr D.M. Jenkins. As with Bryn-du, absentee levels were high. Noel Gibbard notes that the reasons given for not attending school included: the weather, a chapel or *Band of Hope* party, an Eisteddfod, pulling potatoes, hay making and attending Llanelli market. In 1897-98 attendance was further reduced by an outbreak of scarlet fever. Gibbard also notes that the school reflected the close relationship between the village of Tumble and the colliery with these school diary extracts:

> *May 2nd 1898 Several families moved from the Tumble during the last few days owing to colliery stoppage, & consequently the attendance is lower than it otherwise would have been.*

> *6 Feb. 1898 Owing to the unsettled state of affairs of Tumble colliery a large number of children is leaving.*

Wilf Timbrell, who attended Llechyfedach, describes how children from Lower Tumble would walk to school via the entrance to the old Danygraig Farm, along a short lane and then an arduous climb over the top of the Graig to Llechyfedach. He had largely fond memories of the school:

> *They were happy days going through the various forms from the infants to X7. There is only one person still living in the village that accompanied me through all those stages now, Mrs M.A. Evan, 20 Bethania Road. We both well remember the maypole dances we had to do at the annual school concerts or cantata. And the fear when "weaving and unweaving" the gypsy tent, not to incur the displeasure of the headmaster, Mr M. Jenkins. He was a strict disciplinarian, but he meant well for our future. When we reached Form 5 we came under his eye and part instruction, and subject to his cane. On one occasion the entire class could commiserate with each other, after equal treatment. In after years most of us have appreciated the fine primary school education received under his supervision. ... Sometime when in the middle classes an order prohibiting the speaking of Welsh during school hours was introduced. A pupil overheard doing so, was punished by the headmaster. Probably most of them turned a deaf ear, and it was discontinued.*

On 8 September 1913, Llechyfedach School was joined by Tumble County Primary School in Lower Tumble. The new school, with accommodation for 300 children, was needed to relieve the overcrowding at Llechyfedach and Drefach schools. It was built of local stone by Mr. Thomas Morgan of Tumble, at a contract price of about £4,000, to a design described at the time as 'the corridor system.' Mr. H. D. Thomas (formerly at Salem Council School, Llandeilo) was appointed as the school's first headteacher. The Carmarthenshire Education Committee fixed the intake boundary between the new school and Llechyfedach School: all children living below the Tumble Reading Room (halfway up High Street on the west side) were expected to attend the new school, and all living up the street from that point (numbers 50 to 104) were to continue to attend at Llechyfedach. Unsurprisingly, the school log records that on the first day, 'A few children were found in school who had crossed the boundary. These were told to attend Llechyfedach School.'

Figure 86. Llechyfedach School in Upper Tumble before being re-built.

Outbreaks of Scarlet Fever and Measles, along with severe winter weather, impacted on school attendance in the years of the First World War. From 28 October 1918, Tumble and all other schools in the district were closed because of Influenza – the school log noted that, 'the majority of the children are affected either directly or indirectly.' On 30 June 1916, the school log records that: 'The school is closed today for a fortnight's holiday to suit the hay-harvest. The weather proved very unsuitable for the harvest.'

Two 'uncertificated' teachers were killed on the Western Front – Enoch O Davies and Dan Ivor Price. On 5 January 1920: 'The children of Lower Villa were withdrawn at 11.30 on the news being received that Mr. John Davies (their father) had been killed in the colliery. He was the school playground caretaker.' On 19 February 1940: 'The presence of enemy aircraft followed by an aerial combat in the vicinity of the school caused school work to be suspended for a short period. School closed for the afternoon – relaxation for the children.'

These are just a selection of the entries from the school log reproduced in Tumble School's centenary publication.

Figure 87. Building the school in Lower Tumble. Bethel Chapel in the background (the village Hall has yet to be built).

Figure 88. Tumble County Primary School nearing completion.

Education did not end with school, Wilf Timbrell mentions first aid courses held in Drefach, and evening classes, with syllabuses including English, Arithmetic and Book-keeping, at Llechyfedach School (under the tuition for many years of Mr E.R.R. Lewis). Two students earned scholarships at Ruskin College, University of Oxford, from the South Wales Miners' Federation – Jackie Jones (Ostler family) who emigrated to Australia, and John Jones of 18 High Street who became a checkweigher and a pioneer of the Labour movement in the area. Mining classes were held in the Reading Room during winter months. William Jones, Pantglas (later Heol-y-Bryn), was a particularly successful student and went on to become a highly respected manager of the Great Mountain Colliery in around 1911.

Secondary schools were established in Llanelli, Llandeilo and Carmarthen in the 1890s. Tumble and other Gwendraeth Valley villages had to wait over thirty years for the opening of Gwendraeth Valley Secondary School (as it was first known). The new school buildings were formally opened on Saturday 14 January 1928 by the Right Hon. Sir Alfred Mond M.P. (Lord Melchett – chair of Amalgamated Anthracite Companies which had taken over ownership of the Great Mountain Colliery in 1927) with 300 guests and 200 'scholars' attending. The school was intended to serve the secondary education needs of the county and not just the immediate locality. Ahead of the new purpose-built buildings, the school had started in 1923 as a 'Central School' (bridging the gap between the more prestigious grammar schools and the ordinary secondary schools) possibly in Cwm-mawr House which became incorporated within the grounds of the new school. It became recognised as a secondary school on the appointment of Mr Llewellyn Williams as its headmaster in 1925. Originally from Brynamman, he had been teaching science in Kent having served for four years as an officer in France during the First World War. He continued as headmaster for many decades and became well-known latterly for his ever-present companion - his border collie, *Cymro*.

The main school building at Gwendraeth was described in the Western Mail as consisting of 'a large assembly hall to accommodate about 300 people, three spacious well-equipped laboratories, and thirteen classrooms. On another part of the site are the house craft department, the art room, manual instruction rooms, and gymnasium.' The decoration of the classrooms was a special feature - each was painted in a different colour scheme to create an atmosphere suiting the subject to be taught in the room (this innovation was praised nationally by leading educationalists). At the time the school was opened, fields 'eminently suitable for recreation' were in the process of being bought.

Gwendraeth Grammar School, as it became, was joined by its sister secondary schools in Pontyberem and Cefneithin (Maes Yr Yrfa) in the 1950s and 60s. As well as providing high standards of education and sporting opportunity (including as the main conveyor belt of the Welsh No. 10 factory), the three schools served to bring the young people of the Gwendraeth Valley together creating a sense of shared identity beyond their individual villages.

Figure 89. The former Gwendraeth Grammar School (2017 – author's collection)

Figure 90. Gwendraeth Grammar School rugby team 1946-47 with British Lions coach Carwyn James of Cefneithin (captain) and headmaster, Llewellyn Williams (seated).

Recreation

As noted, the Reading Room, provided by the colliery, was opened on Saturday 23 September 1893 by the officer in charge of the Dragoons contingent deployed in the village. Its location was behind the back gardens of High Street reached by a side lane at the middle of the street. By 1913 it had become the Tivoli concert/picture house. Wilf Timbrell gives this description:

> *It was of corrugated sheet structure with well varnished woodwork interior. For many years it served as a reading room, with daily newspapers, weekly papers, magazines and boys' papers. Bagatelle and other games were played there and public meetings were held there when necessary. Concerts, cantatas, with occasional dances were organised by the colliery officials and attended also by the staff of the company's offices at Llanelli. It was used later for showing silent pictures and variety shows. Before the outbreak of the First World War it was the headquarters of the local detachment of the 4th Welsh Regiment, under the command of Captain James Waddell. In 1926 it was demolished because of its unsafe condition.*

On Saturday afternoon 10 July 1915 the New Hall and Workmen's Institute, in what became Heol Y Neuadd, were officially opened by Sir Stafford Howard (Mayor of Llanelli) and Lady Howard-Stepney. The Rev. B. James of Bethel (*chairman of the committee*) presided. Among the speakers were John Waddell Jr. representing the colliery and S.O. Davies and J. Treharne, both checkweighers, representing the colliery workers. The Hall and Institute were designed by Messrs. W. Griffiths and Son, architects, Llanelli, and built by Mr. Tom Morgan of Tumble at a cost of over £3,000. The facilities comprised a hall, accommodating about 900 people, a billiard-room with two tables, committee-rooms, reading room, lavatories, bathrooms and a lending library with about 600 books. The building had electric lighting, a hot-water system for heating the main hall and open fires for the committee rooms. After the opening ceremony, tea was provided for the guests in the billiard-room – the 'general public' could enjoy tea at 6d a cup in the various rooms of the Institute. A piano had been presented to the Committee Secretary and in the evening a grand concert was held under the chairmanship of the Rev. James. The packed audience was entertained by the Ebenezer (Mission) and the Swansea Male Choir which had won first prize at the Abergavenny National Eisteddfod. The programme included patriotic and sentimental songs in both English and Welsh concluding with 'Hen Wlad fy Nhadau.'

The Hall and Institute had been largely paid for by the miners themselves with a contribution of £500 from Lady Howard-Stepney (conditional on alcohol never being found on the premises). The Hall was registered as a Limited Company with members of the community holding the shares. The miners borrowed money to fund their contribution. Four years' later in 1919, the Carmarthen

Journal reported that rapid progress had been made towards reducing the debt with over £400 having been paid off in nine months. To further reduce the debt the workers raised funds through organising entertainments including operetta, drama and an eisteddfod. There were plans to extend the premises to include further baths and recreation fields badly needed for the children of the village. A conservative element of the membership strongly opposed the introduction of the cinema and the holding of dances. However, films of Charlie Chaplin, Mary Pickford and others were being shown by the end of 1917. The Hall was however also used by the people of the village for lessons covering a range of interests and for benefit events when soldiers or miners were injured or killed.

Despite the fund-raising efforts of the miners, up until the World War II the finances of the Hall proved a struggle. Revenue from deductions to miners' wages was lost during the long strikes of 1921 and 1926. A further burden was added by the decision to take on the additional expense of purchasing a field, paid for with a £700 mortgage at an interest rate of 5%, which was then endowed to the new Welfare Park. Wilf Timbrell's account suggests that the challenge of reducing costs proved so onerous that they resulted in the tragic death of one of the committee members. The War surprisingly brought a big uplift in bookings to the extent that the committee was able to pay off the overdraft, shareholders were refunded, and the Hall was transferred to the Welfare Association with a strong bank balance.

Figure 91. Tumble Public Hall with Bethel Chapel in the background.

As well as the new rugby ground (first played on in the 1936/37 season) and changing rooms, the Welfare Park's fine facilities included a smart timber pavilion (used for teas on carnival day), cricket pitch, tennis courts, bowling green and children's play area. It was the site of the annual Tumble carnival and family sports day which, as in other mining villages, was the highlight of the village social calendar. The field endowed by the Welfare Hall committee became the playing pitch for the youth rugby team (long before, in 1897, the same field had been the home ground of the original village rugby team).

It is possible to criticise the colliery owners for not taking greater care of the needs of their workers and tenants, and the village they had effectively built to serve their business interests. However, the Waddell family were by no means among the worst examples of industrialists of their time and there is evidence of engagement with the community particularly on the part of John Waddell Jr. This is one example - his marriage celebrations in the early 1900s recorded by Wilf Timbrell:

> On his homecoming to Ravelston after his wedding there were celebrations and a large bonfire on the Graig with community singing around it. Dan Morgan, of the Cwarau family, sang "penillion" he had composed for the occasion, with the spectators singing the choruses. Every adult received a gift of five shillings in his pay packet and every junior worker two shillings and sixpence at the colliery office.

In the early 1900s, village weddings were also celebrated with style and, as Wilf Timbrell records, a big bang:

> A wedding was always a special and eventful occasion in the village. At daybreak loud explosions would be heard as gunpowder was exploded. The "cannon" was crudely made from an old cast steel tram wheel, and had to be operated well away from residences, but near to a convenient shelter for safety. The time fuse cut at a suitable length to allow sufficient time to reach the shelter. On one occasion misjudgement took place for one person to lose the sight of one eye. This custom had been discontinued for many years but was renewed on one occasion during the early years of the last war. The operator had chosen a spot behind Lower High Street and unfortunately used excessive powder to cause a terrific explosion that frightened people and shattered windows. For this he was nicknamed for some time as "Franco". After a wedding a rope would be stretched across the road to prevent the movement of the horses, and usually the driver would understandably work in our favour, until the bridegroom scattered coins as our reward.

Music and singing, for worship and recreation (with the two often difficult to separate) played a huge role in village life. Wilf Timbrell recalls a time when religious denominations came together for annual Cymanfa Ganu. Operetta, drama, and eisteddfodau were held first at the Tivoli (originally the Reading

Room) which had a musical director and doubled as a *picture house*, and later in the Welfare Hall. In 1971, for a Village Exhibition, Mrs Ceri Evans (Teglan, Upper Tumble) wrote a history of music in Tumble from the year 1900 (*Mor o Gan yw Tymbl o Hyd*). Reproduced by Wilf Timbrell, this provides a rich record of performances by school choirs, choral and operatic societies and solo achievement – including Geraint Davies who won the tenor prize at the National Eisteddfod in Caerphilly in 1947. Tumble also produced notable opera singers: Miss Marion Evans of Cwm-mawr, one of the principal sopranos with the Welsh National Opera Company; and Neville Griffiths of Heol-y-Neuadd, principal tenor with the Doyle Carte Company. From the Drum and Fife Band of 1900 to long-remembered performances of Haydn and Handel and Welsh classics, Tumble's talent and enthusiasm for music shines through the record kept by Mrs Ceri Evans.

NEVILLE GRIFFITHS as ' Frederic ' in ' Pirates of Penzance ' D'Oyly Carte Opera Co.

Figure 92. Neville Griffiths. Theatre Royal 1955 (author's collection).

The village enjoyed many male-voice and mixed choirs over the years including *Bois y Tymbl* and the *Trwbadors*. Some were connected to chapels which also had their own orchestras. The Mynydd Mawr Choir merits special mention. Though drawing from a wider area, it began (or was re-launched) as the Mynydd Mawr Male Voice Party in Tumble in 1913 under the direction of Tom Morgan, Gwendraeth View, Ty-isha Road. There is an earlier record of a choir of the same name dating back to 1908. Early highlights included performing at the official opening of the Cross Hands Public Hall in 1911, and success in competitions at Abergwili and Swansea. Tom Morgan was succeeded by Peter Edwards of Llechyfedach who continued the success of the choir winning fourteen successive first prizes in competitions most notably with its test piece – Protheroe's *Crusaders*. The choir in its original form disbanded in 1948 but the tradition was revived in 1965 initially as 'Bois y Bryniau' before becoming the Mynydd Mawr Choir with success at the National Eisteddfod. The choir also took part in the massed choir festivals for the Welsh Association of Male Choirs at the Royal Albert Hall and performed at Cardiff in front of the Prince of Wales, the Irish President and the Aga Khan.

Figure 93. Tumble Male Voice Party. 1940-41

Commerce

Wilf Timbrell describes Tumble at the start of the early 1900s. He begins in Upper Tumble at the main road junction known as Finger Post Square. At the time, the only buildings on Llannon Road were Brynteg Farm cottage, the old Bryndu Board School and the former Toll House (Bryndu). Proceeding down what became Heol-y-Bryn, the features he mentions include William Richards (Butcher), and the entrance to the old Danygraig Farm. He then gives his not very complimentary description of High Street followed by:

> *Immediately below the churchyard boundary was the road leading into the goods yard siding, with its little office. Here the local grocers collected the heavy sacks of sugar and flour from the railway vans. A short walk under the railway bridge brought one to Daniel's shop and residence. The rapid developments brought increasing trade and compelled shopkeepers to extend their premises. In this case new residential quarters were built almost to the railway embankment and stables and store houses were built at the rear of the premises. He also used the small field below the Workmen's Club, for poultry farming purposes; on the opposite side of the road. Fortunately the traffic on the road then was entirely horse drawn, or there would be many chicken casualties with present conditions ... An amusing incident occurred one morning when a young lad of my age came running around the Greenhill bend with one of*

Daniel's turkeys in pursuit. Of a mischievous type, he probably had annoyed the bird!

Greenhill was owned by Daniel Thomas and his family with a small general store and the village post office. Timbrell recounts how when a customer entered the shop a parrot would immediately call 'Margaret' and would continue to do so until she appeared. The lady being summoned was the daughter of Daniel Thomas. She later married John Lewis of the *Tynton* family (a renowned essayist and musician, he would play the accordion sat on the shop windowsill). After the entrance to the colliery and the Tumble Hotel came Dynant Shop (David Evans) which became the post office. Below Bethel Chapel there were the three cottages of Ty-melin, and a detached property, Lower Villa, the home of John Davies, the first to prospect for coal on the Great Mountain site who became the colliery manager from 1900-1908.

Figure 94. Green Hill Boot Stores

The village inn, latterly known as the Tumble Hotel, was central to village life through much of the 19th and 20th centuries. Strategically located at the intersection of the old Carmarthenshire Railway (Tramroad) and the turnpike road to Nantgaredig, it is shown as *New Inn* in the Llannon parish map of 1813. Noel Gibbard (*Hanes Plwyf Llan-non*) notes that early in the 19th century it was the property of Griffith Thomas of Llanddarog parish and comprised a 'house and garden, cottage and garden' and a 'Gwaun fedach'; and that in 1818-19 it was home to the Simon family with William Simon variously described as a 'gent', 'collier' and 'steward'. In the parish records of 1828, the inn is simply referred to as *Tumble* and is then the home of Samuel Howel ('publican') and his wife Catherine. From 1841, the census returns record the establishment's various names and the individuals who ran it:

- 1841- Tumble Tavern, David Maddox (Publican)
- 1851- Mary Morgan, (Inn Keeper).
- 1861- The Tumble, John Davies (Road Surveyor and Victualler)
- 1871- Tumble Inn, Griffith Evans (Inn Keeper)
- 1881- Tumble Inn, Daniel Thomas (Coal Miner and Inn Keeper)
- 1891- Tumble Inn, Thomas Jones (Inn Keeper)
- 1901- Tumble Hotel, Thomas Jones (Hotel Keeper)

In 1843, during the Rebecca Riots, it was the scene of the capture of the notorious Shoni Scubor Fawr. In the early period of the Great Mountain Colliery, the Tumble Hotel would probably have been where the colliers paid the younger or less experienced men and boys who supported them at the coalface. At this time, and particularly around the disturbances of 1893 and 1906, it had a rough reputation (whether fairly or not) and had its own boxing ring perhaps to help bring some order to the way the early workers tended to settle their disputes. By 1891 it was recorded as the Tumble Hotel, and in 1892 the Llanelly Mercury reported that 'The Tumble, i.e. the old house has been pulled down, and upon its ruins stands a large and convenient hotel, built by Mr. D. Johns of Felinfoel.' The old tavern had probably been a low building in the traditional local form. Its replacement, built in imposing Victorian style, fitted Tumble's new industrial era and its greater connectivity.

Thomas Jones, recorded as Inn/Hotel Keeper in 1891 and 1901, and his wife Margaret (known in the family as *Mummy Jones*) were the grandparents of a well-known Tumble personality – Brinley Jones better known as *Bryn y Barbwr* with his barber's shop in Heol y Neuadd (originally known as Caldy View). He was born at the Tumble Hotel on 10 July 1901, one of seven children who became known as the Temperance Seven because of the family's surprising connections with the temperance movement that arose from the Religious Revival of 1904/05. Consistent with that commitment, when Bryn was aged six in 1907 the family sold the Tumble Hotel and moved to Morawel - a new house they built in Caldy View. As the children grew up a house was built for each of them nearby. Bryn's house, number 12 Caldy View, became his barber's shop. The family sold or donated land formerly held by the Tumble Hotel on which it is believed that Bethel Chapel (next to Morawel), Tumble Primary School, the Welfare Hall and an early village rugby pitch were developed. Bryn's barber's shop (and that of his Upper Tumble contemporary, Jack Wardell) was a feature of Tumble life for many decades. Bryn (who died in 1987) and his family witnessed, and were part of, the intensive growth of the village covered in this story.

The 1911 census records Gwilym Jones as the Licensed Victualler of the Tumble Hotel, though The Cambrian had reported on 1 July 1910 that:

> *Mr. Peter Cairns Guthrie has purchased Tumble Hotel, Tumble., with five acres land, for £ 360. The land, which has a good supply of water, is close to Tumble Colliery and New Dynant and Closyryn Collieries recently opened.*

Figure 95. The Tumble Hotel around 1900 – Thomas Jones, Hotel keeper.

Figure 96 Margaret Jones (born about 1849), of the Tumble Hotel, with her grandson Brinley Jones (Bryn y barbwr) and his sister (about 1912). Courtesy of Lynette Griffiths.

Figure 97. Morawel, home of the Jones family formerly of the Tumble Hotel, pre-1913 (the village Hall has yet to be built next to Bethel Chapel).

Figure 98. The Tumble Hotel in the 1920s

By the 1890s Tumble had outgrown a single pub – workers would struggle to get a drink at busy times let alone a place to stay for the night. To meet the growing need, in 1893 the Great Mountain Workingmen's Club was established with the support of Buckley's Brewery possibly with plans for it to become a hotel. For the next 10 years or so the Club, supported by the brewery, struggled to get a license to sell alcohol (as opposed to providing it for members). In May 1896, John Evans, the Club manager, was found guilty at the Llanelly Police Court of 'selling intoxicants on the club premises.' To be fair he had been subject to an apparent *sting* by the Inland Revenue, as reported by the South Wales Echo:

> *Mr E. Davies, of the Inland Revenue, said that on the 6th instant be went to the Tumble and obtained lodgings there for himself and a friend, Mr Hall, who arrived later on in the day. Mr Hall paid 1s and became, a member of the club. He signed his name on the club book, and then they had drinks. Witness subsequently became a member on the suggestion of Hall. Witness was not elected in accordance with the rules of the club. His name was not placed before the committee. Mr Hall, Inland Revenue officer, also gave evidence. ... The Bench imposed a penalty.*

Figure 99. The founders of the Workingmen's Club.

Noel Gibbard notes that the Club helped its neighbours with the supply of water including Bethel chapel, particularly for use in baptisms. By 1907, it had 281 members and in March 1908, with the support of Buckley's, it made a further attempt to get a license to operate as a public house. The application was heard by a special sitting of the Llanelly Licensing Bench. Those opposed to the grant of the license included the Felinfoel Brewery, owners of the Tumble Hotel, and the Gwendraeth Hotel (Gwendraeth Arms, Cwm-mawr). Thomas Hughes who had made the application on behalf of the Club was represented by Mr Meager. The Felinfoel Brewery and Gwendraeth Hotel were represented by Mr Sankey. Mr Meager gave background to the application explaining that:

> ... the premises in respect of which the application was made cost about £ 3,000. He now applied for a license for a period of two years. In 1892 there were 132 houses in the district, and they had since, increased to 240. Tumble had all along been in the unfortunate position of having only one public house, which did not answer the needs of the district. A petition in favour of a new house had been signed by the vicar, curate, Baptist minister, and the colliery officials at Tumble.

Mr Waddell, on behalf of the colliery, confirmed that in his opinion:

... there was a great need for another public-house at Tumble. Over 600 men were employed at the Great Mountain Colliery alone, and they were at present sinking a new slant, which was nearly completed. This would give employment for another 600 men.

A lively exchange followed with Mr Sankey ridiculing the view that the provision of another public house in the village would reduce the risk of further riots. Thomas Hughes said that there were 280 members of the Club which had sound finances and had not attracted any complaints. Mr Sankey argued that in view of the new Licensing Bill (Asquith's Licensing Bill of 1908 which had special provisions for Wales) it would be a very improper time for the bench to grant an additional license at Tumble. The Bench agreed and the application was refused as was a further one made by the Club in March 1909. Tumble, despite being one of the largest villages in the district, was never to get a second pub though it did benefit from the addition of a further club in Upper Tumble and *Clwb Bach* in Cwm-mawr. Meanwhile, the Gwendraeth Arms had protected its position as the second closest pub to the Great Mountain Colliery.

Wilf Timbrell recalls that one of the most popular amusement features with Club members in those days was the long skittle alley building. This was demolished along with the coach house and stable when the Club was extended in the 1970s. Timbrell ponders '... the confidence which led to the erection of such an enormous building in so small a village as Tumble was then. There must have been ample proof that plentiful "black diamonds" lay buried under the Graig-y-Lletty.'

Figure 100. Early photograph of the Workingmen's Club

The 1911 census record shows that the village enjoyed a wide range of shops and other businesses. These included: Gwalia Stores (David Gealy); National Stores (David Williams, grocers), Siop Daniels (David Daniels, grocer- Grenvill Villa); Draper/Milliner (Lucy Evans – Cloth Hall); Tailors (Evan John – Penllwyn House); Dynant Stores (David Evans); Brynawel (Morgan Williams); Confectioners ('Ma Perkins' – 95 High Street).

Figure 101. Siop Bradbourne

Figure 102. One of the most renowned shops in the Valley – 'Star Supply' c. 1930

Figure 103. Brinley Jones (Bryn y barbwr) with his daughter, Valerie, and the manager of Lloyds Bank. Courtesy of Lynette Griffiths

Other shops and businesses at that time or later included: Green Hill Boot Stores Bradbourne (Ironmongers, animal feeds etc), Star Stores (grocers), Siop Manteg (grocers – Singleton Road), Siop Harold (grocers - Bethesda Road), Siop Jones (High Street), Siop Hafodlan, (Bethania Road), Siop Tommy (newsagent - Railway Terrace), Richards Family Butchers (William Richards – Pen Parc) and Gwyn Williams (garage and coaches). By the early 1960s, shops and other businesses in Heol Y Neuadd included a butchers, shoe shop (Tynton), betting shop, barbers (Bryn's), ladies hairdressers, two banks, chemist, greengrocers, second-hand shop (inevitably know as Steptoe's), fish and chip shop, bakery, Italian Café, a sweet shop (known as the Café) and a post office.

Figure 104. David Thomas (Dai Pantyffynnon) outside his butcher's shop in Heol y Neuadd.
Courtesy of Carmarthenshire Libraries.

Other shops in Upper Tumble included a butcher, newsagent (Elias), Co-op, barbers (Jack Wardell), Siop Annie and a post office. By 1911 Upper Tumble hosted the police station (home to Sergeant Lewis, villain or hero of the 1906 riot his family and two police constables) and a fire station. No doubt, there were many other shops and businesses in Upper and Lower Tumble over the period covered.

By the time the Great Mountain Colliery closed, Tumble had long been well-connected by regular (if rather slow) bus services to local towns. Nevertheless, a variety of village shops (with butchers, bakers, greengrocers, fish mongers, and others also delivering to the home) continued to serve the local community. So, a trip to town could be a Saturday treat, perhaps on one of the distinctive grey double-deckers to Llanelli, rather than a necessity.

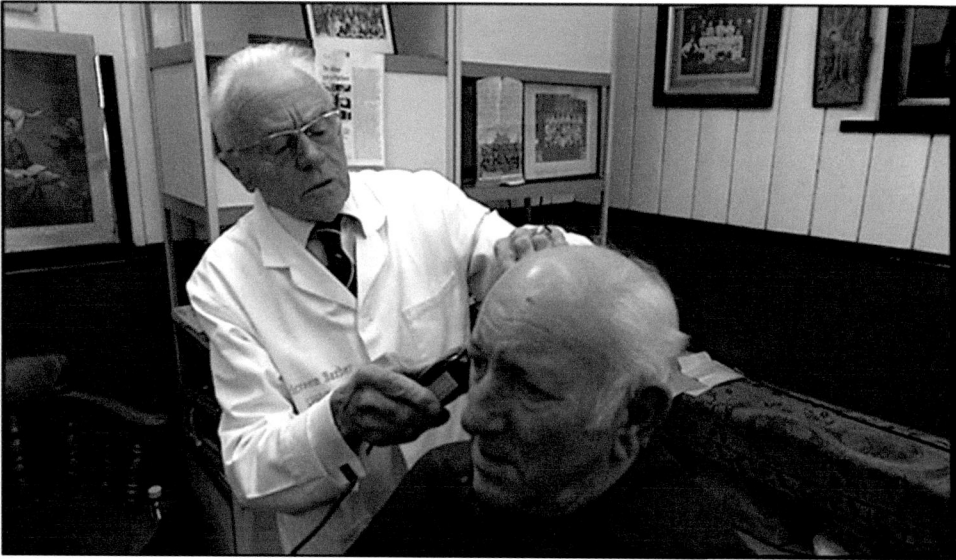

Figure 105. When Jack Wardell retired, aged 91, he was one of the UK's oldest barbers. He cut hair in Upper Tumble for almost 80 years before his death aged 94. 'Going to Jack's wasn't just about the hair cut... his success came from the social experience you had there' (Clive Scourfield, Local councillor. Courtesy of BBC.

Figure 106. 'Siop Tomi' in Railway Terrace (Pen Parc). Courtesy of Helena Jevons (granddaughter of Thomas Elias)

11. 'Coal Dust & Dogma' – Tom Nefyn

On Sunday evening 8 September 1928, 4,000 people gathered on the rugby field in Tumble, where Tir Becca now stands, to say farewell to the Rev. Thomas Williams (Tom Nefyn). The Western Mail the next day reported that the controversial preacher's final words to his supporters were, 'I finish as minister to-night. I do not repent anything I have done. I am quite happy. Stand together! Do good!'

This ended Tom Nefyn's tumultuous three years as minister of Tumble's Calvinistic Methodist (Presbyterian) Church – Ebenezer in Ty-isha Road. During this time, he had shaken the foundations of the Connexion (the Methodist community of connected local churches), caused divisions within families and made national news with his radical views and practices.

On 28 August, Tom Nefyn had been suspended from his ministry for heresy by the Nantgaredig Sassiwn (Calvinistic Methodist Assembly). His *heretical* beliefs included that man had evolved slowly from lowlier creatures – he found the logic of Darwinism far more appealing than a literal interpretation of the Book of Genesis. There are close parallels with the near-contemporary *Scopes Monkey Trial (The State of Tennessee v. John Thomas Scopes)* with the conviction of Scopes for teaching evolutionary theory to a high school class. The case was portrayed in the Hollywood film *Inherit the Wind* - an equally compelling film could have been made about Tom Nefyn and the people of Tumble who followed him all the way to their own excommunication.

The Western Mail provided a blow-by-blow record of the story that shook the Methodist church in Wales and beyond, but it is Glyn Anthony's book, *Coal Dust & Dogma,* that captures what it was like to live through that period in Tumble's history. Anthony was a young man growing up in Tumble at the time and describes, not just the great debate that took place, but the wider social context of Tumble in the 1920s including the impact of the 1926 National Strike.

From North Wales to Tumble via Gallipoli

Tom Nefyn was born in 1895 in the Caernarfonshire village from which he took his name. He left school in 1909 and went straight to work at the Eifle granite quarry. He joined the army in 1914 at the start of the First Word War and served in the disastrous Gallipoli campaign which took the lives of 1,500 Welsh soldiers (he later wrote a book about the landings of the 53rd Welsh Division at Sulva Bay in August 1915). Also serving in France, Egypt and Palestine, he suffered great hardship and, having been wounded, he returned from the War a pacifist. His experiences as a soldier must have influenced his unorthodox religious views *Y Cymro* (a Welsh language publication) commented on Nefyn's writings:

We are not surprised that one who suffered in the Great War writes like this, when we remember the ghastly use made of the Old Testament to justify every horror and to dethrone Christ. We congratulate Tom Nefyn and feel certain that there will be sufficient vision and sense of honour in the Methodist Connexion to appreciate his honest and brave stand for his beliefs. Remember that the old things have passed. Many things fell, besides the boys, never to rise again on the field of slaughter...

In preparation to be a minister, Nefyn attended Porth school in the Rhondda and then the theological colleges at Aberystwyth and Bala. He was selected to be the minister for Ebenezer, Tumble in 1925 and formally inducted in 1926. He later maintained that he had been open about his views to the selection committee - he had, for example, made clear his view that prayer meetings at Ebenezer were at risk of dying out and that the church was failing to secure the interest and attendance of young people. He had also made no secret of the fact that, in addressing this challenge and more generally, his ways of working would be revolutionary. He had made it a condition of accepting the appointment that the church would follow him on his radical path. In response the committee had commented that they 'longed for somebody who could capture the hearts and interests of the young people; that they were willing to venture in any direction that would make the church a healthy power in the district.'

Tom Nefyn achieved early success in Tumble winning the respect of his congregation and the community - he even managed to bring back into his church a number of young men who had been drawn away by left-wing politics.

Figure 107. Tom Nefyn

He did not make a distinction between worship and the day-to-day lives of people. He saw the two as intertwined – he cared for the social and physical well-being of his flock not just their souls. For example, he campaigned hard for improvement to the colliery-owned housing and carried out a thorough survey of conditions to support his case leading to the colliery owners undertaking a programme of improvements (see Chapter 9).

He was also influenced by the impact that the 1926 National strike had on colliery workers and their families in Tumble. As the strike went on, mining communities across South Wales experienced considerable hardship. Glyn Anthony provides a vivid account of *soup kitchens* in the village hall and a fund-raising tour to North Wales made by a Tumble choir. Nefyn did not however win the support of all, either locally or among those who ran the Presbyterian Church in Wales. Four deacons of Ebenezer resigned over his preaching and his refusal to separate social and spiritual matters. In June 1927, these complaints were referred to the South Wales Presbyterian Association.

Figure 108. Great Mountain colliers on strike in 1926.

Tom Nefyn's heresy

In a Welsh-language booklet published for children in 1926, Tom Nefyn gave these answers to questions about God, the Bible and particularly 'Creation':

> *How did God create the World? – Slowly and surely. He took thousands of years to create it. What did man once resemble? – He resembled the animal. He was an animal-man. What is hell? – Impure thoughts, a heart without love, and life without God. What is the Old Testament? – The drama of the Hebrew's life.*

He expanded on these beliefs in preparing to face his challengers at the Treherbert Assembly *(Sassiwn)* in April 1928. His manifesto, *Y Ffordd yr Edrychaf ar Bethau (The Way I Look at Things)* gave a detailed, 80-page, defence of his position in which he denounced beliefs and practices fundamental to Methodism and the wider Christian Church. He rejected the concepts of the holy trinity, the virgin birth and original sin, and dismissed the rituals of baptism, prayer (as a means of influencing God) and of taking Christ's death as atonement for human sin – 'The Cross is nothing in itself, and to adore it is idolatry.' He declared that 'Though Christ was mighty he was not almighty'; denied miracles that flouted natural laws such as the feeding of the five thousand and the raising of the dead (he believed that Christ had possessed strong psychic powers evident in the 'healing' miracles) and saw the resurrection as no more than the disciples emphasising Christ's immortality.

For him the Bible was a record of the experience of the men who wrote it rather than the 'word of God' in a literal sense (he believed that certain passages should be expunged because of their impact on how young people view the relationship between men and women – 'Preserve the truth of the Bible but throw its rubbish ('ysbwrial') over board.' He likened the communion ritual to a reminder, in the same sense as all meals should be, of the power of God (in a sermon he is said to have mused that the bread used in a communion service could as meaningfully be replaced by a piece of coal).

He carried these convictions through to how he ran church services and meetings in Tumble. He thought that week-night chapel meetings should be limited to one a week and have more to do with real life, including the affairs of the pit and other workplaces, than long-winded prayers. He advocated music, novel reading and poetry with children being given the opportunity to chat quietly and play. He promoted a brighter approach with more focus on the vitality of life rather than death - less preaching and more worship and debate. For him, Sunday schools should not be limited to reading the Bible – other books should also be studied, and open-air rambles encouraged.

In summing up his position Nefyn stated that, 'Even if I shall not be called a Methodist, no one, I believe, can call me a pagan. My ideal is to be a Christian and not a person who can carry a denominational label. … Truth is more important than popularity, sincerity in thoughtful quest than office, the rescue of a country's soul than praise and dispraise.' The Western Mail gave a detailed summary of Nefyn's manifesto which generated a strong reaction from traditionalists including this from Dr Cynddylan Jones, 'veteran leader of the "old" school of thought in the Calvinistic Methodist denomination':

> … he is self-condemned and naturally excommunicates himself. There is nothing to be said for him. It is simply gross defiance of the creed of the Universal church for the last 2,000 years. It is simply blasphemy that he reject the baptismal formula laid down by Jesus Christ and substitutes a formula of his own.

But other leading theologians stood by Nefyn including J. Morgan Jones, (head of the Bala-Bangor Congregational College and regarded as 'one of the most brilliant of the younger school of theologians and scholars associated with religious life in Wales') who in condemning Dr Jones' comments stated:

> It [the manifesto] is the personal confession of Tom Nefyn, for my own part I sympathise thoroughly and agree with almost every word in the confession. I believe it is a truly Christian confession in spirit, content, and

form. I know of scores and scores of other ministers who also agree with it to all intents and purposes.

The Rev G.M.L. Davies, former Member of Parliament for the University of Wales agreed stating that Tom Nefyn's confession showed:

> *... an amazing scope and integrity of mind ... this, be it remembered, is not the work of a leisured scholar, excogitated in the quiet of his lonely citadel, but of a private soldier, bruised and maimed in the wars, an almost monoglot Welshman, used to manual labour in field and quarry, and now pastor of a little congregation of colliers in Carmarthenshire. He is the most extraordinary blend of evangelist and modernist, of urgent prophet and playful comrade of children ... The judgment of his orthodoxy by a committee bound to conformity to a trust deed will weigh less in the minds of those who have followed Tom Nefyn closely than the judgment of his fellow soldiers, his fellow-students, his teachers, and, above all, his fellow-members in the Christian society he has built up at Tumble.*

Tom Nefyn stands trial

The Presbyterian Church wanted to be fair to Nefyn and gave him every chance, as they would see it, to redeem himself – this was no witch hunt. Dr Owen Prys, Principal of the Theological College at Aberystwyth and known to be sympathetic to Nefyn, was appointed to lead the investigation. Prys suggested to Nefyn that he take time away from his ministry to contemplate his position but instead Nefyn prepared his manifesto which Prys reluctantly took as a confession of guilt. In his report to the Treherbert Association (Sassiwn), Prys concluded that Nefyn's beliefs were 'fundamentally opposed to the standards of our Connexion and to the historical faith of the Christian Church.' Nefyn was given a stark choice – he could take a year out to contemplate his position or resign from the Presbyterian Ministry.

Tom Nefyn offered his resignation of the pastorate of Ebenezer on Sunday 3 June 1928. The letter was read at a special Church meeting that evening with Nefyn stating that 'He resigned with sorrow, because he saw that in Wales old theological forms were more important than the humanity of the future; that dogma and dead ritual were more beloved than live and searching minds, and that more importance was laid on religious creeds than on character.' Ebenezer members, by a huge majority, refused to accept the resignation and passed a resolution protesting against the action taken at Treherbert. No doubt buoyed by this support, Nefyn dug his heels in at the Nantgaredig Association that followed in August 1928. When challenged on whether he accepted the teachings and standards of the Presbyterian Church he responded, several times, by asking for an explanation of what these were. When the Treherbert 'ultimatum' was put to him, Nefyn was adamant that he would not willingly resign.

This was the last straw for Prys who, despite his sympathies for his former student, moved a resolution to suspend Nefyn from the Presbyterian ministry. This was passed almost unanimously, and a deadline of 9 September 1929 was set for Nefyn to leave Tumble. Nefyn came home to Tumble to a hero's welcome. He was offered opportunities to continue his unorthodox approach but, despite his suspension as a minister, decided to remain in the Presbyterian Church.

Farewell to Tumble

Tom Nefyn's last day as pastor of Ebenezer, 8 September 1928, began appropriately with a children's service described enthusiastically by the Western Mail:

> One was caught wondering what the puritan founders of the Corff would have said had they been present at the Sunday morning service – a gathering at which the deacons were ousted from their seats of honour, and the set fawr monopolised by fiddlers! As became a service for children, it was bright, colourful, vivacious, refreshing, from start to finish. Choice blooms with a dash of red decorated the empty pulpit, while the minister stood between the deacons' pew, close to and facing 200 or more boys and girls, ranging from five to fourteen years of age, all alert and actively participating in every phase of the proceedings. The orchestra consisted of ten string instruments, a trumpet, and clarinet, and a piano, and the players were drawn from amongst the adult members, but they attempted nothing more ambitious than the accompaniments to the hymns. All things savouring of convention and custom were banned.

The whole day was marked by a series of meetings 'remarkable for their fervour and expressions of love and attachment to the minister' culminating with the gathering of 4,000 people for the open-air service. These were not just the people of Tumble – they came 'on foot, in buses, and motor-cars from the surrounding villages, and there were contingents, too, from Carmarthen, Llanelly, Tycroes, and even far off Pembrokeshire.' Nefyn mounted the platform erected near the rugby posts at exactly six o'clock. The Western Mail described the scene:

> ... a typically Welsh gathering, whose melodious voices as they sang one after another a number of soul-stirring Welsh hymns must have carried for miles around. In the stillness of the evening air every word of the sermon could be distinctly heard, even in the streets of the village below. Few present can surely forget the eloquence of the sermon, the inspired appearance of the orator, the marked sincerity of his utterances, the

> *beauty of his Welsh diction, and his dramatic power of oratory. The Welsh hwyl was heard at its best and highest. The preacher's theme was the parable of the Prodigal Son, and his word-pictures were vivid and colourful.*

Nefyn did not mention this suspension from the ministry until near the end of his sermon. He then dropped his voice to low conversational tone and said:

> *I thank you all for your loyalty, your faithfulness. If anyone asks me to return home to North Wales I shall refuse; I feel that my home henceforth is in south Wales (yn y Dde). It was here the fight was fought; it was here the struggle took place. You came with me through thick and thin, through fire and water. I have only one resolve, and it is this: that if ever I see a man down I will try and lift him; if I find anyone lost to the highest life I will try and reclaim him.*
>
> *My future is full of uncertainties without money, without position, without office—but I have one consolation which will ever remain with me—the full assurance that right is might, that service is heaven, that righteousness is strength. And to you, my brothers and sisters, I make this appeal—there are little children in Tumble who seek guides and saviours. Will you be their saviours? God is calling you now to service, not in India or Africa, but here in your very homes.*
>
> *I finish as minister to-night. I do not repent for anything I have done. I am quite happy, I thank God for the opportunity he gave me to help you here. Stand together! Do good! Let your motto be, "Jesus first, others second, self last. Attend all the classes during the coming winter that will broaden your lives, make you richer, and lift you nearer Heaven. And as the church at Ebenezer has resolved to carry on, I appeal to the villagers of Tumble to help them.*

Tom Nefyn's last words as he closed the service and relinquished his ministry were to offer a prayer for the church at Ebenezer, its officers, members, Sunday school, young men and women and for all its activities.

However, despite his stated commitment to South Wales, Nefyn did return to his native North where he had received strong support including a gift of £640 presented at Pwllheli from a testimonial fund 'collected in sums of sixpences and shillings from quarrymen, colliers, and labourers in all parts of Wales' to compensate for the loss of his earnings as a minister. Professor J. J. Jones, of Nefyn, a Calvinistic Methodist minister who was in the trenches with Tom Nefyn during the War, said at the testimonial that 'they were both wounded in the same battle, taken to the same hospital, and had started preaching together after demobilisation … [Nefyn] was a true prophet, but Wales was too engrossed in politics, creed, and doctrines to listen to his message.'

Excommunication, lock-out and funeral

The South Carmarthenshire Presbytery met on 2 October 1928 and determined to dissolve the church in Tumble. When the now former congregation arrived at Ebenezer on Sunday 7 October, they found themselves locked out of the church many of them had founded just 30 years earlier. They had all been excommunicated from the Presbyterian church and told they would not be allowed back in unless they denounced Nefyn and gave a commitment to orthodoxy - *the Confession of Faith*. Their response was to take the bold step of establishing their own independent Fellowship. Having held meetings in the village hall and the new primary school, they purchased a plot of land close to Ebenezer in Ty-isha Road for their own meeting house.

In *Coal Dust and Dogma* Glyn Anthony recalls how Emrys Thomas (renamed Emlyn Price in the book and described as a physical fitness enthusiast) had attended one of Nefyn's *Seiat* (Society) evening meetings and given a fitness exhibition including swinging Indian clubs to a mixed but largely supportive reception. Emrys, one of Nefyn's most faithful followers, died on Whit Sunday 1929 having asked for his former minister to lead his burial service. The young man's father had sought permission to bury his son alongside his mother and brother in the Ebenezer graveyard and had been given permission on the condition that the service at the graveside was performed by a fully ordained minister.

Figure 109. The gravestone of Emrys Thomas at Ebenezer Author's collection).

This was seen by Tom Nefyn's excommunicated flock as taking advantage of someone in distress and the *Nefynites* were determined that their former minister would speak at the service. To satisfy the authorities and orthodox members of Ebenezer, a compromise was found – Tom Nefyn would conduct the main service outside the graveyard wall, and an ordained minister would officiate at the graveside. According to the Western Mail, there were thousands of people present for the service led by

Nefyn who created a deep impression with a 'beautiful address' stating that, 'The time will come when high moral life with a healthy mind like that of our late friend Emrys Thomas, will be far more important than theology. Men hold the key of the graveyard, but God holds the key of Heaven.'

Llain-y-Delyn

The excommunicated Nefynites formed a Fellowship and, emphasising their distinctiveness, built their new meeting place, Llain-y-Delyn, in the style of a single-storey villa rather than a traditional high-ceilinged chapel. Members had themselves excavated the foundations and the first turf was cut in May 1929 by Mr. F. R. Sainty of London, a leader of the Society of Friends. The building, designed by T. Alwyn Lloyd of Cardiff, was built by Lewis Davies of Penygroes at a cost £1,800.

Figure 110. Mr Sainty, a Quaker, cutting the first sod of the foundation of Llain-y-Delyn.

Llain-y-Delyn was formally opened on Saturday 30 November 1929. Tumble residents were joined by sympathisers from the outlying districts for the ceremony performed by Tom Nefyn and Mrs. Jones, Pantycelyn, the oldest member of the group. Mr. Owen Owen, chairman of the building committee, presided over the proceeding. Demonstrating the continuing national interest, Dr Henry T. Gillett of Oxford, who had shown much practical sympathy towards the group, attended the ceremony. In his address he emphasised that the new building stood for pacifism and education not sectarianism. As the Tumble Christian Fellowship, Nefyn's former congregation were committed to the search for truth. They received some support and encouragement from the

Religious Society of Friends (Quakers), but it seems did not formally become part of that movement.

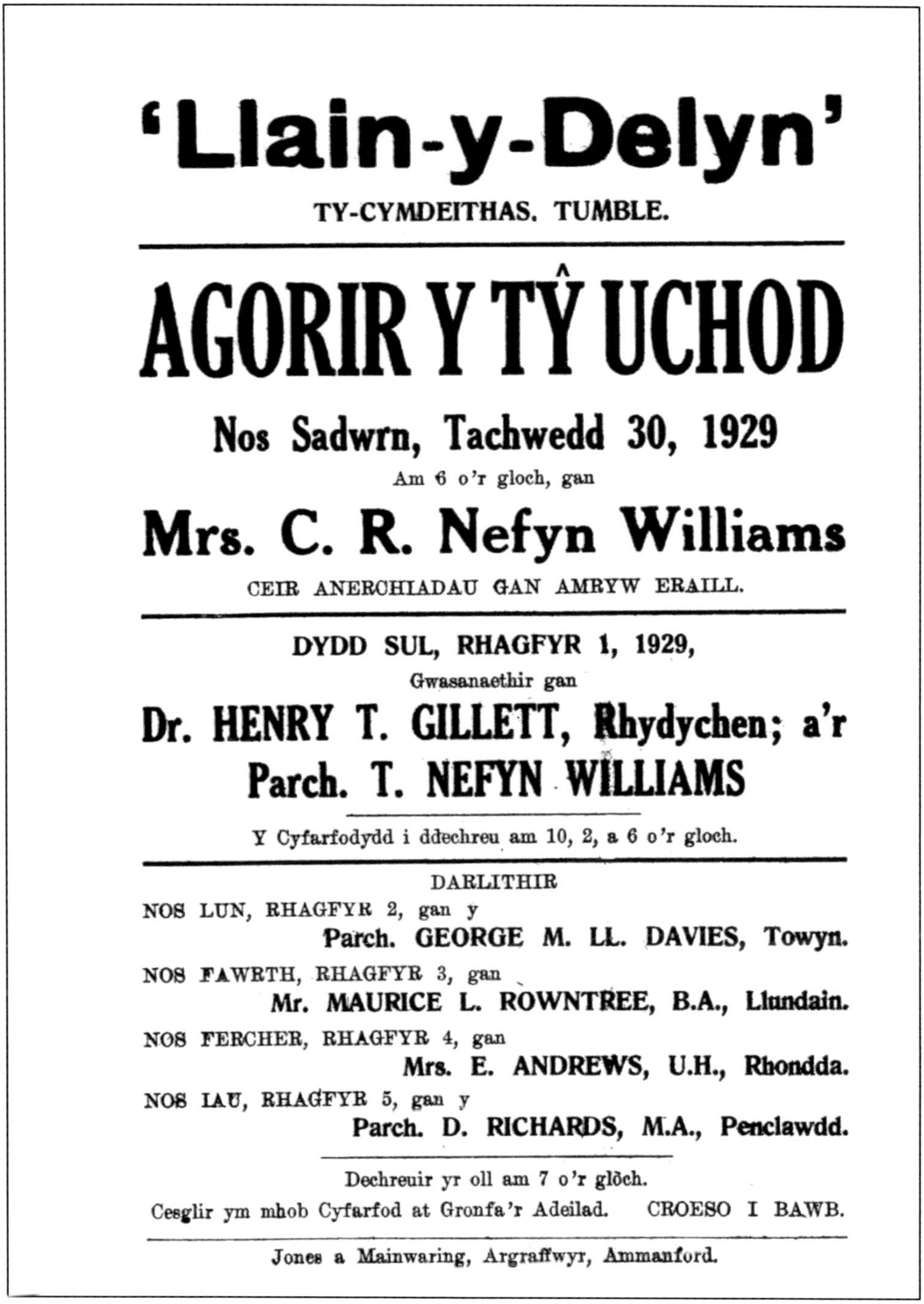

'Llain-y-Delyn'

TY-CYMDEITHAS, TUMBLE.

AGORIR Y TŶ UCHOD

Nos Sadwrn, Tachwedd 30, 1929

Am 6 o'r gloch, gan

Mrs. C. R. Nefyn Williams

CEIR ANEROHIADAU GAN AMRYW ERAILL.

DYDD SUL, RHAGFYR 1, 1929,

Gwasanaethir gan

Dr. HENRY T. GILLETT, Rhydychen; a'r
Parch. T. NEFYN WILLIAMS

Y Cyfarfodydd i ddechreu am 10, 2, a 6 o'r gloch.

DARLITHIR

NOS LUN, RHAGFYR 2, gan y
Parch. GEORGE M. LL. DAVIES, Towyn.

NOS FAWRTH, RHAGFYR 3, gan
Mr. MAURICE L. ROWNTREE, B.A., Llundain.

NOS FERCHER, RHAGFYR 4, gan
Mrs. E. ANDREWS, U.H., Rhondda.

NOS IAU, RHAGFYR 5, gan y
Parch. D. RICHARDS, M.A., Penclawdd.

Dechreuir yr oll am 7 o'r glôch.

Cesglir ym mhob Cyfarfod at Gronfa'r Adeilad.   CROESO I BAWB.

Jones a Mainwaring, Argraffwyr, Ammanford.

Figure 111 Poster announcing the opening of Llain-y-Delyn

Tom Nefyn returned to Tumble to lead early services at Llain-y-Delyn but, with his continuing commitment to the Presbyterian church, despite how he had been treated, declined to be the Fellowship's first minister. In March 1931, Nefyn was received back into the Presbyterian Church of Wales and later reinstated as a minister - he was the last Presbyterian minister to *be tried for heresy.*

The farewell on the rugby pitch and Emrys Jones' funeral were the high points in Nefyn's relationship with his former congregation. Things went downhill from there, culminating in a bitter open letter sent on 20 January 1931 to Nefyn by E.P. Jones, Hon. Secretary of Llain-y Delyn. The letter reminded Nefyn that after the excommunication of his former congregation he had 'eagerly pressed upon them' to keep united and not to make any overtures to be readmitted to the Methodist church adding in uncompromising tones:

> *You are perfectly aware also that we stuck to our principles and to you as our leader through thick and thin. Only about 40 at that time returned to Ebenezer to form a new church on an orthodox basis in accordance with the wishes of the Presbytery. The remaining 210 remained loyal.*
>
> *It might be possible that you mis-interpreted this loyalty as a loyalty to a leader and not to convictions, a group of hero-worshippers and not seekers after truth in all its aspects and aspirations. A road had been prepared for years; then you came along in a majestic way, captivating the young minds, which was appreciated by us all. We are indebted to you for this service, not only to us, but to the would-be seekers for theological emancipation.*
>
> *The first meeting with the object of framing our future was held in the local public hall. You, friend—who had already left us to paddle your own canoe—returned to this meeting. Here again you emphasised the essential desirability that we should cling together at all costs .... you said at that meeting, that you should obtain a building, and get it at once— the sooner the better. An edifice that would convey an impression quite contrary to that of a chapel. A building that would seat about 300: a building in which glass partitions could be placed for different classes in the Sunday school, and for the winter evenings. We accepted your suggestions.*
>
> *In due course we held a committee meeting seeking an avenue as to how to obtain a loan - or an overdraft—to commence building this 'Community House'. You suggested that a friend of yours could easily collect £400 or £500: up to now have received about £6 from your collection towards the building fund, and from your friend—nothing. It is true that you preached to us gratis once a mouth. You repeatedly refused to be remunerated for your services, and we are grateful to you for that.... You have not forgotten to mention the fact in the Welsh press. Many of our great men have helped us—men who were not directly or indirectly*

responsible for our position. They did not promise to give their services free, but they did … these valiant scholars have not reminded us of their generosity.

When the building of Llain-y-Delyn was nearing completion and arrangements commenced as to the procedure for its opening you shocked all of us—without exception—by joining a Methodist Church at Brynbachau. You had not even sent a word to anyone in Tumble of your intentions. When we met you at the meeting of the trustees, held the Sunday after you joined Brynbachau, I asked you, 'In view of the great disappointment and shock our Fellowship felt at your conduct in joining a Methodist Church, would you, in the interests of unity amongst your followers, withdraw your membership from Brynbachau. You answered definitely 'No.' … It became obvious to many of us by your estrangements, your conduct, and your attitude that you were not the Torn Nefyn of yore.

… Never mind friend, you can go your own way, but the noble band of 200 in Llain-y-Delyn are marching on with a load on our backs due to your 'experiment'. We wish you and your family well. Personally, I wish you all the good things possible, and that your path from now on will be smooth, but when you receive messages from Methodist churches in North Wales especially, congratulating you upon 'seeing the light,' think of the band of 200 in Tumble who helped you to hold the light when all doors were locked against you.

This was the rather sad postscript to the story of Tom Nefyn and the forward-thinking people of a small West Wales mining village who together had caused a national storm.

Figure 112. Railway Terrace with Llain-y-Delyn in the distance.

12.Tumble at Play

Tumble has a strong sporting tradition and not just rugby – cricket, football, snooker, boxing, tennis and bowls all feature in the village's story. However, rugby stands out as the great sporting passion bringing unparalleled success to the village and producing great players across many eras.

The Magpies

Tumble Rugby Football Club was established in 1897. In 1920/21 the club adopted its distinctive black and white striped shirts giving it the nickname of the Magpies / Y Piod. Under its first captain, Orphie Evans, the club became one of the most successful teams in the old West Wales Rugby Union. After winning the WRU Challenge Cup for the first time in 1933, Tumble went on to win the trophy a further 11 times setting a record that remains unmatched. In 1937/38 season, the club was crowned West Wales Champions and went on to be champions again 1949/50.

On 12 March 1947, the club officially celebrated its Golden Jubilee with a home match against the mighty Cardiff RFC followed by a dinner with 'well-known celebrities of the rugger world.' To commemorate the occasion, John Myrddin Davies, club secretary and former player, compiled a souvenir booklet, *Tumble Rugby Football Club – 1897-1949,* in which he gave a detailed account of the club's illustrious history. He dedicated his book to the memory of the 'victims of the dreaded disease, Silicosis, and to some who had made the supreme sacrifice in the many wars since 1897.' The following is a summary of Davies' booklet but cannot do justice to the rich detail of the full version. This account draws additional material from Wilf Timbrell who also played for the Club including in the side that won the Carmarthenshire Challenge Cup in 1913. Not very long after that match, Timbrell and several other players left to fight in the First World War with a number not returning.

The club was formed at a meeting held at Bryn Stores Reading Room. Securing a suitable pitch to play on proved a great challenge. In the early days practice was carried out beside a coal tip towards Cross Hands. Later Morgan Hughes of Ty-isha Farm allowed one of his fields to be used before a move to land owned by the Tumble Hotel. This field was also used for other village sporting activities and for Queen Victoria's Diamond Jubilee celebrations. It was situated off Caldy View (Heol y Neuadd) - where the Chemists, Tynton Boot Stores, Bethel Chapel and the Public Hall were later built. The ground appeared overnight with goalposts cut from woodland where the Isolation Hospital was built in the 1930s. Early players included the Walters brothers from Pont Morlais, both international athletes (one competed in the hurdles in the Olympic Games in

Athens), and Tom and David Howells (of 1906 *riot* notoriety) who were also fine athletes.

For its first match, the team, led by Orphie Evans, walked to Pontyberem to play the village team that became one of its fiercest rivals. Tumble won by a try, scored by Watson Welburn, to nil. The team colours were Blue and Gold quarters with the players paying for the jerseys themselves. In 1900, under new captain Harry Rees, the club colours changed to all black except for a white star presented to each player by Edgar Jones the tailor who sewed the emblem on each shirt – the team then became known as Tumble Starlights.

For the 1902-3 season the Club moved to a new field in Bethesda Road near the chapel vestry and the colours changed once more to Gold and Green vertical stripes. A further move in 1904 took the team to a field, owned by Ty-isha Farm, opposite Pistyll Gwyn where homes were later built (it seems that the Club was forced to move its ground as the village grew in the period up to the First World War). One outstanding game of that time was against Dafen. The field was in a terrible state from rain and one of the Tumble players, David Williams, had no *togs* and so turned out in his working boots. From then on he was known as *Dai, Sgidiau Gwaith (Dai, Work Boots)*. In 1905-6 there was another move to Ty-isha field. Few games were played in 1906-7 as a 'wave of religious fervour' had swept over Wales, but the club did mange another change of kit – to All White. One noted player, Evan (Ianto) Penygraig, went on to play for Llanelli and then for Oldham Rugby League, excelling in a tour to Australia in 1920.

In 1907-8 another Tumble rugby team formed which Davies describes as a 'spite' or 'off shoot' of the established team. It played on Danygraig field on the north side of the High Street in Cherry and White. A 'herculean encounter' followed when the Cherry and Whites challenged the Whites to a match. The Whites won and everyone was pleased that the teams then re-united.

Davies identifies the Club's various headquarters and changing rooms as, the 'Old Reading Room, Tumble Hotel a shed alongside Morawel and a room kindly rented by Chalinders at Church Place, better known as the Lodging House.' As well as rugby, team members played and betted on the game of handball which Davies describes as 'this greatest of all pastimes (other than rugby).' Davies also remarks on the more demanding training:

> *Stiffer training was introduced, boxing gloves procured and indeed they became experts at the art. Others whose fitness had to be maintained ran to and from Bryndu flats, even in the dark and dreary evenings. Daylight was only seen at weekends as the boys who were miners toiled underground for 9 1/2 hours a day.*

The next move was to a pitch off Bethesda Road where the factory was built in the 1950s, followed by yet another to a field approached via Tyrhos Farm. Because the pitch was some distance from the dressing rooms, the team trained on *Cae Backs* behind High Street. Baths were set up in the Reading Room on match days for home and away teams. The poor condition of the pitch prompted a move to the Hirwaun field off Blaenhirwaun lane (Wilf Timbrell refers to a Catholic Church once being on this site). The headquarters at that time was *Ma Perkins* - Hannah Perkins' sweet shop at 95 High Street - with *Cae Backs* close at hand for practice. All these pitches suffered from excessively muddy conditions and visiting teams would justifiably complain about them. This prompted a further move in 1912-13 to Lletty Field above Ty-isha Road where Tir-Becca now stands. Originally rented, fund-raising efforts led by committee members, John Tierney and David Lewis, enabled the Club to by the pitch along with further land alongside it. The Lletty Field remained the Club's home until the final move to the Welfare Park and is where Tom Nefyn gave his farewell speech.

Two players, Georgie Davies and Edward Thomas (Tommy Gwag) played for Llanelli in the 1912-13 season. Edward Thomas played on the wing against the all-conquering Springboks who after a rousing game beat 'Sospanville' by a mere point (8-7). The game had been filmed and 'all the local sportsmen filled the Tivoli later on to see their idol once again become famous as the first to be shown in the films, from the village.' This season also saw the first trophy to be brought back to the village - the All Carmarthenshire Cup won at Stradey Park against Amman Rovers in torrential rain.

Davies gives an interesting account of how the team travelled to away matches (they had a reputation for always turning up, once walking the 8 miles to Llanelli when their usual transport broke down):

> *The fulfilling of away fixtures was done under great difficulties for the reliability of the local brake [a horse drawn carriage owned by Daniels' shop] was never guaranteed. This of course meant extra physical demands on the players, especially to walk to Tycroes, Ammanford and Llanelly. The old brake, when available, played an important part in the club's history. The fare was 1/- (one shilling) far or near and the starting point was the 'Finger Post' [the square]. All steep hills and gradients had to be walked, and of course the return journey had to be considered. Invariably on the return journey, especially on Felinfoel and Morlais hills, the horses would nag, on no account would they even pull an empty brake sometime, therefore some coaxing and pushing had to be done. If at last Felinfoel could be conquered their fate still awaited Morlais hill. The boys would sometimes unhitch the wagon and leave it on the roadside to be fetched next morning when the horses would be fresher. They would then ride the horses in relays homeward. The Llanelly clubs who visited Tumble were in a more envious position, they were all catered for by James Mews. It was indeed a glorious sight to see them coming down High Street with their high stepping horses on trot.*

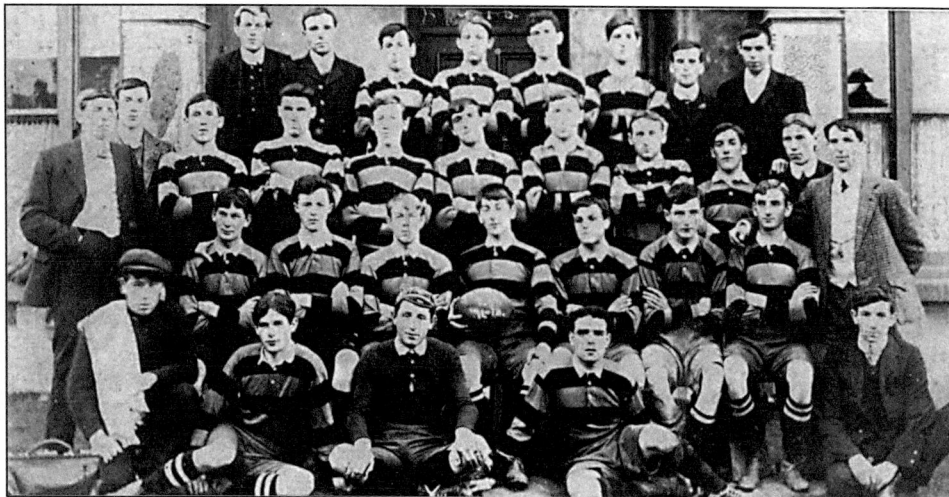

Figure 113. Tumble Rugby Team 1911-12. Back Row: Billo Morgans, Tom Jones, D Davies, W Timbrell. E J Evans, Dai Roberts, E Llewellyn Edwards. Standing: Ben Perkins, D Morgans (Plas Uchaf), Will John Harries, George Davies (Ty Coppa), Vincent Morgan, Albert Richards (Penllwyn-Lleci), W J Harries (Cwmmawr), Will Phipps, Ned Jones, (Pwyllyrodau), Dick Howells. Sitting: Ivor Evans, E R R Lewis, J H Richards (Jacka Bach), George Davies (Captain), Ned Thomas (Gwag), Jack Lewis, Dai Jones (Tymelyn). Front Row: Jack Lewis (Coch), Edwin Stephens, Evan Davies (Penygraig), Evan Jones (Ianto Bach), Dai Jones (Ostler).

Davies also recounts these stories about journeys on the 'Old Brake':

> On the return journey from Llanelly on a very foggy night, the brake under the care of old Billo Lletty, was nearing Brynteg, Billo was guided by two candle lights and was taking extra special care. Inside, covered by the tent, the boys prevailed in a heated discussion. The burning question of the day was 'Home rule for Ireland'. Dai Greenhill and Harry Llifwr were the specialists, both in turn would shout aloud, "Gambwyll Billo" but the brake gradually crept near the gutter. Lo! And behold !! without even warning the brake and its cargo went over the edge. All escaped with only a severe shaking and minor bruises.

> On boxing day 1910, on the way to play Whitland the boys expected to get a train at Carmarthen, Edwards bach, who was in charge of the brake asked one of the boys, "Le byddwn ni cant mlynedd o heno?" ['Where will we be in a hundred years from now?']. A prompt reply came from one of the old wags inside, "Ar yr heol os na shapwn ni." ['on the road if we don't shape up'].

The 1913-14 season saw a notable victory against Llanelly seconds on the Lletty field – Tommy Gwag and George Davies proved too good for the opposition.

Though not covered by Davies, the club also triumphed over the *Scarlets* on 19 May 1917 as the Cambria Daily Reader reported:

> *The Llanelly team journeyed to Tumble on Saturday, when they tried conclusions with the home team, which included such well-known players as Evan Davies, Ned Thomas and Edwin Stephens. Mr. J. Waddell kicked off, and it was noticed that a Soccer ball was being used, no Rugby ball being available in the village. The homesters, whose heavy pack minimised Llanelly's chances of success very materially, were the better team, and before the close of the game Edwin Stephens had scored two tries for them, while a couple of forwards also crossed the visitors' line. Two of the tries were converted, and Dick Edmunds having scored a try for Llanelly, the final was: Tumble, 2 con. Goals 2 tries; Llanelly, 1 try.*

Figure 114. Private Tom Jones (seated) with his brother, Idwal, and sister, May. Courtesy of Lynette Griffiths.

Ten regular members of the team and the young club secretary, Tom Jones (Morawel), served in the First World War. Several, including Wilf Timbrell, were with the 4th Welsh Regiment sent by Winston Churchill in 1915 to attack the Dardanelles (Gallipoli). Of those who served the following 'made the supreme sacrifice': Ivor Evans ('the inside half and one of the cleverest the club has ever produced'), Jacka Richards (Jacka Bach - captain), Jack Thomas, M.M. (Blaennant), Ivor Evans, Will Jones (Shamrock), Evan J. Evans (Ianto Plasucha), Will Davies (Coch), Bertie Treharne and Tom Evans. Tom Jones, brother of Brinley Jones (Bryn y barbwr), was killed in 1918. Before joining the Gloucestershire Regiment in 1914, he was a clerk at Cross Hands Colliery.

Figure 115. Winners of the New Dock Cup, 1917: E Jones, J. Lewis, Tom Jones, T. Lewis, E Stephens, D. J. Matthews, D Davies, E. Davies (Capt.), W. Jones, E Thomas, E. Jones, Will Jones.

In 1919 the club was reorganised with Tom Gwag as captain, but he soon joined Ianto Plasucha in signing professional forms with Oldham, handing the captaincy to George Davies whose son, Myrddin Davies, describes the 1920-21 season as the greatest in the club's history – appropriately marked by the adoption of the now famous Black and White jerseys. The following season, Llanelli brought a full-strength side, including six Welsh internationals, to Tumble and proved to be complete masters beating the village team by 19 points in an 'enjoyable feast of rugby.'

In 1922-23, Tumble went on a Christmas tour of Carmarthen and Tenby. On Christmas day itself they played at Carmarthen Park and Will Lewis scored a 'really amazing try' soon after kick-off (some of the Carmarthen supporters blamed it on the fact that a few of their players had yet to make it onto the pitch from the changing rooms). Will Lewis missed the match against Tenby on Boxing day – he gave priority to going on his honeymoon! That must have been some team – winning all but 6 of their 40 matches and scoring 315 points with just 90 against. The following season back at Carmarthen, with a large crowd of Tumble supporters, the Magpies were winning at half-time and Watt Davies sent a homing pigeon back to the village with the score – unfortunately, Tumble lost the match.

Archie Skym of Drefach made his debut for the club in the 1925-26 season. He went on to play for Llanelli for the first time on Christmas day 1926 having played in the morning for Tumble against Hendy. He was capped 20 times by Wales (16 following his move to Cardiff where he became club captain). He played in every position in the scrum for his country.

Figure 116. Archie Skym - standing, 3rd from left (author's collection).

By the mid-20s the *Old Brake* had been replaced by a *luxury charabanc* (driven by Tom Williams – *Joe Shop*) for away matches. On taking a short cut from Lougher to Penclawdd the vehicle became wedged on a narrow bridge – it eventually got through, but that route was avoided for future trips. In 1929-30 a club record was created when George Davies, in his final match for the club, and his son Myrddin played in the same match against Pontyberem. Sadly in 1931-32 'the brilliant and elusive outside half', Willie Wiltshire, who had been picked to play against Abercrave, was killed at the colliery.

Tumble won the Western Mail Cup in 1933-34 and were perhaps the leading club in the Gwendraeth Valley drawing players from as far afield as Pontyates. By 1936-37 the club played its home matches on the Welfare Park ground (the 'new pavilion' was first used on Saturday 22 April 1939). Tumble became League champions for the first time in 1937-38 defeating Ystradgynlais at

Pontarddulais. During the Second World War, rugby in the village was kept going by the 'Pigstye Rovers' – a local ex-schoolboy club. Thanks to their efforts the senior team were able to rebuild quickly for the 1945-46 season and reached the final of the West Wales Rugby League Cup. The match was played against Amman Utd at Stradey Park on 4 May 1946 in front of a crowd of 10,000. At the end of normal time the score was drawn, and the referee agreed to play an extra 15 minutes each way. After Amman Utd went ahead with an unconverted try, Wyn Jones scored the winning try for Tumble with Jim Wiltshire converting. The Jubilee Season of 1946/47 started well but the club then lost three of its leading players who 'went North' to play Rugby League. This says a lot for the quality of players in the village side at the time.

Figure 117. Three-times Cup winners 1932/33/34.

Figure 118. Tumble Ex-Schoolboys ('Pigsties') 1939/40.

Figure 119. West Wales Cup Champions 1945-46.

Figure 120. Programme for West Wales Cup Final 1945-46.

The Cardiff team that came to Tumble for the Jubilee match included five internationals, one of whom was Bleddyn Williams. Archie Skym was given the honour of kicking off and Tumble's first captain, Orphie Evans, re-started after half time. Another highlight of that season was Peter Rees becoming the second member of the club to be selected by Wales as a full international. He was soon followed by Handel Greville and Desmond Jones. Handel Greville 'proved a tremendous success against the Wallabies at Cardiff Arms Park on December 20th, 1947' and captained the Scarlets in 1948-49.'

Figure 121. The team of 1949.

Figure 122. Des Jones, Wales international 1947.

Figure 123. Handel Greville. Wales international and Scarlets captain.

This summary can only give a flavour of the 'glamorous history of the club' as recorded by Myrddin Davies. Anyone interested in *the Magpies*, or indeed the village of Tumble, should read his booklet in full. It is an important social as well as sporting history of the village. This first half century recorded by Davies laid the foundations for another, later golden era as the Club's website records:

> *The 1980s can be seen as the Golden Era for the club when the Magpies, under the coaching of John 'Coch' Williams and then the John brothers, Clive and Alan, became the dominant force in West Wales rugby. In 1983/84 Tumble were crowned West Wales Champions for the first time in 34 years, a title they reclaimed the following year, along with the Challenge Cup. They held onto the cup for a further four years and in 1987/88 they won the West Wales Championship for the last time before the nationalisation of the league system. 1987/88 season was somewhat of a pinnacle for the club when under the captaincy of scrum half Arwel Davies the 1st, 2nd and Youth XVs had the distinction of wining every competition they were entered in, the fabled 'Grand Slam' season.*

The village produced further internationals including Gareth Davies and Dwayne Peel both of whom also represented the British and Irish Lions. Gareth Davies went on to serve two terms as Chairman of the Welsh Rugby Union.

Tumble Rugby Football Club.

Souvenir ★★ Programme   JUBILEE SEASON

CARDIFF

VERSUS

TUMBLE

at

The Welfare Park, Tumble,

on

Wednesday, March 12th 1947,

P.S. ARCHIE SKYM WILL KICK OFF AT 4.30 P.M
SECOND HALF BY MR. THEO. EVANS - TUMBLE'S FIRST
CAPTAIN.

PRESIDENT - MR. DAN JONES, M.E. F.R.G.S.
CHAIRMAN - MR. DAN JONES.
HON. SEC. - J. MYRDDIN DAVIES.

No. **484** (Prize: 1-cwt. Potatoes)

Price - SIXPENCE.

Printed by Jenkins & Williams, Tumble.

D777/16/38

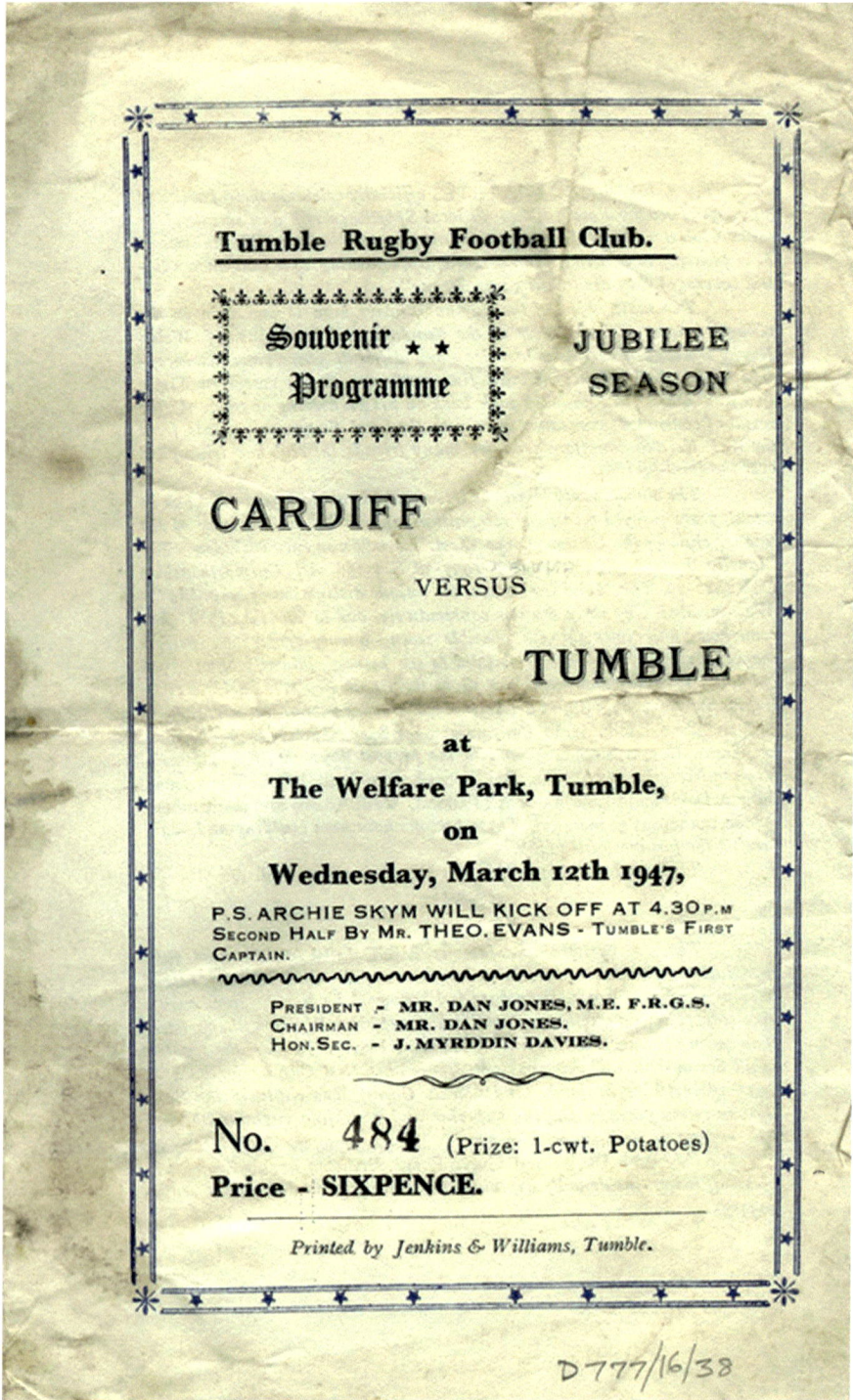

Figure 124. Cardiff v Tumble Programme 194. Courtesy of Glamorganshire Archives.

Today the BLACK & WHITES *officially celebrate their Jubilee of 50 years of Rugby Football, and all local Sportsmen will join in extending to the Club their heartiest congratulations on such a splendid attainment. It is pleasing to note that (in the words appertaining to a well-known liquid beverage) they are "Still going Strong".*

The main object of the club has always been to maintain in the *village a team representative of the standard and traditions of Welsh Rugby Football. There have been lean and difficult years since its inception under the guidance of such fine gentlemen as the evergreen* Theo. Evans. "Ophie" *can proudly look back on his pioneering of 1897. As the result of continued assistance from you, the loyal Supporter, grants from the W.R.U., and donations from its many friends, the club has triumphed over the grim periods.*

The club proudly boasts of its numerous achievements and has in *recent years enjoyed creditable recognition, and is indeed the envy of the smaller clubs of the Union in the West. Its achievements include:- The Llanelly League Championship 1937-38 Season, All Carmarthenshire Cup 1912-13, The Mond Cup 1930, the unique distinction of winning the Western Mail Cup three seasons consecutively, and to date the 'POT' has come home four times out of a possible seven - a truly remarkable performance. Tribute must however be paid to the heroes, stalwarts of the good old days, most of whom have passed to the Great Beyond. Theirs was an impressive story of grit and determination. Such personalities were:-* Elias Bowen, Ianto Bach, Ianto Penygraig, Jack Saer, George Davies, Arthur Williams, Edwin Stephens; *and to the present day:-* Wilfie Timbrell, Vincent Morgan, Day Davies, Dai Topsail, Dan Bach Jones, Tom Ostler, Johnny Davies and Edwin Jones (Tailors), Will Adams and many others, far too numerous to mention. *These persons have been building and maintaining the fortunes of the club.*

The *prowess of* Peter Rees *has been duly recognised.*

———⤬———

Today's Visitors, the famous BLUE & BLACKS, *need little introduction, and the supporters and members of the Club proudly extend to them a warm welcome. Indeed we feel honoured by a visit from such a fine side. This season alone Cardiff has supplied Wales with no fewer than seven players, and the Welsh Captain,* Haydn Tanner, *the greatest of all Scrum-halves of today. Haydn secured his first Cap as far back as 1935 against New Zealand. Undoubtedly Cardiff has captured the limelight in recent years by playing superior and sparkling rugby, with such fine exponents as* Tanner, Bleddyn Williams, Cleaver, Jack Mathews, Tamplin, W.E.N. Davies *and* Gwyn Evans. *Our own* Archie Skym, *who kicks off today, incidentally captained the Cardiff side during the season* 1934-35.

CARDIFF		TUMBLE
	Full Back	
F. Trott		Richie Owen
	Three-Quarters	
From:		
G. Porter		H. Huxtable
H. Lovelock		Glan Jones
W.B. Cleaver		Peter Rees
B. Williams		W.H. Jones
B. Braker		
	Half Backs	
W.D. Darch		J. Wiltshire
G. Martin		T.J. Evans
	Forwards	
From:		
R. Bale		B. Rowlands
M. James		Vernon Jones
J. Beswick		T.J. Rees
R. Carter		Lloyd Morgan *(Capt.)*
S. Bowes		Jack Edwards
W.E.Tamplin		Arthney Davies
Gwyn Evans		Ieuan Jones
G. Williams		Les. Rogers
H.C.Jones		

Referee: Mr TREVOR JONES, *Bridgend.*

———◆◆———

Today's game will surely be greeted with intense enthusiasm, and may it go down in history as the greatest spectacle to be remembered on the Welfare Park.

Croesaw i chwi Gaerdydd, a diolch yn fawr.

There is more to life than rugby?

Y Tymbl Ddoe a Heddiw provides an excellent photographic record of social and sporting activities in Tumble over the period of this story. Here are a few examples:

- In 1919 Tumble had a thriving mixed tennis club and had their photograph taken with John Waddell, owner of the Great Mountain Colliery.

- Football (soccer) teams from at least the 1920s onwards.

- Llechyfedach School had cricket and stoolball teams in the 1930s.

- The Upper Tumble Cricket Club in 1947 included a young Bert Peel (grandfather of Dwayne).

- The Tumble Bowling Club won the David Jennings Bowl in 1939.

- Upper Tumble had a trophy-winning Snooker Team.

- The Tumble Boxing Club was thriving in 1961 (and later produced a heavyweight national champion – Brian Roberts).

Figure 125. Members of Tumble Tennis Club with John Waddell and family (seated), 1919.

Snooker was a popular pastime with tables in the Public Hall and in dedicated snooker hall in Upper Tumble (*Fred's*) which was home to a trophy-winning team. Snooker player Gary Owen was born in Tumble in 1929 and had lived in Railway Terrace. He became world amateur champion for a second time in 1966, beating future world professional champion John Spencer. In 1968 Owen, Spencer and Ray Reardon became the first players in a generation to turn professional. In 1969 Owen reached the final of the reconstituted World Professional Snooker Championship, losing to John Spencer.

Figure 126. Gary Owen of Tumble with Ray Reardon (cueing), 6 times World Snooker Champion. Courtesy of BBC.

Figure 127. Upper Tumble Cricket Team, 1947. Standing: W Richards, W.H. Jones, W. Morgan, W. Jones, M. Thomas, W. Davies, G. Jenkins, E. Thomas. Sitting: B. Peel, J. Edwards, T. Evans, I. Jenkins, R. Owen.

Figure 128. The successful Tumble Bowles Team of 1939.

'Y Tymbl Ddoe a Heddiw'

Ond newid wnaeth y pentre', fel popeth yn ei dro –
Distawodd twrf peiriannau, diflannodd llwch y glo,
Fe gollodd y gymdeithas yr *'agosatrwydd fu'*,
A mawr y cyfnewidiad a welir ar bob tu.

Datblygiad daeth a'i welliant, i harddu a glanhau,
Anghofir yr *'Arferion'*, a'r hiraeth sy'n dyfnhau,
Ym mynwes hen frodorion ar ddiflanedig hynt,
Wrth gofio, yn fyfyrgar, am ffyrdd y *'Dyddiau gynt'*.

Ac er fod carped gwyrddlas dros greithiau'r meysydd glo,
Daw *'Atgof'* a'r Gorfennol I ddeffro'r hynaf go',
A gwelir yr *'Oedolion'* yn ail-fyw llawer awr
drwy adrodd eu helyntion yng nghysgod *'Mynydd Mawr'*.

Hen bentre' diwydiannol – ei ramant – hynos yw,
Lle cafwyd pob brawdoliaeth yn brwydro am gael byw;
Lle nad oedd *'ffiniau'n'* cyfri dyn i ddyn yn frawd
Rol *'Ddoe'* mor *'gymdeithasol'* ... yr *'Heddiw'* sydd yn dlawd.

Closing verses from 'Y Tymbl Ddoe a Heddiw' by Lilian Rees (Cyfle i Bawb).

Figure 129. A modern view of Tumble from Drefach (author's collection)

Bibliography

Published books and articles:

Anthony, Glyn, *Coal Dust and Dogma* (1987).

Bowen, Raymond. E, *The Burry Port and Gwendraeth Valley Railway and its Antecedent Canals: The Canal (2001).*

Cullen, Phil, *Gwendraeth Valley Coal Mines.*

Cullen, Phil, *Outburst: Curse below the Gwendraeth Valley.*

Davies, John, *A history of Wales (1990).*

Davies, John Myrddin, *Tumble Rugby Football Club – 1897-1949*

Dyfed Archaeological Trust, *Turnpike and Pre-Turnpike Roads (2016).*

Gibbard Noel, *The Tumble Strike 1893, The Carmarthenshire Antiquary (1984).*

Gibbard, Noel, *Hanes Plwyf Llan-non, Hen Sir Caerfyrddin (1984).*

Griffiths, Ivor, *Pontarddulais Town Council, Local History.*

Jones, Phyllis M., *They Gave Me A Lamp: Reminiscences of a Colliery Nursing Officer (1992).*

Lewis, Samuel, *Topographical Dictionary of Wales (1843).*

Owen, D Huw, *A History of the Gwendraeth Valleys and Llanelli (Bilingual - 2014).*

Price, M.R.C., *The Coal Industry at Tumble*, The Carmarthenshire Antiquary (2013).

Price, M.R.C., *The Llanelly and Mynydd Mawr Railway (1992).*

Rees, Ronald, *The Black Mystery – Coal-mining in South-West Wales (2008).*

Survey of Great Britain, *The Geology of the South Wales Coal-Field, Part VII, The Country Around Ammanford (1907).*

Timbrell, Wilfred, *Reminiscences of Tumble from 1886 (1974).*

Treharne, K.C., *Glofeydd Cwm Gwendraeth* (1995).

Williams, David, *The Rebecca Riots* (1955).

Ysgol Gynradd Y Tymbl – *Canblwyddiant Ysgol Y Tymbl (Tumble School Centenary).*

Newspapers:

Amman Valley and East Carmarthenshire News

Cambria Daily Reader

Cardiff Times

Carmarthen Journal

Evening Express

Illustrated London News

Llanelli Mercury

Llanelly Star

London Times

Pembrokeshire Herald

South Wales Daily News

South Wales Echo

South Wales Evening Post

South Wales Weekly Post

Tarian Y Gweithiwr

The Amman Valley Chronicle

The Welshman / Y Cymro

Western Mail